Multilayer Corpus Studies

This volume explores the opportunities afforded by the construction and evaluation of multilayer corpora, an emerging methodology within corpus linguistics that brings together multiple independent parallel analyses of the same linguistic phenomena and how the interplay of these concurrent analyses can help to push the field into new frontiers. The first part of the book surveys the theoretical and methodological underpinnings of multilayer corpus work, including an exploration of various technical and data collection issues. The second part builds on the groundwork of the first half to show multilayer corpora applied to different subfields of linguistic study, including information structure research, referentiality, discourse models, and functional theories of discourse analysis, as well as the study of non-standard language. Advancing the multilayer corpus linguistic research paradigm into new and different directions, this volume is an indispensable resource for graduate students and researchers in corpus linguistics, syntax, semantics, construction studies, and cognitive grammar.

Amir Zeldes is Assistant Professor of Computational Linguistics in the Department of Linguistics at Georgetown University, USA.

Routledge Advances in Corpus Linguistics

Edited by Tony McEnery
Lancaster University, UK

Michael Hoey
Liverpool University, UK

For more titles in the series, please visit www.routledge.com

Multilayer Corpus Studies

Amir Zeldes

Routledge
Taylor & Francis Group

NEW YORK AND LONDON

First published 2019
by Routledge
711 Third Avenue, New York, NY 10017

and by Routledge
2 Park Square, Milton Park, Abingdon, Oxon OX14 4RN

Routledge is an imprint of the Taylor & Francis Group, an informa business

Library of Congress Cataloging-in-Publication Data
A catalog record for this book has been requested

ISBN: 978-1-138-08253-3 (hbk)
ISBN: 978-1-315-11247-3 (ebk)

Typeset in Sabon
by Apex CoVantage, LLC

For Clara

Contents

Preface

This book came into being as a result of about ten years of work on building and evaluating increasingly complex corpora. Doing this work alongside some of the most wonderful colleagues I've ever had gradually led to the realization that we often ended up with resources that were much more than the sum of their parts. This seemed especially true for many of the research questions discussed in this book, relating to issues in discourse representation: how entities are introduced and mentioned as a text develops, how referring expressions are realized as particular kinds of pronouns or lexical phrases, how they are ordered and linked to specific grammatical functions in context or how the functional discourse purpose of utterances affects the realization of words and phrases. In project after project, while we were analyzing the same texts again and again using different frameworks and tools, it became apparent that some of the most complex questions we had about interactions between levels of representation, operationalizations of analyses for arbitrary data or even the question of whether some categories were really 'there', could only be answered by annotating data from different perspectives, comparing our results and feeding entire, richly annotated documents to multifactorial models. This meant having growing resources that expanded both horizontally to include more texts, genres and languages, and vertically as more annotations were added successively and needed to be merged with existing resources.

At the same time as doing this research, building tools, negotiating standards and learning what others were doing in related work, it became all the more conspicuous that there are few book-length descriptions of how multilayer corpora are built, why, what we can do with them and the level of predictive accuracy that the application of regression modeling and other machine learning techniques were achieving using such resources in computational and corpus linguistics. As a result, this book was conceived as a synthesis of two goals: going deeper into multilayer corpus architectures, their development and motivation, and showcasing some of the progress in multifactorial modeling, search, visualization and distant reading in ways that go beyond focused multifactorial studies of carefully tabulated cross-sections or excerpts targeting a single narrow phenomenon. The focus of this book is therefore less on multifactorial corpus work in corpus linguistics in general, and more on the unique challenges and opportunities of having complete running corpora annotated on potentially very many layers, both manually and automatically.

This research could not have been done without the support of very many people and organizations, to which I am deeply indebted. I would like to thank my mentors, Anke Lüdeling and Stefan Gries, who made me passionate about corpus building and multifactorial modeling, all while emphasizing the importance of looking at the words behind the data. I am also indebted to the Department of Linguistics and Georgetown College at Georgetown University, not only in general for being a supportive academic home and community, but also for supporting this book with the summer grant which resulted in writing the original book proposal for this volume.

My heartfelt thanks are also due to the many colleagues who discussed parts of this work at different stages and commented on various aspects of the book and the cases studies in it: Piotr Bański, Hans Boas, Richard Eckart de Castilho, Carolin Odebrecht, Anke Lüdeling, Paul Portner, Nathan Schneider, Mark Sicoli, Manfred Stede and Maite Taboada, as well as two anonymous reviewers and the series editors, Tony McEnery and Michael Hoey. Their feedback has been extremely helpful and often opened my eyes to ideas and directions that I completely failed to consider; the usual disclaimers apply, and remaining errors and oversights are, of course, my sole responsibility. I would also like to thank the staff at Routledge for helping to get this volume printed, and especially Elysse Preposi and Allie Simmons for making the publication process go so smoothly. Special thanks are due to my students at Georgetown who helped to prepare, check and improve much of the data used in this book, and in particular to the student annotators who helped to create the GUM corpus described in Chapter 3. The GUM annotation 'team' is fast approaching 100 contributors, of which the most up-to-date list can be found on the GUM corpus website. I would also like to thank Stephen J. Davis, Executive Director of the Yale Monastic Archaeology Project (YMAP), for permission to use the images of the manuscript fragment from the White Monastery in Chapter 7. Finally I would like to thank my family, Nina, Lia and Clara, for always being there for me and continuing to make life wonderful.

Amir Zeldes
Washington, DC, April 2018

Part I
The Multilayer Approach

1 Introduction

This introductory chapter offers both a discussion of definitions and underlying concepts in this book and a brief overview of the development of multilayer corpora in the last few decades. Section 1.1 starts out by delineating the topic and scope of the following chapters, and Section 1.2 discusses the notion of annotation layers in corpora, leading up to a discussion of what exactly constitutes a multilayer corpus in Section 1.3. In Section 1.4, early and prominent multilayer corpora are introduced and discussed, and Section 1.5 lays out the structure of the remaining chapters in this book.

1.1 What This Book Is About

This book is about using systematically annotated collections of running language data that contain a large amount of different types of information at the same time, discussing methodological issues in building such resources and gaining insight from them, particularly in the areas of discourse structure and referentiality. The main objective of the book is to present the current landscape of multilayer corpus work as a research paradigm and practical framework for theoretical and computational corpus linguistics, with its own principles, advantages and pitfalls. To realize this goal, the following chapters will give a detailed overview of the construction and use of corpora with morphological, syntactic, semantic and pragmatic annotations, as well as a range of more specific annotation types. Although the research presented here will focus mainly on discovering discourse-level connections and interactions between different levels of linguistic description, the attempt will be made to present the multilayer paradigm as a generally applicable tool and way of thinking about corpus data in a way that is accessible and usable to researchers working in a variety of areas using annotated textual data.

The term 'multilayer corpora' and the special properties that distinguish them from other types of corpora require some clarification. Multiple layers of annotation can, in principle, simply mean that a corpus resource contains two or more analyses for the same fragment of data. For example, if each word in a corpus is annotated with its part of speech and dictionary entry (i.e. its lemma), we can already speak of multiple layers. However, part of speech tagging and lemmatization are intricately intertwined in important ways: they both apply to the exact same units ('word forms' or, more precisely, tokens, see Chapter 2); determining one often constrains the other (*bent* as a noun has a different lemma than as a verb); in many cases one can be derived from the other (the lemma *materialize* is enough to know that the word was a verb, according to most annotation schemes for English); and consequently it makes sense to let one and the same person or program try to determine both at the same time (otherwise, they may conflict, e.g. annotating *bent* as a noun with the lemma 'bend'). Multilayer corpora are ones that contain mutually independent forms of information, which cannot be derived from one another reliably and can be created independently for the same text by different people in different times and places, a fact that presents a number of opportunities and pitfalls (see Chapter 3). The discussion of what exactly constitutes a multilayer corpus is postponed until Section 1.3.

Multilayer corpora bring with them a range of typical, if not always unique, constraints that deserve attention in contemporary corpus and computational linguistics. Management of parallel, independent annotation projects on the same underlying textual data leads to 'ground truth data' errors – what happens when disagreements arise? How can projects prepare for the increasingly likely circumstance that open-access data will be annotated further in the future by teams not in close contact with the creators of the corpus? How can the corpus design and creation plan ensure sufficiently detailed guidelines and data models to encode a resource at a reasonable cost and accuracy? How can strategies such as crowdsourcing or outsourcing with minimal training, gamification, student involvement in research and classroom annotation projects be combined into a high-quality, maintainable resource? Management plans for long-term multilayer projects need to consider many aspects that are under far less control than when a corpus is created from start to finish by one team at one time within one project and location.

What about the information that makes these corpora so valuable – what kinds of annotation can be carried out and how? For many individual layers of annotation, even in complex corpora such as syntactically annotated treebanks or corpora with intricate forms of discourse analysis, a good deal of information can be found in contemporary work (see e.g. Kübler and Zinsmeister 2015). There is also by now an established methodology of multifactorial models for the description of language data on many levels (Gries 2003, 2009; Szmrecsanyi 2006; Baayen 2008), usually based on manually or automatically annotated tables derived from less richly annotated corpora for a particular study. However, there is a significant gap in the description of corpus work with resources that contain such multiple layers of analysis for the entirety of running texts: What tools are needed for such resources? How can we acquire and process data for a language of interest efficiently? What are the benefits of a multilayer approach as compared to annotating subsets of data with pertinent features? What can we learn about language that we wouldn't know by looking at single layers or very narrowly targeted studies of multiple features?

In order to understand what it is that characterizes multilayer corpora as a methodological approach to doing corpus-based linguistics, it is necessary to consider the context in which multilayer corpus studies have developed within linguistics and extract working definitions that result from these developments. The next section therefore gives a brief historical overview of corpus terminology leading up to the development of multilayer approaches, and the following section discusses issues and definitions specific to multilayer corpora to delimit the scope of this book. Section 4 offers a brief survey of major contemporary resources, and Section 5 lays out the roadmap for the rest of the book.

1.2 Corpora and Annotation Layers

Although a full review of what corpora are and aren't is beyond the scope of this book, some basic previous definitions and their historical development will be briefly outlined here, with the intention of serving as a background against which to delineate multilayer corpora. In the most general terms, corpora have been defined as "a collection of texts or parts of texts upon which some general linguistic analysis can be conducted" (Meyer 2002: xi). This definition and others like it (see Meyer 2008 for discussion) are framed in functional terms, where the intent to perform linguistic analysis is paramount. More specifically, the idea that specific criteria must be involved in the selection of the texts, making them a purposeful sample of some type of language, is often cited: Sinclair (1991: 171), for example, defines a corpus as a "collection of naturally occurring language text, chosen to characterize a state or variety of a language". The idea of characterizing or representing a specific language variety as a kind of sample was later echoed in the formulation that Sinclair proposed for the definition advocated by EAGLES (Expert Advisory Group on Language Engineering Standards) in the 'Preliminary Recommendations on Corpus Typology', which maintains a status as an international standard. There, a corpus is seen as "a collection of pieces of language that are selected and ordered according to explicit linguistic criteria in order to be used as a sample of the language" (see also McEnery et al. 2006: 4–5 for discussion).

In the electronic format, ordering is often flexible, but the initial choice of corpus design is given special prominence: Results based on corpus research will always apply in the first instance to 'more data of the same kind' (Zeldes 2016a: 111). What the sample should be representative of has been debated extensively (see Biber 1993; Hunston 2008), but generally it is understood that the research question or purpose envisioned for a corpus will play a pivotal role in deciding its composition (see Hunston 2008; Lüdeling 2012). As we will see in the next section, design considerations such as these require special care in multilayer resources, but remain relevant as in all corpora.

Annotation layers are often one of the main 'value propositions' or points of attraction for the study of language using empirical data (Leech 1997). Although we can learn substantial amounts of things from ostensibly unannotated text, even just having tokenization, the identification of meaningful basic segments such as words in a corpus (see Section 2.1 in the following chapter), is of immense use, and in fact constitutes a form of analysis, which may be defined as a type of annotation. Formally, we can define corpus annotations in the most general way as follows:

An annotation is a consistent type of analysis, with its own guidelines for the assignment of values in individual cases.

This definition is meant to include forms of tokenization (assigning boundaries consistently based on guidelines, with values such as 'boundary' or 'no boundary' between characters), metadata (annotating the genre of a text out of a set of possible values) or what is perhaps most often meant, the addition of labels (tags from a tag set, numerical values and more) to some parts of corpus data (tokens, sentences or even higher-level constructs, such as adding grammatical functions to syntactic constituents, which are themselves a type of annotation). The stipulation of consistency in the analysis implies that the same analysis should be assigned to cases which are, as far as the guidelines can distinguish, 'the same'.

Some types of annotation layers are very common across corpora, with tag sets being subsequently reused and, ideally, the same guidelines observed. The classic example of this situation is part-of-speech (POS) tagging: Although many languages have a few commonly used tag sets (for English, primarily variants of the Penn Treebank tag set [Santorini 1990] and the CLAWS tag sets; see Garside and Smith 1997), no language has dozens of POS tag sets. Other types of annotations are very specific, with different studies using different schemes depending on a particular research question. For example, a comprehensive annotation scheme for coreference and referentiality which codes, among other things, ambiguity in the reference of anaphora was used in the ARRAU corpus (Poesio and Artstein 2008) but subsequently not widely adopted by other projects (in fact, coreference annotation is a field with particularly diverse guidelines, see Poesio et al. 2016 and Chapter 5). Often to study very specific phenomena, new annotation schemes must be created that cater to a specific research question, and these are regularly combined with more widespread types, resulting in the development of multilayer corpora. As Leech (2005: 20) points out, there is an argument "that the annotations are more useful, the more they are designed to be specific to a particular application". This often means that there is a tension between applying a range of standard annotation layers to help answer a certain research question because they are easy to produce and well understood, and developing new and tailored schemes that are a good fit for a research question but may be idiosyncratic, limited to the text type being investigated and make the resulting corpus less likely to be reused. The former strategy is often realized at least in part by using natural language processinng (NLP) tools and pipelines (for English, often software suites such as CoreNLP, Manning et al. 2014), whereas the latter are usually created manually by researchers, project staff or increasingly via methods such as crowdsourcing or class-sourcing (see Chapter 3).

With these basic definitions and sometimes conflicting motivations in mind, we turn next to consider what multilayer corpora are and what in particular happens when a corpus is designed, or comes to be expanded, to include a potentially unlimited amount of annotation layers.

1.3   What Does Multilayer Mean?

This book focuses on a relatively young paradigm in corpus linguistics and related corpus-based disciplines: the use of very richly annotated corpus resources, in which multiple, independent analyses coexist and can be harnessed together to produce more than the sum of their parts. It is difficult to give necessary and sufficient conditions for being a multilayer corpus. But as a first approximation, we can begin by saying that multilayer corpora are annotated digital collections of textual data (understood broadly to include transcribed conversational data, including sign language, and possibly accompanied by multimodal data), which are collected according to certain design principles (like other corpora, see the previous section) and are explicitly analyzed using multiple, independent annotation schemes. On the face of it, the term 'multilayer' with reference to independent annotation types would seem to imply that any amount of distinct annotations greater than one already satisfies membership in this category – why is a corpus with part of speech and lemma annotations not already 'multilayer'? For these two common annotations, it is relatively easy to show that the independence criterion is not satisfied, at least for common English annotation schemes. For example, the word *reading* can be tagged according to the Penn Treebank tag set (Santorini 1990) as the -ing form of the verb *read* (tag: VBG, lemma: read, e.g. *I am reading*) or as a singular noun (NN), in which case its lemma is the same as its word form (lemma: *reading*, as in *the reading*, plural *readings*); thus the layers are highly interdependent.

At the opposite extreme, we may feel inclined to rule out almost any corpus as multilayer, because some interdependencies can be found between most types of annotations. For example, many multilayer treebanks contain both syntax trees and entity annotation, marking up, for example, nominal phrases and names of people and places. It is easy to see that most named entities correspond to nominal phrases, such as *France* or *the prime minister of Canada*. However, the reason why such corpora are often considered multilayer nonetheless is that, conceptually, the relationship between the layers is not one of necessity, and they can be defined independently, despite the fact that entity annotation guidelines sometimes reference nominal phrases. To see this, consider what happens to nested, non-referential NPs on the one hand and to non-NP entities on the other. In (1), "a number of rocky outcrops" is annotated as a 'place', with no nested entities (i.e. 'rocky outcrops' is not annotated as well by itself). A constituent syntax tree for the same tokens following the Penn Treebank scheme is given in (2), showing the nested NP structure: "a number of rocky outcrops" and "rocky outcrops". It is clear both that a.) not every NP is marked up as an entity and b.) the entity type does not correspond to the head of the syntactic phrase (the entity type corresponds better to 'outcrops' than to the syntactic head 'number'; see Section 4.3 for more on this topic).

(1) *The Chatham islands consist of the main island, (. . .) and [a number of rocky outcrops]*$_{place}$ (GUM corpus)[1]
(2) (NP
    (NP (DT a) (NN number))
    (PP (IN of)
    (NP (JJ rocky) (NNS outcrops))))

As we can see in (2), treebanks annotated in the tradition of the Penn Treebank generally contain at least two layers of annotation in themselves: syntactic phrases (brackets and labels, and sometimes also grammatical functions such as 'NP-SBJ' for subject NPs) and part of speech tags. However, these are not generally regarded as multilayer corpora, and this is in fact congruent with the independence criterion outlined earlier. Although it is certainly possible to annotate corpora with POS tags without treebanking, the opposite is generally not true: There is a direct reliance on POS tags as terminal labels for the treebank, and most decisions cannot be made independently. For example, if we decide that 'hold' in (3) is a noun (tagged NN), then a syntax tree containing it will have an NP above that node, but not if we tag it as a verb particle (tagged RP).

---

1. Examples come from the Georgetown University Multilayer corpus (GUM, Zeldes 2017a, presented in detail in Chapter 3).

(3) *a new obsession is taking hold/RP|NN on the internet.* (GUM)

Conversely, if we are interested in linking mentions of entities for core-ference, such as the anaphoric relation between a pronoun and its ante-cedent, we may be forced to annotate non-nominal spans, which break the mapping between annotating discourse referents and POS tagging. In example (4), it is impossible to link the demonstrative 'this' to an anteced-ent without marking up the verbal antecedent 'count'.[2]

(4) *we [count every day how many ants died]. [This] gives us the data* (GUM)

In light of such examples, when can we speak of multilayer corpora, and what is considered sufficiently independent? In the most extreme case, inde-pendence can mean conflicting annotations of the same ontological types (e.g. multiple tokenizations, multiple part of speech tags, multiple conflicting error annotations or target hypotheses for learner corpora, see Chapter 7). But more often, we simply mean distinct annotation types that are conceptually independent of each other, for example, TimeML annotation for time expres-sions (marking up dates, durations and more, Pustejovsky et al. 2003) and discourse relations (marking one sentence or clause as the 'cause' of another, see Chapter 6). Although many discourse parsing frameworks offer relations that refer to sequential time (e.g. the 'sequence' relation in Rhetorical Struc-ture Theory (RST), Mann and Thompson 1988, or 'narration' in Segmented Discourse Representation Theory (SDRT, Asher and Lascarides 2003), it is intuitively clear that most of the decisions in each of these annotation tasks can be made independently, and it is realistic to expect separate teams at sepa-rate times and places to be able to annotate the same data coherently with-out consulting each other. In practice, although research across annotation layers can move in any direction, researchers employing multilayer corpora are often interested in harnessing 'lower-level', more predictable annotation layers (e.g. POS tagging, syntactic parses, etc.) to discover regularities in less approachable, more complex levels, such as discourse annotations.[3]

---

2. However, it should be noted that annotation guidelines could still refer to syntactic factors, such as selecting the VP without its subject, in this case 'we', as the antecedent. Nevertheless, in practice this type of annotation can be done largely separately from and without consulting a treebank, and in the GUM corpus, which is annotated for dependency rather than constituent syntax, this is also the case (see Section 3.2).

3. Burchardt et al. (2008: 389) echo this trend in exploiting multilayer corpora and point out that "the most common use of such corpora is the acquisition of statistical models that make use of the 'more shallow' levels to predict the 'deeper' levels of annotation". Taboada and Das (2013: 249), who view adding new annotation layers to a corpus as "[o]ne of the most frequent tasks" in corpus and computational linguistics, also note that not 'starting from scratch' is particularly important for "higher-level annotations, those 'beyond semantics', because they tend to rely on annotations at lower levels of discourse".

For multilayer corpora, caution in the choice of corpus design and criteria definitions used to collect the data is even more vital, because the effort involved in creating the rich analyses found in the corpus will be greater than in a corpus with minimal or no annotations. Additionally, the circumstances of annotation projects spanning time and space (later addition of information by other teams who did not create the corpus, see Chapter 3) mean that resources should be selected that are expected to remain relevant over time and are often selected to answer more than one narrow research question. This consideration is central to one of the key differences between a multilayer approach, on the one hand, and multifactorial approaches that extract limited datasets for further annotation, on the other (see Sauer and Lüdeling 2016). As Burchardt et al. (2008: 389) point out, one of the unique foci of multilayer corpus research is "the possibility to empirically investigate the interactions between different levels of linguistic analysis", which means that we gain access to complete, richly annotated texts rather than just a targeted cross-section restricted to certain cases.

The latter type of approach may be exemplified in a series of now-classic studies in multifactorial corpus linguistics on predicting the dative alternation (Bresnan et al. 2007; Bresnan and Ford 2010). Bresnan and colleagues annotated corpus data containing examples of the dative alternation (ditransitive *give Kim the book* vs. prepositional dative *give the book to Kim*) on very many different levels. Significant features used in the studies come from various positions in the construction (the recipient phrase, the theme or the verb itself) and include those outlined in Table 1.1.

Table 1.1 Some features used to predict the dative alternation by Bresnan et al. (2007)

Feature	Locus
animacy	recipient
person	recipient
definiteness	recipient and theme
givenness	recipient and theme
length difference (log scaled)	recipient and theme
pronominality	recipient and theme
pronominality	recipient and theme
number	theme
semantic class (e.g. 'transfer of possession')	verb
structural parallelism (e.g. previous use of a distransitive)	other

The features in the table are extremely successful in predicting the actual variant of the dative alternation that is selected in corpus data, mirroring important facts in the probabilistic grammars that speakers employ.[4] A corpus annotated with these features throughout would be a multilayer corpus (person, number, animacy for every NP are independent features from verb class; parallelism annotation would require some sort of grammatical analysis of every utterance using an independent scheme; etc.). However, the dative alternation data in these studies were annotated only for cases of the constructions in question. This means that the same dataset could not be used to study another phenomenon (e.g. the genitive alternation between *of* and genitive *'s*, see Gries 2002; Szmrecsanyi 2006; Gries and Wulff 2013 for some multifactorial accounts). It also means that we cannot use the same dataset to get baselines for different types of language behavior: Are long phrases generally placed later than short phrases (see Section 4.2)? Is this always mitigated by animacy and, if so, to what extent? In other words, where a targeted multifactorial approach already gives excellent predictions for a specific concern, it does not necessarily tell us whether and to what extent its predictors are surprising above and beyond the general patterns of the language in question.

Another consideration in viewing only a targeted, tabulated slice of the data is that we need to know in advance which cases we will be interested in – it is not possible to use such a table to explore a corpus by searching across annotation layers and inspecting visualizations of entire documents to get intuitive insights on phenomena of interest. In this vein, Redeker et al. (2012: 2823) note that exploring all of the layers in a corpus search makes having complete data available in one interface highly desirable, because "[t]he first thing novel users of a corpus want to do, is browse and explore the data and its annotation". They argue for the necessity of converting and merging layers from multiple formats (in their case, discourse annotations in Rhetorical Structure Theory, coreference annotations and syntax trees for a corpus of Dutch from expository and persuasive genres) in order to explore a unified representation across annotation paradigms.

Although it is probably the default assumption, it is not always the case that all layers cover the entirety of a multilayer corpus resource. For example, the Manually Annotated Sub-Corpus of the Open American

---

4. In fact, in the subsequent study in Bresnan and Ford (2010), it was found that these predictors differ in subtle ways across varieties of English, for example, with Australian English exhibiting greater preference for the prepositional dative, even in the face of length differences between NPs that would promote the other choice for American speakers. This is just one illustration of why having a large number of annotations can be very important.

National Corpus (MASC, Ide et al. 2010) was initially created with full coverage of POS tags and lemmas, syntactic chunks and sentence annotations as well as named entities, but only parts of the corpus were annotated for frame semantics, Head-driven Phrase Structure Grammar (HPSG) and Penn-style parses, discourse annotations, PropBank semantic annotations, TimeBank temporal expression annotation, coreference and more. The goal in such cases is often to grow smaller annotated datasets to the full corpus size, but this can be complicated by difficult annotation layers, especially when resources are scarce. The more crucial property of multilayer data is indiscriminate, broad coverage: annotations in MASC are not restricted to a specific construction, sparsely annotating cases that are chosen selectively. Systematically leaving out certain parts of the data, by contrast, compromises the conceptual ability to analyze the properties of a layer as it applies to unrestricted language within the scope of the corpus. Avoiding this is a prerequisite to studying the properties of an annotation layer as a whole, as well as its interactions with other layers.

A frequent complication arises for the data collection and annotation of multilayer corpora in cases in which it is clear that data processing and exploitation will exceed or outlive the limits of the group or project in which a resource is initially created. From a legal, copyright-sensitive perspective, resources should ideally be chosen that will remain accessible to further teams across international copyright law borders (cf. Hunston 2008). From a technical perspective, too, standard-conformant, well-documented formats are essential to ensuring the success of a resource over time. In the present-day landscape of corpus resources, some of the most used and re-annotated datasets are those that have had high quality, and often very labor-intensive information value, while respecting these principles. Prominent examples are the Switchboard corpus (Godfrey et al. 1992) and the Wall Street Journal corpus (see Marcus et al. 1993) annotated as part of the Penn Treebank project. The underlying texts have been repeatedly annotated to add more and more layers of information, creating richly annotated multilayer resources for users with the right tools to perform the analysis.[5] Table 1.2 gives a (non-exhaustive) selection of prominent expansions to these two corpora.

---

5. In many cases, however, the necessary technology for evaluating the separate layers of information is absent, and users either focus on individual layers for their purposes or use dedicated scripts to traverse the data and extract the information they seek. More often than not, there will actually be inconsistencies in the base text data across annotations done with different tools and at different times, and these may only be discovered through the attempt to merge multiple layers (see Chapter 3 for detailed examples, pitfalls and approaches to solving these).

Table 1.2 Extended annotations of existing treebanks

Corpus	Annotation layers	Reference
Wall Street Journal	Rhetorical Structure Theory	RST Discourse Treebank, Carlson et al. (2001)
	Coreference and named entities	OntoNotes, Hovy et al. (2006)
	Discourse signal markers	RST Signalling corpus (Taboada and Das 2013)
Switchboard	Disfluencies	Meteer et al. (1995)
	Dialog acts	Stolcke et al. (2000)
	Animacy	Zaenen et al. (2004)
	Information status	Nissim et al. (2004)
	Prosody and ToBI breaks[6]	Calhoun et al. (2010)

The data in corpora such as the Penn Treebank is very well documented and understood, and its availability in easily accessible formats facilitates its use. However at the same time, its underlying text is not freely available (Wall Street Journal data, under copyright and licensed by the Linguistic Data Consortium). This means that most institutions using the data rely on an institutional subscription providing access to the underlying resource, which may limit the portability and longevity of a resource. For example, when the Universal Dependencies project launched modern, open-source, dependency-annotated corpora for dozens of languages (Nivre et al. 2017), the English treebank chosen for re-annotation as a gold dependency treebank was the English Web Treebank (Silveira et al. 2014), rather than the more well-known Penn Treebank (Marcus et al. 1993), because only the former could be released under an open Creative Commons license (the data are available under the CC-BY-SA 4.0 license, see http://universaldependencies.org). Although licensing issues have no bearing on what is or isn't a multilayer corpus, there is a strong current trend to prefer open-access resources as underlying data for new projects (see Chapter 3).

In some cases even basic 'ground truth' data (see Chapter 2 for discussion of this concept) is extended in multilayer corpora: For research on continuous speech recognition, portions of the Wall Street Journal corpus were read out loud and recorded, even though the original data were

6. ToBI, or Tones and Breaks Indices, is a minimal annotation scheme for indicating prosodic contours and groups of intonational units, which has been adapted to many languages, see Beckman et al. (2005).

purely written text (Paul and Baker 1992), effectively adding a multimodal layer. Such projects do not necessarily come about because the language of the Wall Street Journal or the Switchboard telephone conversations is the optimal choice as a dataset for working on spoken language, but because the quality and accessibility of an underlying resource (historically, particularly treebanks) bring with them the opportunity of capitalizing on existing annotation layers. The same logic applies to retrofitting existing prominent corpora with annotation layers following the guidelines of another existing project, as in the case of the addition of texts from the Brown corpus (Kučera and Francis 1967) to the Penn Treebank in Version 2 (Marcus et al. 1995).

1.4   A Brief Historical Survey

Although it is impossible to give an exhaustive overview of the corpora to date that qualify as multilayer within the scope of this book, in this section I will review some of the more prominent examples that have driven the development of current multilayer data models historically. At least three English terms have been used more or less interchangeably to refer to multilayer approaches: Early on, we find both 'multilevel' and 'multi-tier' next to multilayer, with the latter term especially in Germany (as well as German *Mehrebenen-* in *Mehrebenenkorpus* 'multilayer corpus'). As far as I am aware, the earliest usage of the term 'multilayer' in the relevant sense comes from early attempts to enrich spoken dialog corpora with annotations above the level of phonetic transcription. Citing orthographic, morphosyntactic, syntactic, prosodic and pragmatics annotation 'levels', Gibbon et al. (2000: 5) assumed "that all the different levels of annotation above need to be integrated in a *multilayer structure*, and linked through relative or absolute time alignment to the sound recording" [my emphasis]. However, many of the same concepts already appear in Gibbon et al. (1997) in the context of the design of the VERBMOBIL corpus (Hess et al. 1995), which was created to support the development of machine translation and simultaneous interpretation for English, German and Japanese. The focus on spoken data was possibly due, on the one hand, to the prominence of corpora in speech research (as opposed to syntax and semantics research, which was more centered on introspective generative grammar at the time), and on the other hand to the fact that time alignment in transcribing and annotating speech naturally harmonizes with the idea of adding independent but aligned annotations at different levels. These ideas were implemented in annotation tools such as PRAAT (Boersma and van Heuven 2001) and other early grid-based tools, such as Partitur (Schiel et al. 1998), which later led to the development of annotation toolkits for multimodal data and field research, such as ELAN (Brugman and Russel 2004), EXMARaLDA (Schmidt 2004) and SIL's Shoebox/Toolbox tools (see http://www-01. sil.org/computing/toolbox/).

The idea to re-annotate corpus data for an unbounded set of layers, including multiple and potentially conflicting part-of-speech layers, appears in Fligelstone et al. (1997: 125), who developed a generic, extensible and reusable tagger:

> [T]he program should support *multiple levels of annotation*, but we did not wish to pre-judge the range of types of annotation [. . .] We see the normal operation of the tagger as accepting text with *n* levels of annotation and allowing the user to add one or more levels of annotation to this [my emphasis].

Of the annotations themselves, they add that the "term 'level' is used here to signify a *type* of information. Just as there is no pre-defined set of levels, nor is there any implicit structure or hierarchy of levels. The user is at liberty to use any number of levels".

In the following years, the development of multilayer resources went hand in hand with advances in textual data representation formats, which were powerful enough to represent extensible corpora with arbitrary collections of annotation layers. Much of the initial work on multilayer corpora was connected to a move from inline annotation strategies, in which running corpus text was interleaved with annotations, first to XML (e.g. TEI XML),[7] which separated markup from primary textual data clearly, and then to stand off XML formats. The specifics of inline vs. stand-off XML and some more recent developments are discussed in detail in Chapter 3. Briefly stated, inline annotation strategies, such as adding the part of speech after each token (e.g. the/DT dog/NN), were sufficient when annotations were relatively few; however, the explosion of annotation possibilities in the 2000s, and particularly of structures that broke XML hierarchies, led to the design of corpora in which annotation layers could be encoded independently in separate files (standing apart from the text, hence 'stand-off').

One of the first openly available multilayer corpora was the HCRC Map Task corpus, originally created at the University of Edinburgh

---

7. TEI XML (http://www.tei-c.org/, see Ide and Sperberg-McQueen 1995 for an early historical overview), the format developed by the Text Encoding Initiative (see also Section 3.2). Although some corpora following multilayer designs have used TEI successfully, the restrictive nature of TEI schemas, which allow only specific combinations of elements with constrained semantics, often makes the format problematic for multilayer data (see Chapter 3).

in the early 1990s (Anderson et al. 1991). The corpus contains fully transcribed, elicited spoken dialogs between an instruction giver and an instruction follower using a map. Over the course of a decade, many annotation layers were added to the corpus, resulting in what the corpus creators then called 'heavily annotated data'.[8] These included POS tagging and syntax trees, but also dialog moves (e.g. instructing, explaining, clarifying, etc.), disfluency annotation and 'reference coding', a scheme referring to mentions of landmarks appearing in the maps used for the elicitation. By virtue of being a multimodal corpus, further annotation layers relating to the Audio/Video (A/V) signal were also possible, including gaze annotation and time-aligned audio. To represent and query the annotations the NITE toolkit and the NITE XML stand-off format were created (see Carletta et al. 2003) as part of the NITE project (Natural Interactivity Tools Engineering, funded by the EU in 2001–2003).

In parallel to annotation formats, annotation tools for multilayer data were developed in the late 1990s beginning with GATE (General Architecture for Text Engineering), designed to provide a "software infrastructure on top of which heterogeneous NLP processing modules may be evaluated and refined individually, or may be combined into larger application systems" (Cunningham et al. 1997: 238), and the MATE Workbench (Multilevel Annotation Tools Engineering), which was designed to "annotate any kind of data, as it is not dependent on any particular annotation scheme" (Isard et al. 2000: 411). The tools also concentrated on development of speech corpora (see Isard et al. 2000).

The developments in re-annotating major reference treebanks such as the Penn Treebank, and specifically the components of the Wall Street Journal and Switchboard corpora already mentioned in the previous section, gained momentum in the 2000s and followed very much the same progression, but using parallel aligned formats rather than stand-off XML. The OntoNotes corpus (Hovy et al. 2006), for example, contains multiple files for each document, giving Penn Treebank–style parses, PropBank proposition annotations, coreference annotations and so on in a mixture of XML and text-based formats, some of which are also given in succession for each sentence within a single file. However, iterative re-annotation is by no means the only path to multilayer data, and many corpora were constructed as multilayer resources from the outset or shortly thereafter, such as the ACE corpora (Mitchell et al. 2003)[9] or MASC (Ide et al. 2010), as well as the GUM corpus (Zeldes 2017a) used for many of the examples in this book.

---

8. See http://groups.inf.ed.ac.uk/maptask/#info, accessed 3 January 2017.
9. The ACE corpora were developed for Automatic Content Extraction applications and contain annotations for syntax, entities, relations between entities, coreference and event annotations.

For languages other than English, the development of multilayer corpora has followed similar patterns, primarily in the more heavily resourced Germanic, Romance and Slavic languages. On the one hand, existing major treebanks have been a hotbed of activity: For example, for German, the Tiger Treebank (Brants et al. 2002) was used as a basis for the SALSA corpus (Burchardt et al. 2006), which was extended from syntax, morphology and grammatical function to include frame-semantic annotations, as well as annotation of idioms, metaphors and light-verb constructions. The Potsdam Commentary corpus (Stede 2004; Stede and Neumann 2014), by contrast, is an early example of a German treebank for which information structure, referring expressions, coreference and rhetorical structure annotations were developed concurrently and merged within the same project (see Chapter 3 on merging issues). For Czech, the Prague Dependency Treebank (Bejček et al. 2013) contains not only POS tags and syntax trees, but also annotations of modality and diathesis (active/passive voice, resultatives and more), and has been more recently extended with coreference and bridging annotations, as well as discourse relations similar to the Penn Discourse Treebank (Prasad et al. 2008). The Rhapsodie Treebank for French (Gerdes et al. 2012) contains speech data annotated at multiple, hierarchically conflicting layers of orthography, phonetic transcription and prosodic information, as well as enriched dependency trees represented as directed acyclic graphs (DAGs), which are subsequently all merged into a single representation for search and visualization.

Multilayer approaches are also becoming widespread in historical and learner corpora. Beyond the use of complex TEI XML to encode manuscript structure around the text, historical corpora are now increasingly merging manuscript representations with syntactic treebanks, either within the TEI standard (e.g. Höder 2012 for Old Swedish) or in several parallel formats (e.g. Heiden 2010 for Old French). For historical German, multilayer corpora include the richly annotated Mercurius Treebank (Demske 2007); T-CODEX (Petrova et al. 2009), which contains grammatical function, information structural annotations, alignment to Latin equivalents and more; as well as the reference corpora of Old, Middle and Early Modern High German (see http://www.linguistics.rub.de/comphist/projects/ref/), which support multiple, conflicting segmentations of data to account for modern and historical orthographic conventions (see Chapter 2 on multiple segmentations and Chapter 7 for consequences for historical data). For Classical Arabic, the Quranic Arabic corpus, which already encompassed a morphologically annotated dependency treebank early on (Dukes and Buckwalter 2010), now contains an entity annotation layer linked to the Ontology of Quranic Concepts. And for the Coptic language of first-millennium Egypt, a richly annotated corpus, including conflicting segmentations, morphological analysis, dependencies and manuscript annotations, is being created as part of the project Coptic Scriptorium (see Schroeder and Zeldes 2016, and Chapter 7 for a case study using this corpus).

Multilayer learner corpora first emerged around the concept of error annotation (see Granger 2003) and target hypotheses (Lüdeling et al. 2005, see also Chapter 7), because multiple versions of the same data (errors and various possible corrections) naturally create unbounded and potentially conflicting data structures. More recent learner corpus work has been incorporating syntax trees next to error annotations, as well as multiple, conflicting annotations of the same layer types. Ragheb and Dickinson (2012) discuss dependency annotation of learner data containing errors, as well as multiple conflicting POS tags for the same data. The Hong Kong City University Corpus of English Learner Academic Drafts (Lee et al. 2015) has tagged and lemmatized successive drafts of essays, annotated for errors by tutors and aligned across versions at the word and sentence level, including annotations for words that were inserted or subsequently deleted across versions. For German as a second language, Falko (Reznicek et al. 2013), the error-annotated learner corpus of German, has multiple independent layers of target hypotheses in addition to tagging and dependency parses of learner texts and target hypotheses, as well as annotations documenting differences between learner data and postulated target data. A very similar architecture has also been applied to comparable L2 data in Czech, German and Italian in the MERLIN corpus (Boyd et al. 2014).

Although this section is only able to give a glimpse of the breadth of corpora currently available, it is hoped that it has illustrated the increasingly wide range of resources and the rapid spread of richly annotated multilayer data to a variety of fields of linguistics. Data models, tools and research methods that support and benefit from this type of approach are becoming much more widely available, and the remainder of this book is meant to survey the underlying concepts that have emerged in the past few years, and then put them to use in a series of multilayer corpus studies.

1.5   Plan for This Book

This book is structured in two parts: the chapters in Part I introduce terminology and methodology, surveying general developments and best practices in work with multilayer corpora. Researchers familiar with recent multilayer corpus data models and technology may wish to skip ahead to Part II, which presents a series of studies showcasing some of the approaches that working with multilayer data makes possible and investigating specific issues in linguistics across layers of information, especially in the domain of inter-sentential phenomena and discourse modeling.

The remaining chapters of Part I give an overview of data models for multilayer annotation before moving on to the detailed case studies in Part II. Chapter 2 discusses the abstract building blocks of data models and unique aspects in applying familiar corpus concepts to the multilayer environment, such as word forms, tokens and annotation graphs; different ontological types of nodes, edges, labels and meta-labels in multilayer corpora; and subgraph types such as trees, directed acyclic graphs (DAGs), and multi-DAGs (or 'forests' of DAGs). Chapter 3 is a more concrete discussion of corpus architectures and handles issues of data collection and primary textual data, white space preservation and aligned multimodal data, formats and standards for the representation and merging of positional annotations and metadata and issues pertaining to visualization as it depends on technical architectural choices. The chapter centers on the case of the GUM corpus used in some of the examples noted earlier, detailing methodological issues in the construction of a complex multilayer resource while merging and validating inputs from multiple tools and formats automatically.

Part II consists of four detailed explorations of multilayer corpus data. Chapter 4 explores the relationship between syntax annotations, morphological agreement, word order and information structure (topicality, focus and givenness). Starting from questions about the competition between givenness, subjecthood, active/passive voice and phrase length in determining word order, a multifactorial model is constructed based on running annotations of all phrases in a corpus. The chapter then continues to construct a predictive model for a highly unpredictable alternation in English morphology: notional agreement for singular/plural anaphora referring back to collective nouns and other unusual NPs. Chapter 5 examines the relationship between different types of discourse referents and the ways in which they are introduced, referred back to and co-indexed across coreference links in a multilayer corpus. The chapter explores the effects of genre on coreferentiality, develops visualizations for distant reading of patterns of coreferentiality and constructs a predictive model for the likelihood of an NP having an antecedent, based on a large number of concurrent annotation layers. Chapter 6 focuses on discourse relations in the framework of Rhetorical Structure Theory (Mann and Thompson 1988). It also explores the interaction of genre with typical patterns of discourse organization and introduces a quantitative framework for identifying 'referential hotspots', in which we may expect referring expressions to be mentioned repeatedly based on the discourse graph. This chapter also presents an interpretable neural network-based model for the identification of markers signaling discourse relations in context, which is compared and contrasted with previous quantitative work on signaling in discourse parses using frequency distributions. Chapter 7 explores applications of multilayer approaches to 'non-standard' language, including historical and non-native data. The former is used in harnessing manuscript structure for the study of Coptic fragments, as well as a Variationist study on the use of Greek loanwords in Coptic. Then in learner corpora we examine non-native use of German compounds through the use of target hypotheses, as well as investigate the phenomenon of textual revision in a corpus of Chinese essay drafts in English as a Foreign Language (EFL) with multiple aligned revisions submitted by the author of each text. Chapter 8 concludes the book and points to some future directions for multilayer corpora.

2 Foundations

In this chapter, key issues of underlying data models for multilayer corpora will be examined in more detail. Although the chapter's primary goal is to discuss the technical infrastructure and limitations of multilayer corpora, readers primarily interested in the results of the studies in the second part of this book may find it useful to refer back to some of the definitions and data modeling assumptions laid out here.

A discussion of corpus linguistics terminology as it applies to multilayer corpora is essential, and potentially tricky, due to the fact that multilayer resources undermine some of the tacit assumptions that most corpus resources work with. These include, for example, the atomicity of word forms as 'tokens', non-overlap of tokens, the negligibility of white space in written data and many other issues that are often not problematic. Because there are many good previous discussions of these concepts (e.g. Meyer 2002; McEnery et al. 2006, and the articles in Lüdeling and Kytö 2008–2009; O'Keeffe and McCarthy 2010), I will focus here on special issues in the design and implementation of data models for multilayer data, as they will be used in the following chapters.

2.1 Words, Tokens, Types and Annotations

Whereas most studies in corpus linguistics are interested in phenomena from the level of the word and up, many others are concerned with phenomena below the word level, and increasingly, it is realized that very many factors in the immediate or long-distance context co-vary with targeted constructions (see e.g. Plag 2010 for a multifactorial account of stress assignment in compounds, or Säily 2011 on the productivity of English affixes and the influence of complex variables, to name just two examples). In such cases, we must contend with a basic segmentation of the data into digitally processable units; for written data, this usually means dealing with tokens that are not words, including not just punctuation, but also morphemes within words, whereas spoken and multimodal data must contend with silences and non-linguistic events between and during linguistic utterances.

For the basic unit of analysis, there is general agreement on the use of the term 'token'. This term has (at least) a twofold meaning: It is used to refer to the running units of a corpus ('word forms') and to distinguish observations of instances ('tokens') from sets of instances ('types', see e.g. McEnery et al. 2006: 52). The latter sense of tokens remains largely the same for multilayer corpora, except that care must be taken to distinguish whether two tokens belong to the same type depending on which annotation layers are considered: Two instances may be identical and belong to the same type with respect to a certain subset of their annotation layers, but if some additional layer is included, they may be construed as belonging to different types by virtue of distinct combinations of features.

The other use of the term 'token', meaning a basic unit of running text, is substantially more complex in a multilayer environment. There is usually agreement on treating tokens as units which are *atomic* (i.e. can contain no sub-units) and above which all forms of analysis may be added. The standard case for most corpora is captured in Schmid's (2008: 527) definition: "Tokens are words, numbers, punctuation marks, parentheses, quotation marks, and similar entities". Krause et al. (2012: 2), by contrast, focus on tokens as any type of indivisible 'atoms', saying: "By definition a token is the smallest unit of a corpus". This means that although tokens are usually the same as word forms, this does not have to be the case. For a morphological or phonological study we may certainly define smaller units, such as morphemes, syllables or phonemes, or even each individual character of the digital text, for example, when we wish to annotate a single letter as an illuminated capital in a historical manuscript (see Chapter 7). In some cases we may have only larger units than words: some studies in Rhetorical Structure Theory (RST), for example, have been concerned with the interrelations of sentence and clause units known as Elementary Discourse Units (EDUs), without necessarily analyzing individual words within them (see Taboada and Mann 2006 and Chapter 6). In fact, one of the most popular formats for representing RST analyses, the rs3 XML format, contains no information about word-form tokenization whatsoever; rather, entire clauses are annotated as having certain rhetorical functions (see Section 3.2). Tokens are therefore not only the smallest units, they also more specifically form the smallest *annotatable* units, making their delimitation all the more crucial for a multilayer data model.

It has been repeatedly noted that in many complex corpora, the simple definition of tokenization as the 'smallest annotatable unit' is insufficient (Chiarcos et al. 2009; Krause et al. 2012), leading to terms such as 'subtokenization' for units below the standard word form (e.g. Guo 1997; Wu 2010: 372) and 'supertokens' for larger units (Lambert and Banchs 2005; Chiarcos et al. 2009). The latter are often white space–containing compounds, multiword expressions or complex names, such as separate 'wall paper' next to orthographically fused 'wallpaper', or 'New York'. Krause et al. (2013) analyze such cases and note that at the level of the underlying data model, issues with complex tokenization typically relate to three problems:

- Visualization
- Adjacency
- Context

In discussing these, I will follow Krause et al. (2012) and reserve the term 'token' from now on for a truly minimal unit in the data model and use 'segmentation' to refer to any layer of annotation that can be considered to supply some alternative basic units of the analysis (cf. Krause and Zeldes 2016).

Of the three problems, visualization is perhaps the simplest, because it only concerns ergonomics for human reading of corpus data containing tokens that do not correspond to word forms. As a simple example, consider the case of page annotations in a historical corpus representing a manuscript or print edition, in which a page break occurs in the middle of a word – for example, the word *everywhere* in Figure 2.1. We may want to display the word in a hyphenated form across two pages if we are visualizing a diplomatic edition of an original artifact (panel A). But in another context, we may just want to reproduce a normalized version of the words in a certain passage, while ignoring page breaks and other distractions (panel B).

We may then wish to store two alternative versions of the split text, with and without a hyphen, or we may have some mechanism to visualize a hyphen when a split occurs. But in either case, in the underlying data model the two split parts of the word must be represented as separate on some level, because otherwise we cannot recover the correct position of the page break. In other words, the span corresponding to the characters

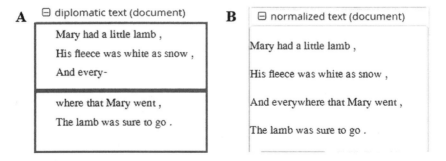

Figure 2.1 Alternative visualizations for a word form segmented by a page break annotation

for 'where' in 'everywhere' must be a separate token in order for us to annotate the page break as occurring before it.

Although this example may seem limited to interests in representing typographical layouting, this type of problem is actually common in a variety of scenarios, including normalization of variants in historical and non-standard or spoken data, whenever clitics are spelled together (if we think of part of speech tags for 'wanna') or in cases of syncope and even in many standard spellings of contractions. A standard spelling of most English contractions, such as *'m* and *n't* already presents problems of normalization and lemmatization, as in (5), but some contractions contain units that are harder to isolate, as in (6), and in some more extreme cases, it is not clear that any segmentation of the base text will produce the desired tokenization, as in (7). Table 2.1 gives some possible segmentations and part-of-speech analyses for these utterances using the Penn Treebank tag set (Santorini 1990), which make it clear that minimal units can be more complex than a segmentation of the surface-form string of an utterance.

(5) *I'll do it*
(6) *I won't do it then*
(7) *I'ma do it* (contracted for *I'm going to do it*)

The problem with (6) is that we postulate a token 'wo' for the sake of consistency with the behavior of the corresponding positive form 'will' or contracted ''ll'. This segment is separated from the negation 'n't', preserving its autonomy, although 'wo' is not a valid segment outside of its connection with 'n't'. The problem with (7) is, however, greater: If we follow the analysis in (7), which is certainly not the only possible solution, we may want to normalize the 'a' segment to two separate units with distinct POS tags: the progressive 'going' and the infinitive marker 'to'. This might be desirable in order, for example, to

Table 2.1 Tokenization, normalization and POS tags for (5)–(7)

(5) transc	I	'll	do	it		
norm	I	will	do	it		
pos	PRP	MD	VB	PRP		
(6) transc	I	wo	n't	do	it	then
norm	I	will	not	do	it	then
pos	PRP	MD	RB	VB	PRP	RB
(7) transc	I	'm	a		do	it
norm	I	am	going	to	do	it
pos	PRP	VBP	VBG	TO	VB	PRP

parse the data using a parser trained on standard written English, or in order to express the functions that the construction shares with the 'going to' construction. If we follow the segmentation in the table, the underlying tokens (i.e. minimal units) are not expressible except by separating the issue of transcription visualization (showing a user the 'a' as transcribed) and the data model tokenization, which requires two units to carry the distinct POS tags.

The second problem associated with tokenization in a multilayer environment is that of adjacency, which follows closely from the previous discussion. For example, should we consider example (6) to contain a word starting with 'w' adjacent to the verb 'do'? If 'won't' is a single word, then this case is a match for a search for words in 'w' followed by 'do'; otherwise, not. The problem initially appears to be related to an unclear formulation of what we mean by 'word'; but it is compounded in the case of (7). If we consider what will happen when we ask whether a progressive verb form is adjacent to a verb in (7), we will see that in terms of both word forms and the basic segmentation of the data, a progressive VBG form is in fact included in a segment adjacent to the VB segment. But VBG does not cover the entire segment preceding the VB. We therefore need to be very precise in our formulation of queries when searching in a multilayer corpus of this type: Items can be adjacent *with respect to a certain segmentation* but not with respect to another. VBG is not adjacent to VB on the 'pos' layer. But it can be regarded as adjacent to the word 'do', or even the tag 'VB', on the 'transc' layer, in the sense that there are no intervening units on the transc layer between the two. They are not perfectly adjacent, in the sense that there exists a segmentation S on which there are filled intervening segments, where S is in this case the 'pos' layer.

The same point applies to intermittent conversation in spoken data. If we are dealing with data from multiple speakers, a similar situation arises, depicted in Table 2.2.

In this case, too, there are multiple ways in which the distinctions noted earlier can be helpful. On the layers of speaker A's transcription, we could say that 'see' and 'but' are adjacent, in the sense that 'but' is the next thing speaker A said after 'see'. However, on the 'time' layer, they are clearly

Table 2.2 Multiple layers for dialog data

spkA	I	see			but	actually		
posA	PRP	VBP			PRP	RB		
spkB							you	know
posB							PRP	VBP
events		[phone rings]						
time	00:03.1	00:04	00:04.2	00:05.6	00:07	00:07.5	00:08	00:08.1

not adjacent: Two other things happened. The first was the second part of a phone ringing, which had begun at the same time as 'see'. The second is a silence of 1.4 seconds, with no filled events except for the timeline itself. The multilayer nature of the data, in which phones ring or are silent completely independently of the uttered words, forces us to be precise and to define the segmentation layer of reference for a term such as 'adjacent'. Other related concepts, such as 'within n words/tokens', overlap, etc., are affected in similar ways and can be discussed with respect to particular layers.

Finally, the problem of context stems directly from the problem of adjacency but has a rather different outward result. It is common when searching in corpora to consider a term of interest within a context of $\pm n$ words or, more precisely, tokens. In working with complex segmentations like those noted earlier, the window size of $\pm n$ words becomes trickier to define. Naively, taking ± 3 tokens, in the sense of minimal units, would produce the following left context for a search for the word 'then' in example (6):

(8) *n't do it then*

In this case, we can easily reconstruct what has happened, but in some more complex cases we may get rather confusing 'half words'. In many languages (notably Semitic languages, such as Arabic or Hebrew), fused elements are not predictable from their continuation, such as prepositions spelled together with nouns. More problematically still, in cases such as (7), when a context word is not entirely within the window but only part of its constituting data model units fall within context, it is not clear what a corpus search result includes. The same applies to the example in Table 2.2: If our context units extend from the target word 'see' to include the timestamp 00:07.5 at 4 units later, should the word 'actually' be considered part of the result? And because any of these spans can be annotated, retrieving and evaluating all annotations within the search area quantitatively will lead to very different results depending on the reference segmentation for determining context.

Here too, the answer is therefore to select a layer on which context is defined: We can get ± 5 time units, ± 5 'Speaker A' units or even more complex computations to get ± 5 words of 'any speaker', where the presence of a speaker word from any speaker 'consumes' a context position, until we reach 5. In all of these cases, inclusion is well defined with respect to the layers in question, even if different numbers of units result on other layers.

2.2 Representing Primary Data

The last section demonstrated some of the challenges involving segmentation of running text, but we have not yet considered properties of what this basic text is and how it is represented in a multilayer environment. All corpora begin with some kind of primary data: the text that we categorize and annotate to express our analyses. However, it is not always trivial to tell what the primary data are: In a newspaper corpus filled with articles, the words or characters of the text as it was printed in the newspaper are generally seen as the primary data. Further details, such as the layout of the newspaper, the fact that some words were in a headline or the position of a picture may be considered annotations from a linguistic standpoint, or may be ignored altogether. But even in the example of a picture placed within a newspaper article, problems crop up: Is a picture not itself a primary datum of the newspaper's contents? Is text within an image part of it? How about multimodal data accompanying a dialog? Is the recording of a conversation the primary data, or is it the transcript of the same conversation? What about translations of texts – is a translation an annotation or is it an equal partner to the source-language text, a piece of primary data in itself?

To each of these questions there can be multiple answers, and we can defend each decision with appropriate reasoning. Unsurprisingly there is no absolute answer, and what ultimately determines a specific answer will be our own research needs or applications. For example, for a biblical historian working on the stemmatology of the Greek New Testament, an English translation is, if at all necessary, merely a convenience attached to the 'real' data, the Greek text. For such a scholar the translation is an annotation and not a primary datum. The same text, for a researcher in translation studies, can be of equal importance in both languages, because the object of study might be the translation process, which depends on properties of both languages. If we wish to annotate data in both languages for such a study, it is reasonable to consider both text streams as sources of primary data. A good data model will be able to express either preference clearly.

To understand the importance of data models for primary data in multilayer corpora, we can look at some problematic cases. One example of primary data being mixed with what is more properly an annotation can be found in the Penn Treebank's (Marcus et al. 1993) bracketing format and its use of special symbols to indicate empty categories, such as *pro* (for dropped subject pronouns), *PRO* (for unexpressed subjects of infinitives), traces (for postulated movement in a deep structure) and more. One dilemma presented by these is that, although they are not visibly present in the text stream, the theoretical framework used to annotate them postulates that they are ordered with respect to the text. For example, in the following tree excerpt from the Wall Street Journal corpus, there are two empty categories at the two next-to-last tokens: a '0' tagged as -NONE- standing in for an omitted *that* (i.e. "*researchers said *that**"), and a trace

'*T*-2', indicating that the direct speech has been fronted (we have a fronted "*crocidolite is . . . resilient . . ., researchers said*", rather than "*researchers said crocidolite . . .*"):

```
( (S
    (S-TPC-2
      (NP-SBJ
...
          (NP (NN crocidolite) )
          (, ,) )
        (VP (VBZ is)
          (ADJP-PRD (RB unusually) (JJ resilient) )
...
      (, ,)
      (NP-SBJ (NNS researchers) )
      (VP (VBD said)
        (SBAR (-NONE- 0)
          (S (-NONE- *T*-2) )))
      (. .) ))
```

For a non-multilayer treebank, this representation is fairly clear, though problems can still occur. There is in fact an instance in the Penn Treebank in which a literal token '0' appears, making it look like an empty category (WSJ, document 1269):

```
(NP
  (NP (DT a) (NN vote) )
  (PP (IN of)
    (NP
      (NP (CD 89) )
      (PP (TO to)
        (NP (CD 0) )))))
```

Although the POS tag 'CD' allows us to recognize the problem, this is not optimal and reveals some of the issues that led to the development of standardized XML formats in which markup and primary data are clearly distinguished. Omitting the distinction at the text level also complicates the application of machine learning algorithms that apply directly to running text (e.g. using character embeddings, see Section 6.4).

Greater problems arise when we try to merge multiple formats with different handling of primary data (see also Section 3.4). For example, Penn Treebank brackets unambiguously encode actual brackets in the text using the sequences -LRB- (for Left Round Bracket) and -RRB- (Right Round Bracket), but tokens containing these may correspond to actual brackets in other formats. Because a bracket is a single character and -LRB- comprises five characters, even offset-based formats not encoding the actual text directly will conflict if we do not take care to encode differences between representations correctly. Another common pitfall is formed by XML escapes: Because XML uses angle brackets to denote elements and ampersands to mark XML entities, these symbols must be replaced by codes such as > (greater-than symbol, for '>') or & for the ampersand, whereas the same characters in a non-XML format are usually represented directly. Software interpreting XML properly will make such conversions automatically, but failing that, errors can occur.

Multimodal data also present substantial difficulties for primary data representation. For a phonetician or a researcher working on signal processing in computational linguistics, an audio signal may be the most pertinent information. For a syntactician or a computational linguist working on automatic question answering, sound files may provide added features for the words they are analyzing in a corresponding transcription. In the construction of multilayer corpora with A/V data, the multimodal signal streams are often understood as an accompanying form of time-aligned annotation, corresponding to time indices such as those in Table 2.2. However much of the discussion presented here will be applicable to some extent to continuous ratio-scaled or numerical annotations that can be applied to audio data, be it categorical schemes assigned to the audio stream such as ToBI (Tones and Break Indices, see Beckman et al. 2005) or exact measurements such as F0 and amplitude taken from the spoken stream itself. A similar conflict can be observed in gesture annotation of transcripts, and even more so in corpora of sign languages (see Crasborn and Sloetjes 2008; Schembri et al. 2013), where a video recording is the most direct representation of language data and the transcription of signs is an exceptional surrogate.

For all of these cases I will nevertheless distinguish a notion of one or more streams of primary data, which will be the subject of 'annotations' or more generally interpretative analyses. Just as primary data can be controversial and multifaceted, so can annotations, and we now turn to examine these in more detail.

2.3   From Markup Spans to Graphs

In the previous two sections, we examined tokenization and multiple segmentations through a mark-up-like lens: Certain spans of the text can be seen as segments, and certain annotation layers coincide with or cover those spans of text. For example, in Table 2.2 a POS annotation with the value 'VBP' spanned the word 'see' and the associated time indices, while the phone's ringing overlapped and overflowed the same position. However, we did not explicitly discuss any interconnections between these layers. For example, it is reasonable to say that the POS annotations 'belong' to the speaker layers on some level, but not to the events layer. In fact, *posA* belongs only to *spkA*, whereas *posB* belongs to *spkB* only. The grid as portrayed in the table does not give this information: The connection between *spkA* and *posA* is just the same as between *spkA* and *events*, and the compatibility of span lengths between the former and not the latter is a coincidence. If we wish to enforce *spkA* and *posA* having equal spans, we must introduce a more complex data model than just aligned spans in a grid, and this model will have the properties of a graph.

As an example of a corpus using an annotation graph model, next I will use GUM, the Georgetown University Multilayer corpus (Zeldes 2017a), which is collected and annotated by students as part of the curriculum at Georgetown University (in other words, it is a 'class-sourced' corpus, see Section 3.1; the corpus itself will be described in more detail in Section 3.2). Much of the discussion in this section therefore follows the organization of Salt (Zipser and Romary 2010), the data model used to represent GUM as well as a variety of other resources, but general terminology and comparisons will be used to establish widespread abstract mechanisms found in multilayer corpus models.

At its most general formulation, a graph is just a set: $G = (V, E)$, where V is a collection of vertices or 'nodes', and E is a set of edges connecting those nodes. More specifically in corpus annotation, we usually also add at least a concept of a set of annotations A (sometimes called labels L, e.g. Zipser 2009; Zipser and Romary 2010), usually containing a simple key–value pair each, but potentially also more complex data types, such as feature structures (see e.g. ISO24612 and Section 2.4). Additionally, some data models add grouping mechanisms to linguistic annotation graphs. Often these are realized as XML namespaces, employed, for example, to distinguish annotation structures coming from one inventory or another, such as using general TEI XML vocabulary (www.tei-c.org/) next to project-specific annotation. For example, Höder (2012) extends existing TEI element and attribute names to annotate a treebank of Old Swedish, with annotation layers representing manuscript structure and phrase structures (using pure TEI tags), and morphological annotations specific to Old Swedish using an additional layer of information containing custom annotation names and values.

Some corpus processing tools offer programmatic (non-XML) constructs to group annotations, such as SLayers (Salt Layers) in Salt or feature structure types in a Common Analysis System (CAS) in Unstructured Information Management Architecture (UIMA, see Götz and Suhre 2004).These often group together data coming from different NLP or annotation tools (e.g. using UIMA CAS in the multilayer NLP tool-chain DKPro, Eckart de Castilho and Gurevych 2014). In a merged multilayer corpus, such grouping mechanisms can be used to delineate annotation layers, including conflicting versions of the same type of annotation – for example, separate layers denoting syntax trees following two different annotation schemes, or produced by different automatic parsers. Layers can also be used to facilitate user access to annotation values, for example, by supplying helper functions to list possible label values within a layer selected by the user (see Diewald et al. 2016). I will use L to denote the set of layers in the following discussion. An annotation graph employing all of these concepts is then:

$$G = (V,E,A,L)$$

Given these basic building blocks, there are many different constraints that can be, and often are, imposed on the combinations of these elements. Some data models allow us to attach annotations only to nodes or also to edges; some data models even allow annotations of annotations (e.g. Dipper 2005), which opens up the possibility of annotation subgraphs expressing, for example, certainty or provenance of annotations (see Eckart de Castilho et al. 2017). Layers, too, can have different ontological constraints, including whether layers can be applied only to nodes or also to edges and annotations and whether layer-to-element mapping is 1:1 (e.g. DKPro's data model) or whether an element can belong to multiple layers (e.g. Salt).

Figure 2.2 gives an illustration of the annotation graph of a corpus fragment taken from GUM for the two tokens "I know" and showing a large part of GUM's multiple layers: multiple POS tags and lemmatization, sentence segmentation and rough speech act, document structure in TEI XML (paragraphs, headings, figures, etc.), separate constituent and dependency syntax graphs, information status annotations (given, accessible, new), entity and coreference annotation and Rhetorical Structure Theory analyses. All of these are interwoven to produce a rich annotation graph.

At an abstract level, the boxes in Figure 2.2 represent general graph nodes from the set V. The two tokens in the boxes at the bottom of the image are somewhat special nodes in that they carry both a variety of annotations (part of the set A) and references to textual data (I and *know*). Their annotations include three distinct POS tags based on different tag sets, as well as the lemma and grammatical function annotations. The token nodes also function as anchors for the remaining nodes in the graph: Every other node in the figure is attached directly or indirectly to the tokens via edges from E. Layers from L are represented by ovals; in this case, the tokens have not been placed in any layer, but all other nodes and edges belong to exactly one layer. For example, there is a dependency edge at the bottom of the figure connecting the two tokens and carrying a label (func=nsubj, because I is the subject of *know*). This layer contains only an edge and no nodes. Conversely, a single-sentence node above the tokens is annotated as s_type=decl (declarative sentence) and is attached to both tokens, but the edges attaching it to the tokens

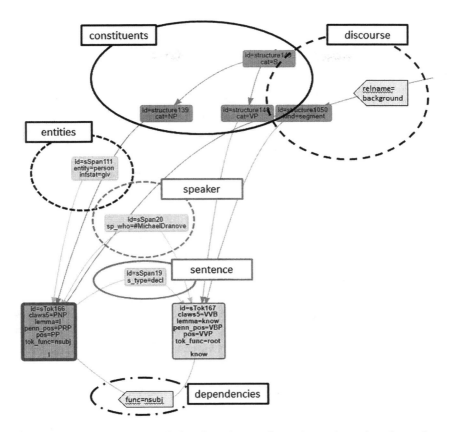

Figure 2.2 Annotation graph for the tokens *I know* in an interview from the GUM corpus

are unannotated. Finally, some layers, such as the constituent layer, contain a complex subgraph: an NP node is attached to the token *I*, and a VP node to *know*, and together they attach to the *S* node denoting the clause. Similarly, the discourse layer, of which we only see one incoming edge, is the entry point into the discourse-parse part of the graph, which places multiple tokens in segments and then constructs a subgraph made of sentences and clauses based on RST (Mann and Thompson 1988; see Chapter 6).

Another point of interest in Figure 2.2 is that it is strictly the corpus designer's decision which elements are grouped under a single layer. For example, the constituent annotation *S* for the clause has a very similar meaning to the sentence annotation in the layer just above the tokens, but these have been modeled as separate (and in fact annotated separately). As a result, it is at least technically possible for the corpus to have conflicting constituent trees and sentence span borders. Similarly, a speaker annotation is attached to both tokens, as is the sentence annotation, but it is conceivable that these may conflict hierarchically: A single sentence annotation may theoretically cover tokens belonging to different speakers, which may or may not be desirable (e.g. for annotating one speaker completing another's sentence). This is the technical realization of the notion of independent layers on the data model side, mirroring the theoretical distinction outlined in Section 1.3.

The graph structure presented here is quite complex, but its creation can actually be kept comparatively simple through the use of multiple, simple annotation tools and automatic merging (see Section 3.4). Although the data model does not force us to use single, mutually exclusive layers, in practice the layers used in GUM are created in different interfaces and source formats: The dependency annotations were edited using the Arborator (Gerdes 2013), entity annotations come from the WebAnno tool (Yimam et al. 2013) and RST annotations from rstWeb (Zeldes 2016b). Because the same primary data were analyzed in all tools, merging the subgraphs into a larger graph anchored in the same underlying text can be done without manual intervention.

Using a graph structure can simplify the way we think about complex corpora, because different kinds of information can all be reduced to the same types of objects: labeled nodes and edges. However, some aspects of different annotation layers still mandate ontological differences between types of annotations. We have already seen that tokens have a special place in the ontology of nodes, because they are minimal units and carry implications for ordering, adjacency and context. Similarly, other nodes and edges may have special properties: For example, constituent syntax trees contain hierarchical nodes such that if a phrase points to another phrase or token, we may want to say that it *contains* it. Other types of edges imply no such containment: For example, coreference relations annotating that 'she' may be a reference to 'Mary Poppins' do imply a relationship between these expressions, but we would not say that the node corresponding to 'she' *contains* 'Mary Poppins'. Differences of this kind are sometimes expressed in graph-based models of corpus annotation, and it is to these that we turn next.

2.4   Ontological Types of Within-Document Annotations

In this section I will discuss some of the different types of objects that multilayer corpora often contain, with a focus on graph-topological consequences for corpus architecture. The focus here is not on particular XML formats, etc., but on abstract data model categories (for discussion of specific serialized representations, see Chapter 3). As in the previous section, the point of view largely follows the Salt data model perspective of Zipser and Romary (2010).

Tokens and Token Annotations

One of the earliest and most common types of annotations is the addition of some categories to each token in the corpus. Common examples of token annotations are part of speech tags and lemmatization, giving a morphosyntactic category and uninflected dictionary entry form for each unit in the corpus (see Newman and Cox, to appear, for an overview). In most multilayer architectures, it is possible to assign some annotations to only some tokens, and this can make sense, for example, for morphological categories: If we have a tense annotation, it is usually applied only to verbs. However, often all tokens in a corpus will have the same range of annotations, and either empty values will be assigned to tokens not carrying an attribute (e.g. tense="-"), or compound tags will be used which only fill certain categories for each kind of token. For example, in the MULTEXT-East Morphosyntactic tag set for Russian (see Erjavec 2012), hyphens are used for unfilled categories. A Russian plural demonstrative pronoun эти 'these' can be tagged 'P---pna' using only 4/7 possible inflectional slots: the first 'P' identifies it as a pronoun, and the final 'pna' designates a plural nominative used adjectivally. The three hyphens are place-holders for the categories pronoun type, person and gender, which are left underspecified based on guidelines.

Although token annotations are relatively simple, there are some non-trivial design decisions in modeling them, which can lead to different results. First, annotations can be attached either directly to tokens (true token annotations) or they can be attached to non-terminal elements directly above each token (single-token spans). A key difference between these strategies is that multiple true token annotations are necessarily attached to the same node in the graph (the token), whereas single-token spans can be applied again and again to the same token, creating a set of distinct graph nodes that merely happen to cover the same token set. Depending on the format and software used to evaluate the data, these will produce different results. In particular, true token annotations can form part of a query path beginning at a higher-level node, such as a syntactic phrase (see later on syntax trees). A syntactic node, such as an NP, will then dominate not just the token, but also its annotations – this case is portrayed on the left in Figure 2.3(A). In this example, because 'loud'

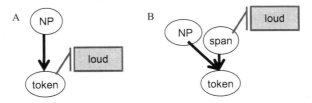

Figure 2.3 A true token annotation in A is dominated by an NP. In B, the annotation is placed on a separate single-token span and is not dominated by the NP

is a feature of the token itself, we can say that the NP node dominates a 'loud' annotation (or more precisely, the node to which that annotation is attached). Adding a single-token span above a syntactically dominated token will not have this effect, as shown in (B): An NP's dominance over a token will not directly reveal that it is dominating something 'loud', because that property actually belongs to the separate span node above the token.

Span Annotations

After token annotations, spans are the most common type of annotation found in corpora in general. When spans are allowed to conflict, they also form the basis of many multilayer corpora, because conflicting spans allow us to annotate any number of phenomena that apply to any contiguous sequence of tokens. This paradigm is implemented in most grid-based annotation tools, such as ELAN (Brugman and Russel 2004) or EXMARaLDA (Schmidt 2004), and produces data structures similar to Table 2.1.

Rows in such a table can correspond to logically distinct annotation layers, and generally speaking, there is no special order to spans of this kind: Although we may have a preferred viewing order for grid rows, we cannot assume that a larger span in a high row of the table 'dominates' the annotations of smaller spans lower in the table. In other words, an annotated span merely implies that some property applies along a specific segment of text. For example, if a token, or several tokens, are annotated with a span indicating that they were uttered loudly (as in Figure 2.3), and a separate span indicates that some tokens overlapping the first span were providing new information unfamiliar to the hearer, we could not say that the 'newness' annotation contained the 'loud' annotation, or vice versa. In fact, their spans may only overlap partially and can conflict in such a way that we cannot say which one might contain the other.

More complex types of spans that are less frequent but sometimes found in multilayer corpora include discontinuous spans and spans not matching tokenization borders. In the former case (supported e.g. by formats such as PAULA XML, Dipper 2005), we can still speak of a single annotatable span covering some tokens, but the token indices need not be consecutive. The property being annotated applies only to the covered token indices. The latter case occurs in formats that allow a span to refer to independent character offsets, without 'snapping' to token borders (e.g. WebAnno, Yimam et al. 2013). Although there can be practical applications for such representations, they are usually the result of using the 'token' concept to model what is really more like a 'word form', with other span borders converging with some smaller unit of analysis (e.g. individual letters within a word). Based on our working definition of tokens as 'atomic' or minimal units of analysis earlier in this chapter, the actual tokenization in such data models corresponds to the most granular character-offset borders used in the corpus, that is, to the span borders in this case. Another possibility is that in such a data model, each character can be viewed as a token (see Lüdeling et al. 2005).

In cases where multiple borders are of interest as basic units of analysis (e.g. space-delimited word forms vs. smaller tokens, including clitics spelled together with adjacent units), we can think of specific spans as offering alternative segmentations of the same data (see Krause and Zeldes 2016). As mentioned earlier, architectures supporting multiple segmentations can treat such spans as the relevant unit of measurement when specifying search context sizes ('all occurrences within ±5 space-delimited word forms/morphemes/other types of tokens', etc.) and similarly for visualization purposes (showing a context size of ±5 units of some span). Spans therefore play an important role in defining the unit of measurement for distances in such applications.

Trees and Dominance Relations

Whereas spans are unordered elements that merely 'cover' an area of the data, some annotation layers integrally require the concept of ordered 'containment'. Formally, we refer to this type of connection between a superordinate and a subordinate unit as 'dominance', but the concept can informally be thought of as stating that a complex higher unit 'consists' of lower units. For example, in constituent syntax trees, a sentence can consist of an NP and a VP node, which may consist of other syntactic nodes, all the way down to token nodes (which are atomic and therefore may not dominate other nodes).

Some simpler formats for syntax annotation, such as Penn Treebank brackets, treat labels such as 'NP' as if they literally are the non-terminal nodes; however, multilayer corpora recast such structures in a more generalized approach, treating phrase nodes as underspecified nodes, to which a phrase category annotation is attached (e.g. a non-terminal structure carrying an annotation cat="NP"). This allows us to add more than one annotation to each node. The same applies to dominance edges, which can carry annotations as well, depending on the way in which our corpus is modeled: For example, we can mark that a phrase is the subject of the sentence on the NP node (e.g. in the Penn Treebank, a label such as 'NP-SBJ'), or we can annotate the edge connecting the higher sentence node (in a Penn-style tree, the category 'S') to the NP with an edge annotation denoting its function, for example, func="SBJ".

Properly speaking, trees may never include structure sharing (a node being dominated by two different parents in the graph) or crossing edges, but these are in fact used in many multilayer corpora. If the graph contains violations of these tree constraints but does not contain any cycles, we can speak of a directed acyclic graph (DAG). Although the overwhelming majority of corpora preclude cycles (not least of which because these make the evaluation of the corpus very complex – which nodes can be said to dominate which?), some architectures allow different types of edges to form cycles. For example, as shown in Figure 2.4, a syntax tree may contain an NP ('a buyer') dominating a relative clause ('who') which contains a pronoun ('his'), while a coreference edge (dashed arrow) links that pronoun back to the NP head. If we take the syntax tree to mean that the NP points to its constituents, then we have a cycle formed of syntactic dominance edges pointing downward from the NP all the way to the pronoun and then back up by means of the coreference edge. In this situation, we speak of a Multi-DAG (or Forest of DAGs): Each edge type component is acyclic within itself, but cycles may form across edge types. Some corpus search systems that support this type of structure do not allow for indirect dominance queries across multiple cycling edge types, for example, the ANNIS search and visualization platform, which was used to generate Figure 2.4 (see Krause and Zeldes 2016 and Section 3.5 for more information).

Pointing Relations and Alignment

Although spans and dominance graphs cover a substantial portion of the data modeling needs for building and evaluating multilayer corpora, not all annotation graphs express the notion of 'dominance' or 'containment'

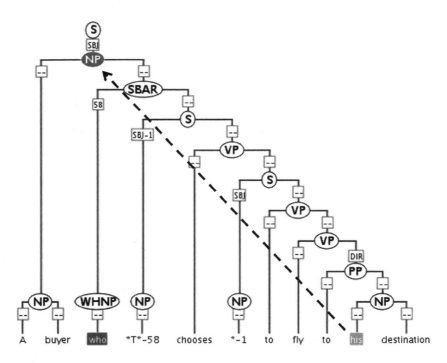

Figure 2.4 Syntax tree for an NP from the Penn Treebank, which contains a pronoun that can be annotated as referring back to the entire NP

described in the previous section. In fact, the example of a coreference edge provided earlier already violates that definition: We would not say the word 'his' in Figure 2.4 'contains' or 'consists of' the NP that it is pointing too. Edges of this type, which do not imply containment, are referred to as 'pointing relations' – instead of dominating, they merely connect a source node and a target node (see Chiarcos et al. 2008).

At this point we may ask whether all edges might not be representable as pointing relations: Why should the syntax tree above not also consist of pointing relations? The answer is that for constituent trees, we expect different behavior from our corpus data model. If we want to know the text that the highest NP corresponds to, we expect to be given the entire text ('A buyer who chooses to fly to his destination'). This is because we wish to retrieve any text covered by any node dominated (directly or indirectly) by the NP. The same is not true for the coreference relation: If we wish to retrieve all text dominated by the token 'his', we would not expect to get back 'A buyer'. This is because dominance relations imply inherited text coverage, but pointing relations do not. Although some data models do not distinguish ontological edge types (e.g. GrAF, Ide and Suderman 2007) and leave the interpretation of different edge annotation names to software processing–specific edge names, other data models explicitly distinguish such relation types (e.g. Salt, or PAULA XML; see Chapter 3 for more on specific formats).

Another special type of relation that is sometimes treated as a pointing relation is alignment edges. Alignment between data in different translations of the same text (in parallel corpora) or other types of alignment (e.g. of the same words in different versions or revisions of the same text, see Lee et al. 2015) also do not imply inherited textual coverage or constituency. For example, if French *maison* is aligned to an English translation *house* in some text, we would not say that *maison* 'consists' of *house* in any way. Alignment edges can be seen as directed, in which case we might have separate edges from French to English and from English to French, or they may be bidirectional (e.g. the data model for the Stockholm TreeAligner, Lundborg et al. 2007, an annotation tool used to align parallel treebanks). In a generalized multilayer corpus architecture, we will treat all edges as directed in order to avoid cycle issues; as a result, we follow Zeldes et al. (2013) in treating parallel alignment as a type of directed pointing relation, and bidirectional alignments as pairs of edges with distinct types.

Feature Structures and Meta-Annotation

So far we have mainly treated annotations as simple key–value pairs, possibly grouped into layers. For example, a morphosyntactic annotation layer may contain a case annotation and a number annotation, both of which hold some string values (e.g. 'nominative' and 'plural'). However, some data models allow for more complex annotations, which are themselves structured. The broadest class of such annotations is formalized in the concept of feature structures, which are a properly nested subgraph of nodes, possibly carrying key–value pairs, which are subsequently attached to nodes within the document graph. For example, in GrAF (Ide and Suderman 2007), feature structure values are used to combine morphological features into single complex annotations, such as verbal morphology tags for verb chunks, as in the following excerpt from the MASC corpus (Ide et al. 2010, using tags from the Verb Group Chunker component of GATE, Cunningham et al. 1997):

```
<node xml:id="vc-n24"/>
<a xml:id="vc-N65979" label="vchunk" ref="vc-n24" as="anc">
  <fs>
    <f name="voice" value="active"/>
    <f name="tense" value="SimFut"/>
    <f name="type" value="FVG"/>
  </fs>
</a>
```

This feature structure denotes an active voice, simple future, finite verb group. Substantially more complex feature structures are generated by LFG and HPSG parsers, which analyze entire utterances in terms of a complex feature structure (e.g. CoreGram, Müller 2015).

Additionally, some data models allow annotations of annotations (e.g. Dipper 2005), sometimes referred to as 'meta-annotations' (not to be confused with metadata, see the next section). Meta-annotations also implement a form of annotation subgraph, because an annotation of an annotation can be seen as dominating (or being dominated by) that annotation. Although such devices are not frequent, they are sometimes used to express concepts such as provenance (see Eckart de Castilho et al. 2017), that is, marking the source of an annotation (e.g. a label with an annotator's name or an anonymized identifier) or conveying the certainty of an annotation (either a categorical label such as 'uncertain' or a numerical likelihood estimate of annotation accuracy).

In many cases, the same kinds of information we find in annotation subgraphs can be expressed using regular annotations and/or layers: For example, the Stockholm TreeAligner mentioned in the previous section uses regular edge annotations to express annotation certainty using the labels 'fuzzy' versus 'good' for the alignment. Annotation sources are often marked using a grouping layer rather than a meta-annotation, for example, a layer denoting all output from an annotator or NLP tool, such as a 'Stanford' layer for POS tags and parse trees coming from the Stanford Parser (Socher et al. 2013).

2.5 Document and Corpus Metadata

Although metadata is, in the first instance, any kind of 'data about data' (Lehmberg 2008: 492), the term is usually applied to properties of entire corpora, documents or perhaps speakers within documents (Schmidt and Wörner 2009: 572). In principle, we can think of a complete corpus as one big annotation graph, starting with the main corpus node at the top, potentially subcorpora below that and then documents, each of which can contain a multilayer annotation graph. In such a view, there is no special reason to distinguish between annotations within a document and metadata. However, in practice, virtually all corpus architectures encapsulate within-document annotations and metadata separately, so that the term metadata is not applied to annotations of elements within the document graph, such as phrase labels or token annotations.

Some of the concepts described for other annotations earlier may nevertheless be applied to metadata: Metadata is sometimes grouped into layers or a similar concept; some architectures may allow multiple, conflicting values of the same metadatum for the same document (for example, multiple 'language' annotations if a document contains multiple languages or code switching). Frameworks with highly complex metadata, such as the TEI standard (http://www.tei-c.org/), use nesting and feature structures within metadata, resulting in a metadata subgraph (in TEI, the contents of the 'header') set apart from the document body's annotation graph.

In the context of multilayer corpora, care must be taken that metadata coming from tools generating a single annotation layer are not unintentionally mixed with metadata originating in other layers. As a trivial example, consider a 'tool' metadatum giving the source annotation tool: in a merged corpus, we may wish to include information about all source tools involved in the creation of the dataset, but we may need to rename this metadatum, or at the very least ensure that multiple values are adequately represented. In some cases, conversion and merging can render certain metadata fields incorrect or misleading: If there is a 'format' metadatum in one source format out of many used in a multilayer corpus, we will almost certainly want to rename or possibly even archive this information, because the final corpus will no longer be in the format specified in the original metadata.

2.6 Interim Conclusion

As we have seen, many of the basic notions and enduring debates in corpus linguistics apply to multilayer corpora as well, but complications can become compounded when multiple layers coalesce to form a multilayer corpus. Although the scope of the present discussion cannot do justice to many of these debates, there is extensive literature on the abstract concepts involved in previous works (e.g. Reppen et al. 2002; McEnery et al. 2006; Biber and Conrad 2009; O'Keeffe and McCarthy 2010; and for a recent overview of complex annotation types see especially Kübler and Zinsmeister 2015).

In practice, a large portion of the modeling choices that go into multilayer data and subsequently influence the types of studies that can be undertaken is often co-determined by the choice of available annotation tools and the properties of their corresponding formats. Choosing to compromise data model integrity can be justified if it means working with a more suitable tool, and as we will see in the studies in the second part of this book, some inconvenient concessions often result. For example, many spoken corpora containing dialog do not model speaker overlap, and instead place overlapping utterances in the order in which they begin. This may not influence studies of the vocabulary in a corpus, but it can have an effect when larger contexts are examined, especially in the context of discourse studies. Because of the centrality of concrete corpus serialization formats and merging data from different annotation tools, Chapter 3 will discuss these next by dissecting the construction of the GUM corpus as an example, which will also be used for several of the studies in the later chapters of this book.

3 Tools, Formats and Multilayer Data Collection

In this chapter I will apply the abstract concepts presented in Chapter 2 to some concrete corpus models, looking at specific formats, tools and data collection strategies. Much of the discussion will be informed by the architecture and construction process of one of the main corpora used in this book, the Georgetown University Multilayer corpus (GUM, Zeldes 2017a), and other corpora will be used for pertinent aspects and challenges of multilayer methodology not addressed in that corpus.

3.1 Collecting and Annotating Multilayer Data

Raw data collection and corpus design for multilayer corpora are initially no different from how we collect data for all corpora: Representativeness and balance with respect to a target population (Biber 1993; Crowdy 1993; Hunston 2008) should be considered when choosing texts, and the relationship between the data and the research questions they can answer is critical (cf. Reppen 2010; Lüdeling 2012). As there is excellent literature on corpus design for a variety of data types (see the chapters in part II of O'Keeffe and McCarthy 2010), I will not reiterate the topics here, but rather focus on several aspects that specifically affect multilayer corpora: licensing for multilayer data, the use of interoperable standards to scale datasets, broadening the scope of annotations using NLP tools, crowdsourcing and class-sourcing and special issues in the handling of non-standard data from historical and non-native texts.

Licensing and Multilayer Data

Making corpora freely available is becoming a frequent goal of corpus designers (e.g. Broda et al. 2012; Habernal et al. 2016),[1] although

---

1. Habernal et al. (2016: 914) write about corpus data for the development of NLP tools specifically that "[o]ne of the big obstacles for the current research is the lack of large-scale freely-licensed heterogeneous corpora in multiple languages, which can be re-distributed in the form of entire documents".

determining copyright conditions as they apply to any given text is non-trivial (see McEnery et al. 2006: 77–79). An astoundingly large portion of the work using multilayer corpora uses just a handful of well-known or easy-to-obtain resources, such as the LDC (Linguistic Data Consortium) licensed OntoNotes corpus (Hovy et al. 2006, for English, Chinese and Arabic) or the freely available ANC/MASC corpora (English only, Ide et al. 2010).[2]

One of the reasons why freely available data are particularly important for multilayer corpora is the issue of reusability: Many complex corpora come into existence by a gradual process of adding new annotations to existing resources. Although few research groups have the resources to annotate a sizable amount of data for ten different categories, a group wanting to examine one specific type of annotation can benefit immensely from concurrent existing annotations when they select an already available corpus for further annotation. This is most often the case when researchers choose an existing treebank, with complete syntactic analyses, as the basis for a further annotation project (e.g. the use of the Wall Street Journal corpus in OntoNotes, or of the tagged and constituent parsed English Web Treebank in the Universal Dependencies project, http://universaldependencies.org/). However, this situation is only possible if the latest research group has access not only to previous annotations (which are sometimes released separately from the text) but also to the underlying raw data.

The easiest way to ensure that we are allowed to re-annotate existing data is to select corpora with explicit open-access licenses, such as Creative Commons licenses (https://creativecommons.org/), and conversely, choosing such licenses for our data ensures that others can extend our corpora in the future. This ultimately benefits both researchers adding annotations to the corpus and the original corpus designers, who may now benefit from further layers of annotation. Although working with freely available data is desirable, for some research questions it is often not possible: Spontaneous conversation data must almost always be collected by researchers (see Adolphs and Knight 2010), and written public-domain data are often old and unsuitable for studying contemporary language (McEnery et al. 2006: 77). However, for many research questions, very recent data from the Web is often used as a form of fair academic use (usually for non-commercial applications). Web data often also offer text types not found anywhere else, making them irreplaceable for some linguistic research questions. A prominent example, which is also widespread due to its easy availability, is tweets

2. Van den Bosch (2009: 863–864) argues that "the distribution of corpora in the literature follows the Pareto '80%-20%' rule: 80% of all work uses 20% of the available corpora". He refers to the Penn Treebank (Marcus et al. 1993) as the most widely used dataset. In multilayer work, OntoNotes, which is partly based on the Penn Treebank, probably assumes this role in a similar way.

from Twitter, which represent a rather unique genre with unique annotation challenges (see Gimpel et al. 2011). However the licensing situation of Twitter data is problematic, and often leads to anntoations being distributed with only tweet IDs, meaning that researchers must recover the raw text themselves. On the other hand, many kinds of web data, including Twitter,also have the advantage of offering an indelible, replenishing supply of text, meaning that corpus size can be gradually expanded as needed.

Standards and Scalability

A second important consideration in making multilayer data available for further annotation is the use of well-documented, accepted standards, which make the interchange of data and its conversion for use with new annotation tools easier. Many corpus projects use annotation tools developed within the same group producing the corpus, which are tailored to the task that interested the group. A potential problem with this situation is the danger of using highly idiosyncratic data models or representations, which make it less likely that further researchers will be able to extend the data.

Some technical considerations already discussed in Chapter 2 feed into this issue: For example, source data integrity and white space preservation can be crucial if further annotation layers will require more exact representations of the underlying text than a previous annotation step makes available. For this reason, it is important to maintain representations that are as raw as possible of the source data (or, failing that, at least to retain copies of original sources) and to use formats which allow access to this information (see Section 3.3 for a comparison of some formats). Another technical issue is the use of annotation scheme-specific devices in ways that are not well separated from the source text. A typical example is the use of empty category tokens, such as traces and empty pronouns, in the Penn Treebank scheme, shown in Section 2.2. Although a syntax tree can be built to integrate such categories in a sensible way, further annotation layers that assign categories to 'every token' may not have sensible values to assign to these empty categories, and even if they are skipped, they will interfere when searching for adjacent cases annotated with the new annotation layer (cf. Section 2.1).

Using standard conformant formats can also be crucial for the scalability of a multilayer corpus: Standard formats make working with automatic NLP tools easier, such as taggers, parsers and Named Entity Recognition (NER). Such tools are often a good way of expanding layers of manual annotation, which are costly to prepare, with roughly accurate syntactic, morphological or shallow semantic information, which automatic tools are increasingly able to provide. Using idiosyncratic representations will lower the potential for compatibility with such tools, making further annotation difficult for both humans and machines.

Crowdsourcing, Class-Sourcing, Gamification and NLP

NLP tool chains can increasingly give us a range of useful annotation layers 'out of the box', especially for research on standard English. For example, CoreNLP (Manning et al. 2014) can automatically produce tagged, dependency and constituent parsed data with added NER and coreference annotation (although the accuracy of the latter two annotation types is not yet as good as the former). However, for many interesting annotation layers, some amount of human annotation or correction will be required. The particular issue for multilayer corpora is that the breadth of information that we want may exceed our ability to annotate by ourselves, both for single researchers and small research groups. As a result, multilayer corpora often require bringing in a larger workforce than just a local research team.

Two prominent ways of expanding an annotation project to a broader set of annotators are crowdsourcing and class-sourcing. Crowdsourcing (see Fort 2016) relies on the distribution of work in the form of relatively simple annotation tasks to a large workforce of online annotators, each of which is not considered completely reliable on their own. Crowdsourcing platforms, such as Amazon Mechanical Turk (www.mturk.com/) or CrowdFlower (www.crowdflower.com/), provide interfaces for training annotators, adjudicating their disagreements and evaluating performance on a variety of tasks (see Sabou et al. 2014 for an overview of projects and best practices). Tasks themselves are usually fairly simple or have to be broken down into simplified subtasks, corresponding both to the low level of compensation per annotation task for annotators and the amount of training that is feasible for lay annotators. Crowdsource workers (or 'Turkers' in Amazon Mechanical Turk) generally have no linguistics training and little time to learn complicated guidelines, making the usability of their work limited when compared to expert annotators. For example, Snow et al. (2008) report good results for crowdsourcing textual entailment and word sense disambiguation, and similarly Hsueh et al. (2009) for sentiment analysis. However, even for a relatively intuitive task such as binary sentiment analysis (negative/positive), Hsueh et al. (2009: 30) report a gold-standard average accuracy of 0.974 for expert annotators versus just 0.714 for Mechanical Turk. For more complex tasks, such as syntax annotation, crowdsourcing is less feasible (though in some cases, subtasks can be simplified sufficiently, see Jha et al. 2010 on using Mechanical Turk for PP attachment disambiguation).

An alternative to working with non-linguistically trained annotators is class-sourcing – working with a classroom of linguists or computational linguistics students and annotating data as part of the curriculum (pioneered by Blackwell and Martin 2009, Gerdes 2013 and others). A key advantage of class-sourcing as a source of information is that students of linguistics are, of course, nascent experts in the domain of study, and their performance is often excellent compared with NLP tools (see Zeldes 2017a and Zeldes and Simonson 2016 for evaluation on various tasks). For example, whereas manual syntax annotation is not feasible in a crowdsourcing paradigm, it is for class-sourcing. Limitations of class-sourcing are, however, a smaller scale than crowdsourcing (we may work with thousands of Turkers but only dozens of students every year) and the need to meet the pedagogical requirements of the curriculum: Class-sourcing is only viable if it logically forms an integral part of some curriculum which contributes to students' knowledge.[3]

Another alternative to these two forms of 'crowds' is found in gamification strategies (see Stieglitz et al. 2017), sometimes called 'Games With A Purpose' (GWAP). These can be targeted at either a lay population, similar to crowdsourcing, or at domain populations, more similar to class-sourcing. Although approaches vary in many respects, the general idea is to embed an annotation task within the context of a game, which makes it more enjoyable and motivates participants. This is often done by introducing a competitive aspect, such as leader boards, or matching players in pairs or larger groups to determine the winner. One of the earliest successful applications of the concept to linguistic annotation was Phrase Detectives (Chamberlain et al. 2008), which challenged players to perform anaphora resolution as 'detectives' searching for pronoun antecedents. Gamification has been used both on crowdsourcing platforms and on the Web to collect data on word sense disambiguation (Rumshisky et al. 2012; Venhuizen et al. 2013), term and relation extraction (Dumitrache et al. 2013), argumentation mining (Habernal and Gurevych 2017) and more. Beyond motivating annotators, a key advantage of gamification is the ability to introduce a longer training period for participants, because an engaging game may be played for a comparatively long time. Additionally, games can be constructed in a way that combines or alternates between different tasks, contributing multiple related layers of annotation. However, the disadvantage is often in the development effort required to create an engaging game: Constructing annotation interfaces is a challenging task to begin with, meaning that gamifying complex annotations is often hard to realize in a successful way.

Historical Data and Non-Native Language

Special mention should be made with regard to handling 'non-standard' data, especially with a view to some of the case studies described in

---

3. Although this is certainly non-trivial, my own experience has been that well-planned class-sourcing work is received very positively by students, and is well suited precisely for complex tasks that students find challenging; see the next section for details.

Chapter 7 on historical and non-native speaker language. Although these two types of data initially seem very different, they share some of the same challenges in corpus building, particularly when a more complex multilayer architecture is needed. The basic difficulty uniting these cases is the discrepancy between the representation that linguists wish to search in and a faithful rendition of the primary data – be it a potentially ungrammatical learner utterance or an orthographically non-standard or even partial representation of content in historical texts with potential lacunae. As an example, consider the following two utterances taken from a multilayer historical corpus of early German botanical prints (RIDGES, Odebrecht et al. 2017) and a learner corpus of English with aligned revisions after tutor corrections (Hong Kong City University Corpus of English Learner Academic Drafts, Lee et al. 2015; images rendered using ANNIS, see Section 3.5).

The first example in Figure 3.1 reads 'were put together from many small leaves', or literally in German word order 'from many small leaves together put were'. Segmentation and alignment problems for the primary data emerge from two sources in this example: 1. The diminutive of the word 'leaves' is spelled across two lines with a line break marked by a diagonal double hyphen: 'Blåt⸗lein'. Because this corpus also includes line break annotations on a separate layer, the word form must contain the boundary in the middle of the word on the 'dipl' layer (diplomatic transcription). A cleaned-up layer called 'clean' does not include this break and normalizes some non-standard characters (e.g. the 'a' with raised 'e' above). The third 'norm' layer goes a step further and also merges tokens which are spelled together in Modern German, such as the word 'put together' (*zusammengesetzt*). This is made possible by an architecture that considers the various representations of word forms to be aligned annotation layers on a single timeline of events (cf. Section 2.2).

The second example shows corrected learner language, where a text originally used the verb 'try' in the present tense (the tag VBP), but where the learner intended to say 'tried' (simple past, the tag VBD). In this case, the correction was made by the same learner who produced the error, following comments from a tutor (the corpus contains learners' own revisions

dipl	aus	vielen	kleinen	Blåt⸗	lein	zuſammen	geſetzet	wåren	/
clean	aus	vielen	kleinen	Blätlein		zusammen	gesetzet	wåren	/
norm	aus	vielen	kleinen	Blättlein		zusammengesetzt		wåren	/

a	result	,	when	I	try	to	make	my	website	,
DT	NN	,	WRB	PRP	VBP	TO	VB	PRP$	NN	,
a	result	,	when	I	tried	to	make	my	website	,
DT	NN	,	WRB	PRP	VBD	TO	VB	PRP$	NN	,

Figure 3.1 Multilayer examples of primary data representation for historical and L2 texts

of their texts, see Chapter 7). However, the same type of situation can apply in learner corpora containing target hypotheses (see Reznicek et al. 2013), in which expert annotators annotate L2 data with a grammatically correct version of what they believe the speaker is trying to say.

Thus in both of these cases, linguists often choose to prepare some form of 'normalized' version of the text before proceeding with higher annotations, such as POS tagging, parsing, etc., leading to similar opportunities but also challenges. The main motivations for this are at least twofold: From a theoretical point of view, we may be uncertain what tags to apply to non-standard utterances, especially if we are using 'standard' tag sets intended for a more or less normative conforming text. Normalizing the text and providing annotations for the normalized data allow for more predictable application of annotation schemes and easier search through the data, because we have a better idea of what to expect (e.g. we can predict normalized spellings, but we may not guess some aberrant ones). Beyond this, from a practical point of view, normalization allows NLP tools to provide a first approximation of some annotation layers, such as tagging, because the normalized data will often be similar enough to their training data (see Piotrowski 2012 for an overview of NLP for historical data). In some cases, we may even be able to project tags from normalized tagged text back to the underlying original. Even then, though, higher error rates may require more manual correction than would otherwise be needed.

An additional challenge for historical data is digitization, which is usually not necessary in learner corpora collected using electronic means (though handwritten learner data still need to be transcribed). In such cases, optical character recognition (OCR) may or may not be an option, and usually only for printed texts available in sufficiently high quality. For data from the more recent print era, Odebrecht et al. (2017: 698) advocate using "freely available, good quality scans of historical books", either from open-access digital libraries or if not available then often under license from Google Books. Some specialized OCR efforts have recently been able to approach even difficult scripts, such as early Gothic prints (i.e. Fraktur typefaces, see Springmann and Lüdeling 2017) and non-Latin scripts, such as Coptic (Miyagawa et al. 2017). Using a multilayer architecture, it is even conceivable to indicate uncertain regions of text recognition in larger, automatically acquired corpora (see Section 2.4 on meta-annotations of provenance and certainty).

3.2   Leveraging Tools and Formats: The Case of GUM

In this section we will explore the creation process of a single multilayer corpus project in detail, with two goals in mind: First, the aim is to complement the cross-sectional presentation of multilayer corpus architecture in Chapter 2 with an end-to-end example of how the multilayer methodology is applied in corpus construction. Second, the corpus presented here will be used extensively in Chapters 4–6 to carry out studies on discourse-level phenomena which relate to many layers of annotation for syntax, information structure, entity models, coreference resolution and discourse parsing. The corpus in question is GUM, the Georgetown University Multilayer corpus (described in Zeldes 2017a), which is collected and expanded yearly as part of the Computational Linguistics curriculum at Georgetown University.

A Closer Look at Acquiring Data in the Classroom

The idea to collect and annotate digital corpus data in the classroom iteratively as part of a standing curriculum is by now almost a decade old and goes back at least to Blackwell and Martin (2009), who allowed undergraduate students in Classics to apply their growing knowledge in Classical Greek to the acquisition and annotation of primary sources. Blackwell and Martin stressed the problematic nature of essay assignments with "an audience of one" (the lecturer) and advocated the promotion of curricular models that put student work in a position to enjoy an audience of more than one, both in the form of traditional scholarly publications and through the release of online materials in the digital information age. Their ideas fed into the formation of the Homer Multitext project (http://www.homermultitext.org/), an online corpus of aligned Homeric manuscripts with searchable text and facsimiles. The idea of integrating the classroom into a publication workflow was developed further in subsequent years, and was also at the basis of the historical corpus of German scientific texts, RIDGES (Register in Diachronic German Science, Odebrecht et al. 2017), described in the previous section: Students collected and digitized early prints of herbal texts and annotated them as part of the curriculum on multiple layers, which were later merged for online publication.

The GUM corpus, which began collection in 2014, follows very much the same design and motivation. Based on a mixed undergraduate/graduate introduction to corpus linguistics, data are collected as part of the curriculum at the beginning of every fall semester at Georgetown University in a course usually attended by about 20 students. In parallel to learning about corpus design methodology, preprocessing, search and evaluation, students select their own texts, which they then work with for the entire semester, annotating and re-annotating their data using different tools and schemes every few weeks, as new types of annotation are learned in the course. The ability to choose one's own text means that topical interests can be explored to some extent (students are free to work on whatever topic they like, which positively affects motivation),[4] though

---

4. It has been pointed out (see Zeldes 2017a) that Computer-Assisted Language Learning (CALL) tools often follow the same strategy of allowing learners to work on a text of their own choosing in the target language, often from the Web, using a browser extension (see the REAP project, http://boston.lti.cs.cmu.edu/reap/ and VIEW, http://sifnos.sfs.uni-tuebingen.de/VIEW/).

there are some limitations. The choice of text in GUM is constrained by two principles: The first is that data should come from openly available sources, preferably licensed under a Creative Commons license (cf. Section 3.1). Although this means that GUM will realistically contain only data from the Web, this ensures that, should students wish to publish their data online at the end of the course (which is purely voluntary), that data will be made available under an open license that is as permissive as possible. Open licenses directly promote 'an audience larger than one' in that anyone interested in the corpus is free to access and use it, and using web data means that a base text to work on is already available in digital form, and the limited time of a semester's course work need not be spent on transcribing from non-digital sources.

The second constraint concerns the actual websites from which GUM is collected. Although a corpus collected in the classroom is not likely to achieve the proportions of truly representative and/or balanced national corpus projects, a certain degree of stratification is desirable: Having a corpus of 100 totally heterogeneous texts is less valuable than having 10 texts in each of ten genres, because the former scenario allows for no grouping or studying of genre effects beyond the idiosyncratic properties of individual texts. Based on this line of reasoning, GUM data were restricted to four websites in its first three years of collection (2014–2016). Table 3.1 shows the distribution of data from these sources as of 2017.[5]

As the table shows, text types are not quite equally divided both in number of texts and number of tokens. This is partly due to the

Table 3.1 Proportions of texts in GUM in 2017

Text type	Source	Texts	Tokens
Interviews (conversational)	Wikinews	19	18,037
News (narrative)	Wikinews	21	14,093
Travel guides (informative)	Wikivoyage	17	14,955
How-tos (instructional)	wikiHow	19	16,920
Total		76	64,005

5. Text types are set to change after every three iterations; for example, in 2017, shortly before this book was typeset, we collected biographies, academic papers, fiction and discussion threads from online forums. The complete GUM data are available online in multiple formats at http://corpling.uis.georgetown.edu/gum. The underlying documents from the Wikimedia foundation, including the News, Interview and Travel subcorpora, are available under Creative Commons attribution (CC-BY) licenses, including for commercial use, and wikiHow makes its texts available under a CC-BY-NC-SA license (noncommercial, share alike). The annotations themselves are all licensed under CC-BY.

unpredictable nature of course participation (students sometimes drop out or join the class late) and the unknown exact number of tokens when collection begins. Students are instructed to select texts between 500 and 1000 words long based on a word-processor word count, but after a more rigorous tokenization is complete, this number invariably changes. Nevertheless, as we will see in Chapters 4–6, the amount of data in the different subcorpora is sufficient to study certain aspects of genre variation.

The selection of the text types in Table 3.1 was made to maximize variability in communicative intent (cf. Biber 1993), and is also motivated by the intended use of GUM to study variation in discourse structure (see Chapters 5–6): We want to compare spoken and written communications, informative and instructional communicative purposes, etc. Covering some form of interlocutive, conversational data is particularly difficult when relying on open-access texts from the Web, the more so if we are not prepared to devote time to transcribing audio data (e.g. podcasts). To meet this challenge, we opted to use online interviews as a proxy for conversational exchanges. Although interviews are a very particular type of conversation, with one participant (the interviewee) dominating the conversation, they do offer some of the most important properties of conversational data, such as situational deixis and interpersonal pronouns, dynamic common ground management, digressions and potentially false starts, back-channeling and disfluencies. The latter types of situations depend directly on whether interviews are transcribed by the online publisher from actual speech or rather come from e-mail interviews, in which the interviewee receives written questions and responds in writing. GUM contains both types of data, which can look rather different, as the following examples show:

(9) —*What is the most important aspect of your background that voters should know about?*

—*I am [. . .] the only candidate who embodies both physically and philosophically the growing diversity of the commonwealth. (I am mixed-race [half-Chinese] and in an interracial marriage.)* (GUM_interview_libertarian)

(10) Bill: *It's portrayed as though it's dark, black and evil. And—*

Rebecca: *Oh man, well?*
Bill: *What's up?*
Rebecca: *I do wear a lot of black.* (GUM_interview_dungeon)

The first example comes from a written interview with a Libertarian politician, Robert Sarvis, and shows a good example of the mixed nature of such data: From a discursive perspective, we have a question and answer pair in a second person–first person interlocutive framework, much like in a face-to-face interview. At the same time, we see relatively long sentences, and even use of parentheses, in this case even including a nested parenthetical, which would have likely been expressed differently in speech. The second example comes from an interview with a couple who operates a recreational dungeon, resulting in three-way conversation between the interviewer and the two interviewees. Because this is a spoken face-to-face interview, there is a chance for speakers to interrupt each other, we see incomplete utterances ("And—") and there are some very short sentences as a result. At the same time, because this interview was transcribed at the source and not by GUM annotators, the corpus relies on the interpretation of the original transcriber, who is in all likelihood not a trained linguist. For example, we have interpretive use of sentence segmentation and capitalization (the interrupted "And" could still be part of the previous utterance), question marks and commas and perhaps most importantly, the necessary serialization of overlapping speech. This substantially simplifies the corpus data model (no concurrent speakers, one token at a time), but compromises some possible research questions on dialog interaction.

A second important question in acquiring documents is what exactly to include in the primary data, because web pages typically include navigation elements, such as links and menus, and in the case of many wiki resources, interactive buttons, for example, to edit the text. Enforcing consistency for this type of collection in a classroom setting is challenging, because the number of annotators is rather large, and time is limited by the progression of the course. This is somewhat mitigated by the ability to discuss decisions as a group in the classroom so that participants benefit from each other's experiences and have a chance to reach a consensus.[6] Additionally, we wish for decisions to remain consistent from year to year of the data collection, which means that decisions need to be documented. In the case of GUM, this is done using a wiki interface which course participants can edit and use for the discussion (see http://corpling.uis.georgetown.edu/wiki/doku.php).

In practice the attempt is made in GUM to preserve as much meaningful markup as possible as a form of annotation, which means anything that is not automatically predictable or external to the document at hand. For example, navigation elements present in any travel guide on Wikivoyage are completely dropped, such as the "view history" button of each page or the sidebar navigation menu or edit buttons

---

6. For larger corpora, automatic boilerplate removal must be used instead, which, thanks to recent advances, can often reach high accuracy levels (see Schäfer 2017) but is not easily configurable to different design decisions.

next to each section. These are automatically included by the website and are therefore viewed as not belonging to the document in question (and, in fact, with any given stylesheet change, they can become radically different). Another argument for excluding such sections is that they are not created by document authors intentionally and do not constitute a voluntary part of the author's message. Other forms of graphical arrangements in the document which are not predictable and can be assumed to have been contributed by authors are captured using TEI XML tags (www.tei-c.org/), which will be discussed in the next section.

Tokenization, Sentence Segmentation and Basic Markup

Tokenization and part of speech tagging are done completely manually for GUM, which serves as a hands-on exercise in how to apply a tag set, as well as the realization that tokenization is a non-trivial form of analysis. Classroom discussion often leads to interesting cases spotted by some participants, for example, the need for intricate handling of punctuation: In cases such as 'Bill Clinton-Al Gore connections', splitting the hyphen seems obvious (otherwise we have a token 'Clinton-Al'), whereas for 'seven-day program' a strong case can be made for keeping 'seven-day' together as a complex nominal modifier (notice it is not pluralized 'seven-days'). The need to POS tag concurrently with tokenization also informs segmentation decisions: For a token such as the last word in 'you and your friend(s)', it may be tempting to split off the 's'. However, knowing that we must also tag the data, we may prefer to tag the complex 'friends(s)' as a plural (tag NNS) rather than having a singular 'friend' (NN) and not knowing how to tag the remainder (is '(s)' a plural, taggable as NNS?). Decisions on these layers are therefore interdependent.

The tag set used for tagging is the extended version of the Penn Treebank tag set (Santorini 1990), as used by the TreeTagger Schmid (1994). Main additions in the extended tag set are special tags for the verbs *be* (VB*) and *have* (VH*) versus lexical verbs (VV*), more tags for punctuation and a special tag for the word *that* as a complementizer (IN/that). However, in a multilayer framework, there is no need to be restricted to one tag set, and the data are automatically extended with the original Penn tags (which are predictable from TreeTagger tags), as well as automatically assigned tags from the UCREL CLAWS5 tag set (Garside and Smith 1997), to allow for comparison and combined searching. For example, CLAWS distinguishes a tag for ordinal numbers ORD, regardless of their use as adjectives or adverbs, whereas the Penn tags make only the latter distinction. Having both kinds of tags allows for conjoined searches, for example, for an ordinal used adverbially, as in the following examples from GUM[7]:

(11) *What **first** attracted you to researching ants?*
(12) *Did you see those guys when they **last** came to town?*

Having access to multiple tagging schemes concurrently can thus expose information that is not available to any one of the tag sets by itself. Additionally, as we will see in Section 3.4, the multiple tags will allow us to perform certain kinds of validation by leveraging differences between multiple annotation layers applying to the same tokens.

In addition to segmenting and POS tagging tokens, sentence segmentation and tagging are also performed at this stage: Each token must belong to exactly one sentence, and sentence types are assigned from a tag set based on an extended version of the form labels assigned to C-units[8] in the SPAAC annotation scheme (SPeech Act Annotated Corpus, Leech et al. 2003). The types distinguished are given in Table 3.2.

Sentence types are attached to the type attribute of <s> tags using the TEI's vocabulary of elements. Note that sentence annotation 'tiles' the text, meaning that there is no hierarchy of clauses; this layer therefore constitutes a span annotation in the sense of Section 2.4. We will use these

Table 3.2 Sentence type annotation in GUM

Tag	Type	Example
q	polar yes/no question	*Did she see it?*
wh	WH question	*What did you see?*
decl	declarative (indicative)	*He was there.*
imp	imperative	*Do it!*
sub	subjunctive (incl. modals)	*I could go*
inf	infinitival	*How to Dance*
ger	gerund-headed clause	*Finding Nemo*
intj	interjection	*Hello!*
frag	fragment	*The End.*
other	other predication or a combination	*Nice, that!' Or: 'I've had it, go!'* (decl+imp)

7. These can be retrieved in GUM using the ANNIS web interface and the query `pos="RB" _=_ claws5="ORD"`, finding cases where these tags apply covering the same tokens. See Section 3.5 for more on ANNIS and the ANNIS Query Language (AQL).
8. C-units are defined as fully independent syntactic units in (spoken) English, i.e. utterances (see Biber et al. 1999: 1069–1082).

sentence types to help predict several alternation phenomena in the second part of this book.

Finally, the structural markup of the document also encompasses a subset of TEI XML tags, such as paragraph tags (<p>), speaker turn tags (<sp who="#somespeaker">), non-linguistic events (e.g. <incident type="cough">) and more (see https://corpling.uis.georgetown.edu/gum/ for an up-to-date list, which is added to as necessary with each class iteration). The XML tags are then merged with the tokenized and POS tagged data, using the widely used Corpus Workbench vertical format (CWB, Christ 1994, also used by the popular CQPWeb interface, Hardie 2012). The format of this initial result is shown here:

```
<text id="GUM_voyage_lodz" type="voyage">
<head rend="bold">
<s type="frag">
Łódź  NP
</s>
</head>
<p>
<s type="decl">
<ref target="http://en.turystyczna.lodz.pl/page/">
Łódź  NP
</ref>
(     (
Pronounced    VVN
:     :
<hi rend="italics">
Wootch NP
</hi>
)     )
is    VBZ
<ref target="https://en.wikivoyage.org/wiki/Poland">
Poland NP
</ref>
's    POS
third RB
biggest JJS
city  NN
. . .
```

Although this representation is no longer TEI XML, it retains much of the vocabulary used by the TEI standard, such as rendering annotations (e.g. <hi> for highlighting, with a 'rend' attribute designating bold or italics for emphasis), and similarly images (<figure>), captions, bulleted or numbered lists, etc.

In order to validate the data, annotators work with the online XML editor GitDox (Zhang and Zeldes 2017), which uses XML Schema Definition (XSD) files and configurable validation functionality to check for valid POS tags, XML elements, nesting, etc. Validation at this first data collection step is crucial, because further layers of annotation created subsequently with different tools will rely on the tokenization, and in part on the sentence segmentation created at this stage.

Syntactic Annotation

Syntax trees are among the most useful annotation layers, because they allow us to detect phrase boundaries to address questions regarding entity mentions in discourse (e.g. people, places and things, see Chapters 4–5), and also give information about key grammatical functions such as subjecthood, event structure of predicates and more. This is especially true if we have labeled dependency information, which loosely represents argument structure at the syntactic annotation level. Although syntax annotation is a highly complex task, the class-sourcing setting with linguistics students as annotators offers a unique opportunity, but also a challenge, for collecting consistent syntactic analyses.

The syntax annotation layers in GUM are done in a separate environment than TEI annotation, but two implicit constraints are inherited from the previous layer. First, tokenization is assumed to remain identical, and second, sentence borders are assumed to converge with <s> elements in the XML data. Using these segmentations as input, as well as the gold POS tag information, the data are initially parsed automatically using the Stanford Parser (Manning et al. 2014) for both constituents and dependencies (using Stanford basic dependencies, de Marneffe and Manning 2013). The resulting constituent trees are retained in the corpus unaltered in the Penn Treebank bracketing format (https://github.com/amir-zeldes/gum/tree/master/const), to be merged with other formats in a later step. The dependency trees are imported into an online annotation interface called Arborator (Gerdes 2013), shown in Figure 3.2. Because both types of parses use the same underlying tokens, it will later be possible to merge them (see Section 3.4): Constituents will form dominance structures using

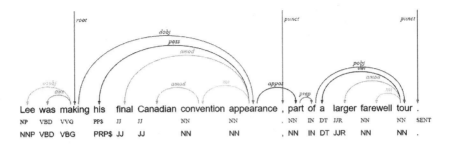

Figure 3.2 Annotating dependencies in the Arborator. Edges can be dragged from token to token, and labels can be selected for each edge from a dropdown list

phrase nodes above the tokens, which are also linked via pointing relations expressing the dependencies.

Both the focus on dependencies and the decision to correct parser output rather than annotate from scratch are largely motivated by time constraints: Dependencies are faster to teach, automatic dependency parsing already has fair quality but can be improved on substantially by student corrections and exploring dependencies in a linguistics curriculum nicely complements existing curricular foci on constituent parsing. Annotation from scratch would offer an even stronger learning focus but is very time consuming, leaving little time to learn other annotations, and overall quality is likely to be lower. Gerdes (2013: 94), for example, suggests that student annotation of dependencies from scratch can achieve a rather low 79% average attachment accuracy for French; for GUM, students achieve labeled accuracy of about 95.5% attachment accuracy and 93.6% labeled attachment accuracy in corrected parser output, as compared to 84.8% and only 81.2% for the initial automatic parse result (Zeldes 2017a).[9] After correction by instructors, accuracy of the data should be even higher, though some errors inevitably persist. The final corrected dependency data are available online in the CoNLLU tabular format (version 2, see http://universaldependencies. org/format.html), enriched with speaker and sentence type information during merging (see Section 3.4), which appears sentence by sentence as shown here:

```
# s_type=decl
# speaker=MichaelDranove
1   I        I       PP    PRP    _   3    nsubj     _   _
2   just     just    RB    RB     _   3    advmod    _   _
3   wanted   want    VVD   VBD    _   27   ccomp     _   _
4   to       to      TO    TO     _   5    aux       _   _
5   know     know    VV    VB     _   3    xcomp     _   _
. . .
```

The format gives token values, two of the three POS tags available in GUM and lemmas, which are added during merging. Grammatical function labels and dependency parent IDs are given in the last two filled

---

9. Although parser performance may seem substantially lower than accuracy rates reported in reference papers on parsing (about 92% attachment and 90% labeled attachment accuracy in Chen and Manning 2014), it should be noted that reported scores always refer to Penn Treebank data from the Wall Street Journal (specifically section 23, the test partition); degradation on unrestricted web data is therefore not surprising, and considerably worse numbers can be expected for more diverse web genres, especially social media (cf. Silveira et al. 2014 on the need for more diverse gold web data).

columns on the right, that is, '3 nsubj' in line 1 means that the token 'I' is governed by #3 ('wanted') as its nominal subject ('nsubj'). Errors detected in this data are corrected and re-released periodically, with version control via GitHub (for a genre-by-genre breakdown and further analysis of errors, see also Zeldes and Simonson 2016).

Entities, Information Status and Coreference Annotation

With a high-quality parse at hand, it is relatively simple to detect entity mention borders, that is, spans of text referring to people, places and other things. Although we do not have correct constituent parses for the data, we can infer correct stretches of text for each span using the dependencies. All nominal heads and their dependents recursively form a potential entity mention, as shown in Figure 3.3. The token corresponding to the word 'fox' can be identified as a nominal expression by its POS tag, 'NN'. The dependency arcs emanating from this token (in black) are pointing relations (cf. Section 2.4), which indicate that 'big' and 'the' are parts of the referring expression. The word 'ran', by contrast, is pointing at 'fox' as a target, and is therefore not part of the phrase – this token is excluded from the entity mention span (see Section 4.3 for another application of this filtering procedure).

Using this procedure and the gold POS tagged and parsed data, all documents in the corpus are fed to an automatic (non-)named entity recognition and coreference resolution system called xrenner (Zeldes and Zhang 2016, https://corpling.uis.georgetown.edu/xrenner/), which gives a first guess at the entity type of each span (e.g. 'animal' for fox) and links any suspected coreferring expressions (e.g. a subsequent 'it') with a new pointing relation. The output of the system is then imported into the WebAnno annotation interface (Yimam et al. 2013) for correction by students (Figure 3.4).

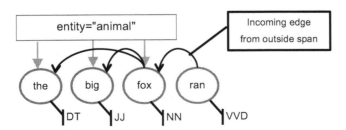

Figure 3.3 Using dependencies and POS tags to recognize span borders for entity mentions

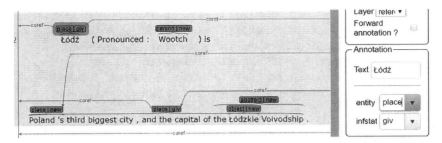

Figure 3.4 Initial view of automatic entity and coreference annotation in WebAnno

Although the data initially contain many errors (especially with foreign words as shown in Figure 3.4 for some Polish place names), correcting automatic output is still much faster than annotating from scratch. Especially in cases where mention borders are correct, annotators only have to edit entity types and potentially coreference edges. For the entity types we used a collapsed version of the OntoNotes annotation scheme (Weischedel et al. 2012), which is used by many Named Entity Recognition tools, but reduced from 22 to 11 types, due to time constraints in the classroom setting. For example, very specific and relatively rare types, such as LAW or WORK OF ART, were reduced to either ABSTRACT or a physical OBJECT type, thereby giving up some fine-grained distinctions in favor of an easier annotation scheme to learn and apply. Table 3.3 gives the mapping between OntoNotes and GUM categories.

Note that whereas annotations in OntoNotes are restricted to named entities (headed by tokens tagged as proper nouns), annotations in GUM are applied to any referring expression. For example, an unnamed 'a reporter' is tagged as a PERSON. Non-referring nominal expressions, such as '(on) the other hand', are not annotated. The exhaustive annotation of referring expressions will be crucial for studying the relationship between referentiality and syntax in Part II of this book, and especially in Chapter 5.

Most of the collapsed categories are a straightforward simplification of the OntoNotes guidelines, such as not distinguishing different kinds of locational entities or time expressions (though dates are specifically annotated on the TEI layer outlined earlier, making them distinct). The categories OBJECT and ABSTRACT were introduced in order to cover a variety of non-named entity NPs that are generally unannotated in OntoNotes. These two categories are very frequent in GUM, covering about a third of all entity mentions, but they refer to common rather than proper noun expressions in 89.9% and 94.3% of cases, respectively. Corresponding OntoNotes categories, such as LAW, DISEASE, PRODUCT and WORK OF ART, are probably quite rare in GUM and were collapsed into these

Table 3.3 Entity types in GUM versus OntoNotes

GUM	OntoNotes equivalent
PERSON	PERSON, NORP *(when nominal)*
PLACE	GPE, LOCATION, FACILITY
ORGANIZATION	ORGANIZATION
OBJECT	PRODUCT, WORK OF ART and all other concrete objects
EVENT	EVENT
TIME	DATE, TIME
SUBSTANCE	SUBSTANCE
ANIMAL	ANIMAL
PLANT	PLANT
ABSTRACT	LANGUAGE, DISEASE, LAW and all other abstractions
QUANTITY	PERCENT, MONEY and all other quantities
(variable)	ORDINAL, CARDINAL

two categories as well. The OntoNotes categories ORDINAL and CAR-DINAL are not annotated, and instead where a more complete NP is absent, they are annotated as the respective type of the referent being counted. For example, an 'MMPI form' (a kind of personality test) was annotated as an OBJECT, so a subsequent mention as 'one' is annotated in the same way:

(13) [*a mini-MMPI*]$_{\text{OBJECT}}$ *that I developed . . . if you'd like to see* [*one*]$_{\text{OBJECT}}$

Although the scheme diverges from OntoNotes entity tags in the respects listed earlier, annotators were given the OntoNotes guidelines as a point of reference, both for pedagogical value in getting acquainted with a major annotation scheme for NER and as a first authority on question-able cases.

In addition to entity types, annotators corrected the automatic coreference layer, which extends coreference annotation as found in OntoNotes in a number of ways (see Zeldes and Zhang 2016 for dis-cussion). Beyond identical mention coreference and appositions, which are distinguished in OntoNotes, the GUM scheme adds cataphora and bridging annotation, inspired by the German coreference scheme in the TüBa-D/Z corpus (Telljohann et al. 2012) and the English GNOME corpus (Poesio 2004). Cataphora refers to forward-pointing pronouns whose reference can only be resolved by reading on (see Gernsbacher

Table 3.4 Coreference types in GUM

Type	Direction	Description
ana	back	anaphoric pronoun
cata	forward	cataphoric pronoun
appos	back	apposition
bridge	back	bridging
coref	back	all other types of coreference (e.g. nominal re-mention)

and Jescheniak 1995; Naumann 2006), and bridging (Asher and Lascarides 1998) denotes entities that are accessible in context by virtue of a previous mention of a related referent (e.g. part-whole: *[a car]* <-bridge-*[the wheels]*).[10] These two types are illustrated in context in (14)–(15), taken from GUM.

(14) *In [her] opening remarks for attendees, [Waters] pointed out those features to attendees*

(15) *One side of [the memorial] is scenes made by student groups [. . .] at the main entrance to [the grounds]* (=of the memorial)

Table 3.4 gives an overview of the annotation types in the coreference layer of the corpus. Note that although all relations are pointing relations (cf. Section 2.4), cataphora have the unique property of pointing forward. Thus edge direction represents the source and target of information that can be used to resolve the reference of an antecedent or, for cataphora, a postcedent.

Finally, knowledge about the coreference chain allows us to identify when an entity is introduced into discourse (its first mention, when it is 'discourse new') and which mentions refer to already given entities. This type of information is initially added as an information status ('infstat') annotation based on the automatic coreference resolution, and is then corrected by students in a three-way distinction: 'new', 'giv(en)', and 'acc(essible)', following Dipper et al. (2007). The 'acc' category refers to entities that require no introduction at their first mention, for example, generic or uniquely identifiable entities, such as 'the sun'; deictic or indexical expressions, such as '(give me) that' (where 'that' is visible to the

---

10. The term *bridging* has also been used in pragmatics with a broader sense to cover pragmatic inferences (Clark and Haviland 1977: 6–7); here the discussion is restricted to the entity-bridging sense discussed by Asher and Lascarides.

listener); interlocutive pronouns such as 'I'; etc.[11] All three types of annotation (i.e. entity types, coreference and information status) are tightly
intertwined and were done using the same tool (WebAnno) – the data
are downloadable from https://github.com/amir-zeldes/gum/tree/master/
coref in several formats, including the WebAnno TSV format (Version 3)
shown here:

```
#Text=Tulsa
1-1   0-5     Tulsa       place       new       coref 2-1

#Text=Tulsa is in the Green Country region of Oklahoma.
2-1   6-11    Tulsa       place       giv       ana   3-1
2-2   12-14   is          _           _         _     _
2-3   15-17   in          _           _         _     _
2-4   18-21   the         place[3]    new[3]    _     _
2-5   22-27   Green       place[3]    new[3]    _     _
2-6   28-35   Country     place[3]    new[3]    _     _
2-7   36-42   region      place[3]    new[3]    _     _
2-8   43-45   of          place[3]    new[3]    _     _
2-9   46-54   Oklahoma    place[3]|place[4]           new[3]|new[4]
                                                      coref|bridge
                                                      8-8[33_4]|7-4[23_4]
2-10  54-55   .           _           _         _     _
```

This format represents the sentence's primary textual data as comments
above each sentence and tokens in individual lines below these, using IDs
composed of the sentence number and token number (e.g. 2–1 means sentence 2, token 1). Character offsets in the second column refer to the text
of each sentence and allow for white space preservation. The third column
gives token strings, and subsequent columns are reserved for annotations,
such as the entity type (e.g. *place*) and information status (*giv*, *new* or
acc) in GUM. Annotation spans are co-indexed using numbers in square
brackets, indicating, for example, that a span [3] stretches across "the
Green Country region of Oklahoma". Multiple spans are separated by a
vertical line, for example, in 2–9, where "Oklahoma" is given a nested
span [4] inside "the Green Country region of Oklahoma". Finally, incoming pointing relations and their annotations are expressed in the last two
columns: line 1–1 has an incoming coreference relation (*coref*) emanating
from a node beginning in line 2–1. If the source of the relation spans
more than one token, its span ID is also given in square brackets, as in
2–9 (8–8[33_4], which means that the first incoming coref relation comes

11. Dipper et al. also suggest a more fine-grained tag set, with subtypes such as given-active/
    inactive to model recent mention, or accessible-generic vs. accessible-situational and
    more, in order to distinguish different reasons for discourse accessibility. These types
    of annotations were not used due to time limitations in the curriculum. For another
    example of information status annotation, see also the RefLex scheme, Baumann and
    Riester (2012).

from token 8–8, entity [33], pointing to entity [4]). For a comparison of this format with other formats, see Section 3.4.

Discourse Parsing

To explore relationships between propositions above the sentence level, discourse relations are also added to GUM. In choosing the annotation scheme to work with, several frameworks were considered: Rhetorical Structure Theory (RST, Mann and Thompson 1988), Segmented Discourse Representation Theory (SDRT, Asher 1993) and the more recent Penn Discourse Treebank's annotation scheme (PDTB, Prasad et al. 2008) have all been implemented in annotated corpora. What these frameworks have in common is expressing a kind of graph, with discourse segments (often sentences or clauses) as nodes and discourse relations between these, such as 'causality' or other relations that are often signaled by conjunctions or prepositions, such as *because*. For GUM, the framework of RST was chosen, but see Section 7.1 for a comparison of some main features of these three frameworks.

RST analyses consist of a document graph in which Elementary Discourse Units (EDUs), such as utterances or clauses, form a hierarchy of nodes, which are joined together based on the discourse function that each unit (or group of units) plays with respect to other parts of the text (see Taboada and Mann 2006 for an overview). The inventory of relations varies across implementations of RST, but often a distinction is made between presentational relations, which attempt to alter the reader's (or listener's) state of mind (e.g. a *motivation* relation, using a unit to convince someone to do something), and subject matter relations, which merely signal information to be recognized (e.g. *condition*, which simply states that one unit specifies a condition for another unit to apply). Structurally, RST graphs form trees with ordered leaves (the EDUs), which in some corpora possibly contain crossing edges. Additionally, two different kinds of discourse relations are distinguished: satellite–nucleus relations, which are asymmetric, with the nucleus node being more prominent or indispensable for the text, and multinuclear relations, which coordinate multiple nodes with the same degree of prominence. Figure 3.5 gives a fragment from a longer analysis in GUM, which illustrates the structure of the graph.

The set of EDUs in the figure is reporting on a stampede, starting with the bottom-left unit, numbered [9]. The nucleus in unit [9] is being expanded upon with a satellite using the *cause* relation to explain the cause of a stampede that is being reported on. Unit [12], by contrast, is placed in a coordinating multinuclear relation called *sequence* with the block of nodes [9–11]: the stampede first begins, and then people were injured, a progression signaled among other things by the word 'then' in [12]. Finally, note that some nodes in the graph are used purely for

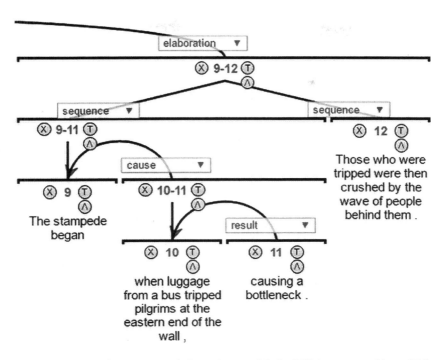

Figure 3.5 Part of an RST graph for a news article in GUM, annotated in rstWeb (Zeldes 2016b)

grouping purposes to form the backbone of the discourse constituent tree: the span labeled [10–11] merely serves to group [10] and [11] together, indicating that both of these units together form the *cause* of [9].

In the construction of GUM, RST annotation forms the last unit in the curriculum. The fact that RST graphs resemble complete constituent trees made out of clauses facilitates instruction for students, because the analogy to syntax trees can be used to quickly grasp the underlying structure (see Section 7.1 for a discussion of different graph structures for discourse annotation). In addition, if we ensure that EDUs may never cross sentence boundaries as annotated for syntax, we can use the sentence boundaries from the first step again to offer annotators an initial segmentation of the data into EDUs. Although students manually segment smaller EDUs (e.g. clauses below the sentence level), they are instructed not to merge sentences into larger EDUs, but to use joining relations in RST if necessary (the semantically underspecified multinuclear relation *joint* can serve this purpose). This creates a certain amount of interdependence between layers (see "Merging and Validation" later), but offers some benefits which we will take advantage of in the following chapters, because knowing that

EDUs never cross sentences means that we can examine the interaction of sentence-level annotations with RST annotations more easily. For example, each RST EDU is guaranteed to be nested within exactly one sentence type (declarative, imperative, etc.), and we can know whether it covers a complete sentence, whether it contains the dependency graph's root token or what the local root token's function was in subordinate clauses (e.g. that an EDU's root token dependency is 'advcl', an adverbial clause). We will use these interrelations to study interactions between syntactic structure and discourse structure in Chapter 7.

The annotation tool used to annotate RST analyses in GUM is rstWeb (Zeldes 2016b), a web interface which again allows annotators to work using only a web browser, and without the need to submit or exchange files. The interface allows users to segment and merge EDUs and to construct the hierarchical tree of relations, the inventory for which can be configured by administrators. The set of 20 relations used in GUM (Table 3.5) is much smaller than the detailed set of 78 relations used in the largest corpus of RST, the RST Discourse Treebank (Carlson et al. 2003), as achieving reasonable annotation quality and agreement for such a large inventory was not feasible in the framework of just a few weeks of course work. However, this reduced inventory corresponds fairly closely to the 16 top-level distinctions used to group together fine-grained relations in the RST-DT,[12] and is very similar to the inventory used by other smaller RST projects (e.g. the German Potsdam

Table 3.5 RST relations in GUM

Relation	Structure	Relation	Structure
antithesis	satellite–nucleus	*motivation*	satellite–nucleus
background	satellite–nucleus	*preparation*	satellite–nucleus
cause	satellite–nucleus	*purpose*	satellite–nucleus
circumstance	satellite–nucleus	*result*	satellite–nucleus
concession	satellite–nucleus	*solutionhood*	satellite–nucleus
condition	satellite–nucleus	*contrast*	multinuclear
elaboration	satellite–nucleus	*joint*	multinuclear
evaluation	satellite–nucleus	*sequence*	multinuclear
evidence	satellite–nucleus	*restatement*	multinuclear or
justify	satellite–nucleus		satellite–nucleus

12. For example, the RST-DT top-level category 'elaboration' includes eight subtypes such as *elaboration-additional*, *elaboration-general-specific* and *elaboration-part-whole*.

Commentary Corpus, Stede and Neumann 2014, or the Dutch RST corpus, Redeker et al. 2012). Most relations are either multinuclear or satellite–nucleus, but note that the 'restatement' relation has a multi-nuclear and a satellite–nucleus version.

The data format for RST analyses is the rs3 XML format developed for the desktop interface RSTTool (O'Donnell 2000), which contains no explicit tokenization below the EDU level, as shown in Figure 3.6. It is easiest to separate tokens with spaces matching the tokenization in other formats, but it is also possible to use a merging approach to align the graphs to the base text in other formats (see Section 3.4). EDUs are wrapped with the tag, which specifies the parent node and the relation name, whereas groups of EDUs are represented by <group> tags and contain no text. The tree structure is represented using the 'parent' attributes, which correspond to the 'id' attribute of the parent node.

```
<rst>
<header>
  <relations>
      <rel name="antithesis" type="rst"/>
      <rel name="background" type="rst"/>
      <rel name="cause" type="rst"/>
. . .
  </relations>
</header>
<body>
. . .
    <segment id="9" parent="40" relname="span">The
stampede began</segment>
    <segment id="10" parent="25" relname="span">when
luggage from a bus tripped pilgrims at the eastern end
of the wall ,</segment>
    <segment id="11" parent="10"
relname="result">causing a bottleneck .</segment>
    <segment id="12" parent="39"
relname="sequence">Those who were tripped were then
crushed by the wave of people behind them .</segment>
. . .
    <group id="25" type="span" parent="9"
relname="cause"/>
    <group id="40" type="span" parent="39"
relname="sequence"/>
  </body>
</rst>
```

Figure 3.6 XML data for RST annotations in GUM, using the rs3 format

The Complete Corpus

After following the collection of the annotations from GUM, at this point data exist in five source formats, all of which contain the same underlying text for each document:

- CWB format data containing tagged tokens and sentence spans, as well as structural markup using the TEI's inventory
- Constituent parses in the PTB format, produced automatically using gold tagged data as input for a parser
- Manually corrected dependency parses in the CoNLLU format
- Entity and coreference annotation, exportable in WebAnno's TSV format
- Rhetorical Structure Theory analyses in the .rs3 format

To bring these formats together as a multilayer corpus, we must first ensure that the data are valid: The primary data must match across formats, and some other constraints need to be checked as well. Then we can merge annotations from all layers and represent them in a multilayer format as a single corpus. Finally, we need to be able to use the corpus to search in and visualize the results. The next section deals with direct serializations of multilayer data. Section 3.4 discusses validation and merging from different formats, and Section 3.5 explores search and visualization in more detail.

3.3   Multilayer Representations

Although there have been some efforts to produce tools capable of annotating unrestricted multilayer data directly (e.g. Atomic, Druskat et al. 2014 or FLAT, http://flat.science.ru.nl/, using the FoLiA format, and to some extent WebAnno using UIMA XMI; see below), most multilayer corpora have been created in a more piecemeal fashion, either over a long period, with annotations gradually being added, or as a concerted effort but using multiple different tools (see Section 1.4 for examples). This is not surprising considering that the possibility of independence between annotation layers is what sets multilayer corpora apart from datasets that contain multiple but tightly intertwined annotations, such as POS tags and phrases in treebanks. One of the most exciting features of multilayer corpora is the ability to analyze annotation layers independently and in tandem, to modify, add or remove information at a later time without disrupting other parts of the corpus annotation. This ability hinges on a conceptual separation of annotation layers, but also on technical formats that allow easy retroactive modification of the data. In this section I will review some of the main characteristics of multilayer formats, and especially stand-off XML representations, as they are used to encode GUM and similar datasets, such as MASC.

A first distinction worth exploring is between inline formats, stand-off formats and stand-off/inline formats, which I will also refer to as 'hybrid' formats. Inline formats are the classic form of annotation found initially in token-wise annotation (e.g. suffixing each token with its annotations, separated by separators), as well as simple forms of XML spans (e.g. multiple tokens are 'wrapped' with an annotation) as in the popular Corpus Workbench format (CWB, Christ 1994, also the back end of the widely used CQPWeb interface, Hardie 2012). Hierarchical inline annotations are also used often, such as Penn Treebank brackets or basic XML formats. In such formats, annotations directly accompany the tokens, and although use of XML can make it somewhat clearer which parts belong to the text and which parts are annotations, the conceptual difference between these options is not large, as shown in the example here:

(16) Inline POS annotation:

*This*_DT *is*_VBZ *an*_DT *example*_NN

(17) Inline hierarchical bracketing tree:

```
(ROOT
  (S
    (NP (DT This))
    (VP (VBZ is)
      (NP (DT an) (NN example)))
    (. .)))
```

(18) Inline hierarchical TEI XML tree:

```
<s>
    <phr type="NP">
        <w type="DT">This</w>
    </phr>
    <phr type="VP">
        <w type="VBZ">is</w>
        <phr type="NP">
            <w type="DT">an</w>
            <w type="NN">example</w>
        </phr>
    </phr>
</s>
```

In essence, the TEI XML representation of a syntax tree in (18) is no different from the one in (17), except that XML tags in angle brackets are used as separators instead of round brackets and spaces. However, the XML representation uses a widely agreed upon standard for separating markup from primary data content, and thus may have some advantages for interoperability and machine readability of the data. In the case of TEI XML, the inventory of tags is also standardized, for example, the use of <s> to mean sentence, <phr> for phrase nodes and <w> for word forms. Yet all of these representations are not easy to add further layers of annotation to, because even if no hierarchy conflicts break the data's bracketing structure, it is still necessary to interlace new annotations with the existing graph structure.

Lai and Bird (2004) found that inline representations were insufficient for the expression of the type of complex annotation graphs and corresponding queries that early multilayer corpora were beginning to demand, especially for non-tree structures.[13] They presented and advocated the use of stand-off formats as used in NITE XML (Carletta et al. 2003) for the multilayer representation of resources such as the HCRC Map Task corpus (Anderson et al. 1991). The stand-off approach entails storing primary data and annotations in separate files and then using referencing mechanisms, such as XML XPointers, to reference elements in other files. In NITE XML this is done by reference to timed units, giving time indices at which primary data are uttered. This is shown for data from one speaker in the HCRC Map Task corpus in Figure 3.7. In the first part (file ending in *timed-units. xml*), actual uttered tokens are given IDs and start and end times. Time indices and IDs are also given to non-linguistic events (e.g. 'inbreath') and multiple word forms uttered in a way that cannot be separated ('does that', pronounced like 'zat'). Token indices are assigned to all time-unit sequences, and special separate tokens are given to cases such as the instance of 'does that', in the second file, using the *turef* (time-unit reference) attribute. In the third file, POS annotations refer back to these identifiers, for example, the POS tag 'nn' applies to the word 'forest' at ID "q1ec4f.123".

Although this format is difficult for human reading, it can be processed automatically, and there is no limit to the amount of annotation layers that we can apply to the data by referring to the relevant identifiers. Another advantage of the time-alignment scheme in NITE XML is the ability to represent primary data from multiple speakers separately, because any amount of time-unit events can be added for multiple concurrent speakers (see Section 2.2). Similar issues apply to the representation of parallel corpora (i.e. corpora containing texts and their translations): There may be more than one primary text datum occupying each 'position' from a logical point of view.

At the same time, this form of time-aligned representation is less natural for monolingual written data, because the primary text is not

---

13. In fact, Lai and Bird (2004: 145) regarded the presence of co-indexed traces in the Penn Treebank as already expressing secondary edges which violate tree structure. If the relationship between traces and their co-indexed phrases needs to be searched for, this point of view is certainly justified.

```
Contents of q1ec4.f.timed-units.xml
<nite:root xmlns:nite="http://nite.sourceforge.net/"
id="tu.q1ec4.f">
...
<tu id="q1ec4f.118" start="107.5593" end="107.7371"
utt="34">like</tu>
<tu id="q1ec4f.119" start="107.7372" end="107.9273"
utt="34">have</tu>
<tu id="q1ec4f.120" start="107.9273" end="108.0361"
utt="34">you</tu>
<tu id="q1ec4f.121" start="108.0361" end="108.1061"
utt="34">got</tu>
<tu id="q1ec4f.122" start="108.1061" end="108.1515"
utt="34">a</tu>
<tu id="q1ec4f.123" start="108.1516" end="108.4561"
utt="34">forest</tu>
<tu id="q1ec4f.124" start="108.4561" end="108.8274"
utt="34">stream</tu>
. . .
<noi id="q1ec4f.221" start="199.8607" end="199.9693"
type="inbreath"/>
<tu id="q1ec4f.227" start="200.7741" end="200.9585">does
that</tu>
. . .
</nite:root>

Contents of q1ec4f.tokens.xml
<nite:root xmlns:nite="http://nite.sourceforge.net/"
id="tok.q1ec4.f">
. . .
<tuseq id="q1ec4f.tok.10"><nite:child href="q1ec4.f.timed-
units.xml#id(q1ec4f.154)..id(q1ec4f.226)"/></tuseq>
<token turef="q1ec4f.227" estimated="end" end="200.9585"
start="200.7741" id="q1ec4f.tok.11">does</token>
<token turef="q1ec4f.227" estimated="start" end="200.9585"
start="200.7741" id="q1ec4f.tok.12">that</token>
. . .
</nite:root>

Contents of q1ec4.f.pos.xml
<nite:root xmlns:nite="http://nite.sourceforge.net/"
id="pos.q1ec4.f">
. . .
```

Figure 3.7 Stand-off data in NITE XML showing excerpts from three XML files

```
<tw   tag="hv"   id="q1ec4f.pos.105"   cited="not_
cited"><nite:child   href="q1ec4.f.timed-units.
xml#id(q1ec4f.119)"/></tw>
<tw   tag="ppss"   id="q1ec4f.pos.106"   cited="not_
cited"><nite:child   href="q1ec4.f.timed-units.
xml#id(q1ec4f.120)"/></tw>
<tw   tag="vbn"   id="q1ec4f.pos.107"   cited="not_
cited"><nite:child   href="q1ec4.f.timed-units.
xml#id(q1ec4f.121)"/></tw>
<tw   tag="at"   id="q1ec4f.pos.108"   cited="not_
cited"><nite:child   href="q1ec4.f.timed-units.
xml#id(q1ec4f.122)"/></tw>
<tw   tag="nn"   id="q1ec4f.pos.109"   cited="not_
cited"><nite:child   href="q1ec4.f.timed-units.
xml#id(q1ec4f.123)"/></tw>
<tw   tag="nn"   id="q1ec4f.pos.110"   cited="not_
cited"><nite:child   href="q1ec4.f.timed-units.
xml#id(q1ec4f.124)"/></tw>
. . .
</nite:root>
```

Figure 3.7 (Continued)

available in any one place: It can only be reconstructed from the timeline by concatenating units adjacent in time. Some stand-off formats reserve a special file for this purpose, representing the underlying textual data as a sequence of characters and using character offsets to define token and annotation positions. This can be done using a plain text file, for example, in the GrAF stand-off format (Ide and Suderman 2007, the format of the American National Corpus, codified as a standard in ISO 24612) or an XML file, as in PAULA XML (Dipper 2005). PAULA XML is also the format used to represent the merged data from all formats in GUM, and will therefore be described in some more detail. The following example illustrates the basic principles used in PAULA. The primary data are represented in *doc1.text.xml* inside the <body> tag, as shown in Figure 3.8. Tokens are delimited in *doc1.tok.xml*: Note how character ranges define token positions (e.g. tok_1 occurs from character 1, for four characters, using an XPointer range) and not all characters are part of a token. For example, tok_2 begins at character 6, whereas the preceding space, character 5, is untokenized. The final period in tok_5 is directly adjacent to the preceding word 'example', and therefore it begins at character 19, directly after the end of the token 'example'. Finally, annotations are created which refer back to the tokens created in *doc1.tok.xml*. Again, any number of annotations can be created or added retroactively (see Zeldes et al. 2013 for detailed documentation).

```
Contents of doc1.text.xml
<paula version="1.1">
<header paula_id="mycorpus.doc1_text" type="text"/>
<body>This is an example.</body>
</paula>

Contents of doc1.tok.xml
<paula version="1.1">
<header paula_id="mycorpus.doc1_tok"/>
<markList xmlns:xlink="http://www.w3.org/1999/xlink"
type="tok"
xml:base="mycorpus.doc1.text.xml">
<mark id="tok_1" xlink:href="#xpointer(string-range(//
body,'',1,4))"/><!-- This -->
<mark id="tok_2" xlink:href="#xpointer(string-range(//
body,'',6,2))"/><!-- is -->
<mark id="tok_3" xlink:href="#xpointer(string-range(//
body,'',9,2))"/><!-- an -->
<mark id="tok_4" xlink:href="#xpointer(string-range(//
body,'',12,7))"/><!--example-->
<mark id="tok_5" xlink:href="#xpointer(string-range(//
body,'',19,1))"/><!-- . -->
</markList>
</paula>

Contents of doc1.tok_pos.xml
<header paula_id="mycorpus_pos"/>
<featList xmlns:xlink="http://www.w3.org/1999/xlink"
type="pos" xml:base="mycorpus.tok.xml">
<feat xlink:href="#tok_1" value="DT"/><!-- This -->
<feat xlink:href="#tok_2" value="VBZ"/><!-- is -->
<feat xlink:href="#tok_3" value="DT"/><!-- an -->
<feat xlink:href="#tok_4" value="NN"/><!-- example -->
<feat xlink:href="#tok_5" value="SENT"/><!-- . -->

. . .
```

Figure 3.8 Stand-off annotation in PAULA XML

Complete merged data for GUM in PAULA XML can be found at https://github.com/amir-zeldes/gum/tree/master/paula/.

True stand-off formats, such as NITE XML or PAULA XML, are very powerful in terms of the data models that they can represent but are also highly complex and require the proliferation of very many XML files. However, there is no principled reason why the same information represented in the examples shown earlier cannot be placed in a single XML file. This is the logic behind the use of 'hybrid' representations, or 'inline/

```
<text>Karin flies to New York. She wants to go on vacation
there.</text>
<tokens>
    <token ID="t_0">Karin</token>
    <token ID="t_1">flies</token>
    <token ID="t_2">to</token>
    <token ID="t_3">New</token>
    <token ID="t_4">York</token>
    <token ID="t_5">.</token>
    <token ID="t_6">She</token>
    <token ID="t_7">wants</token>
    . . .
</tokens>
<sentences>
    <sentence ID="s_0" tokenIDs="t_0 t_1 t_2 t_3 t_4
t_5"></sentence>
    <sentence ID="s_1" tokenIDs="t_6 t_7 ... "></sentence>
</sentences>
<POStags tagset="PTB">
    <tag ID="pt_0" tokenIDs="t_0">NNP</tag>
    <tag ID="pt_1" tokenIDs="t_1">VBP</tag>
    <tag ID="pt_2" tokenIDs="t_2">TO</tag>
    . . .
```

Figure 3.9 Inline/stand-off data in TCF XML

stand-off' formats. In such formats, a concept such as a timeline or set of tokens is defined in one area of the file, and annotations referring back to these are added in another region. Often, however, the number and types of annotations that can be added are not arbitrarily large. For example, in the TCF format (Hinrichs et al. 2010), a single XML file has dedicated elements for the expression of primary data, tokens, sentence segmentation, syntax trees and entity annotations. This format is explicitly white space preserving and allows for multiple annotation layers but does not allow the addition of arbitrary annotations (Figure 3.9).

Other inline/stand-off formats allow arbitrary annotations of varying degrees of complexity. For example, the XML formats for the EXMA-RaLDA (Schmidt 2004) and ELAN (Brugman and Russel 2004) grid editing tools define timelines for events and then align any number of span annotations to any sequence of timeline events. Some complex annotation formats take this idea to the level of hierarchical graphs, including syntax trees, such as the tiger2 format for syntactic annotation (Romary et al. 2015), which is also codified in an ISO standard (ISO 24615). A complete overview of annotation formats for multilayer corpora is beyond the scope of the current discussion, but Table 3.6 gives a summary of the

Table 3.6 Overview of properties of some popular annotation formats

	Whitespace	Stand-off	Hierarchy	Confl. spans	Discontinuous	Parallel	Dialog overlap	Metadata	Subcorpora	Multimodal
CoNLLU	yes	no	dep[14]	no	no	no	no	no	no	no
CWB	no	no	no	yes	no	yes	no	yes	no	no
Elan	yes	inline	no	yes	no	no	yes	yes	yes	yes
EXMARaLDA	yes	inline	no	yes	no	no	yes	yes	yes	yes
FoLiA	yes	inline	yes	yes	yes	no	no	yes	yes	no
GrAF	yes	yes	yes	yes	yes	no[15]	no[15]	yes	yes	no
PAULA XML	yes	yes	yes	yes	yes	yes	yes	yes	yes	yes
PTB	no	no	yes	no	no	no	no	no	no	no
TCF	yes	inline	yes	yes	yes	no	no	yes	no	no
TEI XML	yes	yes[16]	yes	no[16]	no[16]	yes	yes	yes	yes	yes
TigerXML	no	no	yes	no	yes	no[17]	no	yes[17]	yes	no
tiger2	yes	yes	yes	yes	yes	no	no	yes	yes	no
WebAnno TSV	yes	inline	dep[14]	yes	no[18]	no	no	no	no	no

14. The value 'dep' indicates formats with some capacity to express pointing relations or dependency edges between flat units (including, e.g. syntactic dependency or coreference annotation) but without complex non-terminal node hierarchies.
15. Although GrAF does not explicitly support multiple overlapping speakers or parallel corpora, there are some conceivable ways of representing these using the available graph structure. However, I am not aware of any corpus or tool implementing these with GrAF.
16. Stand-off annotation has been implemented in TEI XML (see Chapter 20.5 of the TEI p5 guidelines, www.tei-c.org/) and can cover a wide range of use cases for discontinuous annotations and hierarchy conflicts. However, it is not frequently used in the TEI community, and there are some limitations (see Bański 2010; Bański et al. 2016 for analysis).
17. TigerXML itself does not implement parallel alignment, but an extension format known as STAX has been developed for parallel treebanking in the Stockholm TreeAligner (Lundborg et al. 2007). Metadata in TigerXML are limited to a pre-determined set of fields, such as 'author', 'date' and 'description'.
18. The WebAnno TSV format may be capable of representing discontinuous spans, but because the WebAnno interface does not support them, they are not produced in practice.

relevant properties and capabilities of some popular annotation formats discussed here. The list in the table is only a small sample and in no way exhaustive, but the focus is deliberately on formats that are either official or de facto standards and in use in multiple projects.

3.4   Merging and Validation

Retaining multiple source formats, as in the final stage of the GUM source data described at the end of Section 3.2, can be very useful for several reasons:

- Formats from original source tools can be fed back to those tools for correction.
- Errors can be traced more directly back to the formats they arose in.
- Users interested only in a subset of layers available in one format may find it easier to interact with a more familiar, simpler format with fewer layers.

However, for many purposes, including validation across layers, simple search over multiple layers and merged visualizations, having a single-format, authoritative representation of a multilayer corpus can be useful. Stand-off XML formats are often a good basis for such a merged representation, but getting data from different sources into such a format is a non-trivial task. Under the best circumstances, data structures of annotations from different sources (annotation interfaces, NLP tools) are all compatible, meaning that minimally, they reference the same basic text, and ideally also share the same tokenization of the data. The first step in approaching the merging task is therefore validating the data's integrity and alerting corpus editors to errors or problems in the data.

Two types of validity can be distinguished for the merging task: structural (sometimes referred to as syntactic) validity and content (or semantic) validity. The structural validity of the data consists of each format being valid in itself (e.g. no broken bracketing structures in PTB trees, well-formed XML in XML formats, etc.), but also in the validity of any aspect that is a prerequisite to the technical possibility of the data representations being merged. For GUM, this means in the first instance that for each document we have all annotation layers, that the document names match across layers and that the token counts in each and every format match. The GUM Buildbot (see https://corpling.uis.georgetown.edu/gum/build.html) ensures this by going into each directory in the GUM repository, counting the files in each and verifying that names match: for example, a document named GUM_interview_chomsky has a

PTB file called GUM_interview_chomsky.ptb and a CWB file containing TEI markup called GUM_interview_chomsky.xml, and both have exactly as many tokens. Once this validation is passed, the text of the documents is compared, ensuring that merging annotations for these documents will not fail.

Already at this level, some discrepancies are inevitably found, because, for example, as noted in Section 3.2, the PTB format cannot directly represent tokens which are themselves brackets. Our validation script must therefore recognize that an escape sequence such as -LRB- (Left Round Bracket) is a valid correspondent of a token '('. The final structural validation carried out in the data is then a comparison of sentence borders, because GUM guidelines dictate, for example, that RST EDUs may not cross sentence boundaries (see Section 3.2 on discourse parsing). Although this would not necessarily lead to an unmergeable corpus, because there are no annotations depending on this identity of boundaries, we would still like to ensure that this guideline has been followed. We can also issue a warning and force-adjust any conflicting boundaries by favoring the version found in whichever format we feel is more likely to be correct. Alternatively, it is possible to construct an adjudication interface to manually resolve conflicts.

After structural validation is passed, we can apply content validation by checking for annotation constellations that are implausible or clearly erroneous, even though they do not constitute structurally invalid data. In many cases, invalid annotation values can be detected within a single annotation file (see Dickinson 2015 for an overview of methods). For example, forms of the English verb 'have' are annotated in the TreeTagger's extended Penn Treebank tag set using tags with 'H', such as 'VHP' for present tense verb 'have', or 'VHD' for the past 'had' (instead of 'VBP' and 'VBD' for the lemma 'be'). As a result, cases of the token 'have' with a tag such as 'VBP' can immediately be flagged as semantic errors.[19] Similarly, some dependency annotations must obey categorical rules, such as multiword-expression edges in dependency syntax trees (the label 'mwe') always pointing to the right (by convention, mwe tokens such as 'as well as' are dominated by the leftmost token). Such expressions are also limited to a closed list, which is maintained and expanded as necessary. Violations of these semantic constraints can be found simply by looking at the dependency annotation files.

---

19. This particular error is, however, infrequent, because 'have' and 'be' have a closed set of forms – most violations for this rule arise due to non-standard apostrophe glyphs (e.g. in the form *'ve*) or due to non-standard spelling omitting them (e.g. *shouldve*, which can be tokenized *should + ve*).

Another possibility is to look for rare or unusual patterns and especially identical sequences of tokens which receive multiple inconsistent analyses. Dickinson and Meurers (2003) suggest setting an n-gram window (e.g. looking at all trigrams) and creating frequency tables for their annotations (e.g. POS tag trigrams), which can help to flag rare and therefore unlikely analyses. The advantage is that errors can be found that were not envisioned from the start, but the disadvantage is the need for manual evaluation of the detected anomalies. Dickinson and Meurers' approach is implemented in the DECCA (Detection of Errors and Correction in Corpus Annotation) tool suite (http://decca.osu.edu/), which inspects POS tags, dependencies and constituent annotation layers in sequence (but not jointly). Although this has not yet been implemented, we plan to apply DECCA to GUM as well.

In more complex cases, we can leverage the multilayer corpus by looking at multiple formats at the same time. The GUM Buildbot compares dependency annotation files, POS tags and sentence type annotations to flag unlikely combinations, such as negations not having the 'neg' dependency label or imperative sentences (the SPAAC type 'imp', Section 3.2) having a subject dependent of the root token (because imperatives should have no subject). Some of the automatically generated annotations in GUM are also corrected in this way. For example, CLAWS POS tags, which are added automatically to the PTB tags in GUM, are cross-checked to ensure consistency. CLAWS distinguishes the use of 'to' as a preposition (the tag 'PRP') and as an infinitive marker ('TO0'), but automatic tagging is not always correct. Because gold PTB tags do not make this distinction (always 'TO'), they cannot tell us which is correct; however, the dependency trees should have the 'prep' dependency in prepositional cases, meaning that we can catch such errors. The result of all of these automatic validation processes is that there are fewer errors in total, and noticing a new error should ideally lead to considering whether it, and similar cases, could be identified automatically and added to the Buildbot's validation routine (see https://github.com/amir-zeldes/gum/blob/master/_build/ for source code).

Another useful improvement of the original data's separate formats can be undertaken by projecting annotations from one format into others, provided that they have ways of representing this information. An enriched copy of the source annotations can then be produced automatically whenever the source annotations change. For example, the CWB format data contains a column for each token's POS tag, but it can be extended with any number of columns adding other token annotations automatically, such as the dependency function of each token as found in the syntactic annotation files. Conversely, we could take information about sentence types and speaker information from the CWB files and enrich the dependency annotation files. The final published data in individual formats for GUM have such annotations added, as shown in the following excerpt, which has columns not just for POS tags and lemmas, but also for added CLAWS tags and dependency functions:

```
<s type="decl">
<ref target="http://en.turystyczna.lodz.pl/page/">
Łódź    NP     Łódź   NP0    nsubj
</ref>
(        (      (      PUL    punct
Pronounced      VVN    pronounce      VVN     vmod
:        :      :      PUN    punct
<hi rend="italics">
Wootch NP       Wootch NP0    xcomp
</hi>
)        )      )      PUR    punct
is       VBZ    be     VBZ    cop
```

Because the added data are automatically projected, they can never conflict with the same annotation layers as expressed in parallel in a different format.

Once validation is complete and annotation quality has been checked as best as possible, the actual merging step can be carried out. In principle, given a stand-off format it would be possible to build dedicated converters to transform each annotation layer in a corpus such as GUM directly into the target format, in this case, PAULA XML. However, this process is both error prone and difficult to maintain: If there is no merged representation of the data in a programmatic data model at any point, nothing guarantees that the result of merging is valid, and changes to one component could make the process fall out of sync with other components. In addition, if we wish to convert to other formats than just PAULA XML (which we will likely want to do in order to search through and visualize the data, see Section 3.5), then we would need another set of dedicated converters targeting those different output formats.

Instead, Zipser and Romary (2010) suggest a meta-model-based methodology, in which data are represented in a central data model that is abstracted from any specific format. The data model used by Zipser and Romary is Salt, a Java-based graph modeling framework for corpus data which is powerful enough to contain all types of annotations used in GUM, and more. A converter framework called Pepper (https://corpus-tools/pepper) is provided, which incorporates plugin modules that convert data from and to a variety of formats via Salt. This circumvents the need to convert data between specific pairs of formats. All formats used in GUM as described in Section 3.2 are supported by Pepper, meaning that we can directly import them into the data model, which represents all formats as a graph of nodes and edges of the types described in Section 2.4: spans and node hierarchies connected to tokens above a primary textual data source, all linked into one graph using different types of edges, such as potentially annotated dominance and pointing relations.

With the different source format graphs now in memory as a Salt representation, information from the different datasets needs to be merged in order to allow output in a single stand-off XML format and for joint queries to work across layers (see Section 3.5). In the case of GUM, this is not difficult, because tokens are already guaranteed to match across formats thanks to validation. Pepper includes a merging module that can simply treat the tokens from all source formats as the same set of nodes and attach the different non-terminal graphs above them. When this is done, two main options need to be chosen from for the non-terminals: either *node-copying* is chosen, which means all non-terminal nodes from all source datasets will be represented, or *node-merging* can be chosen, which means that as many non-terminal nodes as possible will be fused. These two options are represented in Figure 3.10.

The node-merging option attempts to collapse as many nodes as possible based on dominating the exact same sequence of tokens. In some cases this is desirable, because the corpus graph will be smaller, leading to smaller files and better performance in search engines. However, the resulting graph is often harder to interpret, because any given node can have an unpredictable combination of annotations (e.g. some nodes will carry entity annotations and syntactic category annotations, whereas others will only carry one or the other). It also becomes impossible to assign unique layers to nodes (if desired; cf. Section 2.3), and in some cases, cycles may arise which cannot be exported into certain cycle-free target formats. In GUM, node-copying is chosen, and each set of nodes from a single-source dataset receives its own layer, as previously shown in Figure 2.2 in Section 2.3.

In more complex cases of merging, tokenization will be different in each format. This often happens in cases where one layer annotates units

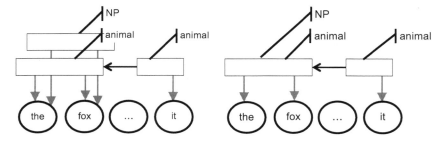

Figure 3.10 Merging syntax and entity annotations with node-copying (left) and node-merging (right)

below the word form (morphological analysis, or typographical information about individual letters), but another layer is created in a word-based annotation tool. A typical example is a historical treebank preserving diplomatic manuscript information (illuminated letters inside words, which are leaves in a syntax tree). In such cases, automatic merging can still take place, provided that the primary textual data matches across representations. Pepper can then simply create a minimal tokenization based on all needed boundaries and form 'super tokens' (actually ordinary nonterminal nodes) to represent the original tokens of a less granular format – the 'smallest' tokens then correspond to the timestamp-based segments in Section 2.1 (e.g. in Table 2.2). This is illustrated in Figure 3.11 for a

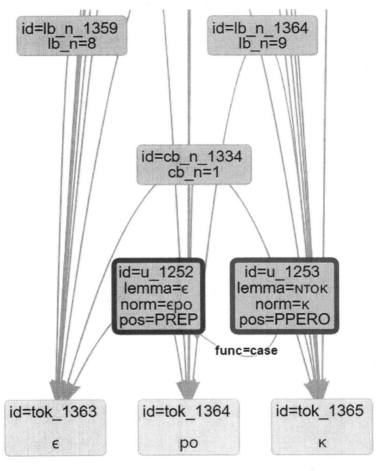

Figure 3.11 Merged annotation graph for two words/three tokens in a multilayer historical treebank

corpus of ancient Coptic manuscripts, which will be presented in more detail in Chapter 7 (image generated from a Salt model by the ANNIS visualization platform, see the next section).

The figure shows three minimal tokens at the bottom, corresponding to a sequence of Coptic characters ⲉⲣⲟⲕ <erok> 'to you'. The normal segmentation of this word form would only require two tokens: the preposition ero- 'to' and the pronoun -k 'you'. However, the manuscript containing this word has a line break in the middle of the first part after e- (lb_n=8 represents line number 8, followed by lb_n=9). As a result, the tool in which manuscript structure was annotated required a token boundary here. At the same time, the data are annotated for dependency syntax, with a pointing relation annotated 'func=case'. This edge connects two 'super tokens', generated during merging above the necessary minimal tokens, even though the dependency annotated data (in the CoNNLU format shown in Section 3.2) treat these higher super tokens as the only and minimal tokens in that format. As a result, these higher nodes also carry the annotations from the CoNLLU format, such as the POS tags (e.g. pos=PREP) and lemmas. Although this data representation is quite complex, it is necessary in order to search for patterns across all layers at once – for example, we can use such a graph to examine which POS tags or grammatical functions scribes felt more willing to interrupt by line breaks in the middle of a word. However, in order to pose questions such as these, we need search and visualization facilities to comb through the data. The discussion of tools and formats concludes with this next topic.

3.5   Search and Visualization

Many designers and some users of multilayer corpora use programmatic means to traverse merged or unmerged datasets and extract desired subsets of annotations or derive new datasets from the corpus, often using a scripting language such as Python or R. Such programming languages also offer very flexible visualization facilities to plot aggregated data from corpora, as we will do at multiple points in the second part of this book. However, extracting data using dedicated scripts can be laborious, and often new scripts would have to be written for each type of data extraction we wish to run. As a result, we may end up 're-inventing the wheel' quite often, creating multiple scripts which all have to read tokens, check for some relations and construct some sort of output.

A better option is to use a more generic architecture that can retrieve arbitrary subgraphs from a multilayer corpus, defined as paths of nodes and edges instantiating some properties and formalized in some sort of corpus query language. The requirements for corpus query languages have been discussed extensively in the literature, both in proprietary solutions tailored for one or a few corpora and generic architectures meant to include many new corpora (see Lai and Bird 2004; Dipper and Götze 2005; Ghodke and Bird 2010; Bański and Witt 2011; Evert and Hardie 2011; Frick et al. 2012; Krause and Zeldes 2016; Diewald et al. 2016). For the purpose of querying multilayer corpora, architectures capable of representing the data model objects outlined in Section 2.4 are essential and have been implemented with more or less intricate possibilities in several systems. Although in some cases it is possible to use general-purpose XML tools, such as XPath and XQuery (www.w3.org/XML/Query/) to extract data, in many cases a dedicated tool is more convenient or even indispensable.

Some support for multilayer corpora is found in systems capable of expressing an unrestricted set of potentially conflicting spans. The Corpus Workbench (Christ 1994) and its web interface CQPWeb (Hardie 2012) are among the most popular tools of this kind, as are grid-based tools such as EXMARaLDA or ELAN, already mentioned earlier. EXMARaLDA and ELAN files can be indexed for search using EXMARaLDA's search engine, EXAKT (http://exmaralda.org/en/exakt-en/). However, all of these tools are not capable of representing hierarchical data, and therefore they cannot be used to query treebanks. For treebanks, aside from command-line tools such as TGrep2 (http://tedlab.mit.edu/~dr/Tgrep2/) or Tregex (https://nlp.stanford.edu/software/tregex.shtml), there are also a few freely available search interfaces, such as TigerSearch (Lezius 2002, a local application with support for crossing edges), or Fangorn (Ghodke and Bird 2012, which only supports projective, unlabeled constituent trees). For dependency trees, PML-TQ (Štěpánek and Pajas 2010) offers a freely available query and visualization solution. Some applications support both constituent and dependency trees simultaneously, such as TüNDRA (the Tübingen aNnotated Data Retrieval Application, Martens 2013).

For corpora such as GUM, more complex search architectures are required, such as ANNIS (http://corpus-tools.org/annis/) or KorAP (Diewald et al. 2016). Pepper is capable of exporting data in the ANNIS format (called relANNIS), and a version of GUM in this format is available online (https://github.com/amir-zeldes/gum/tree/master/annis). The ANNIS Query Language (AQL) is based on the idea of declaring search nodes in terms of the annotations they must carry and then specifying relations between these nodes.[20] For example, the

---

20. AQL is, in many ways, an extension of concepts developed in TigerSearch (Lezius 2002) and NQL (Carletta et al. 2003), which use similar concepts and query syntax. See Krause and Zeldes (2016) for more details and Frick et al. (2012) for a comparison with several other corpus query languages.

query in (19) declares two annotated nodes, identified by carrying a lemma annotation and a POS annotation, respectively. The two nodes, #1 and #2, are then connected via a pointing relation (the operator ->) carrying a type label 'dep'. This query therefore finds noun dependents of the verb "sleep".

(19) `lemma="sleep" & pos="NN" & #1 ->dep #2`

A variety of operators can be used instead of '->' in (19), and they can also be placed directly between search terms. For example, the dot operator '.' is used to search for two adjacent nodes whose rightmost and leftmost tokens are consecutive, as in (20).

(20) `lemma="sleep" . pos="NN"`

This query finds the lemma sleep directly followed by a noun. Other operators indicate that an annotation covers the same tokens as another (the operator '_=_'), begins or ends at the same position ('_l_' and '_r_'), dominates another annotation's node ('>'), etc. (for a complete list of operators see http://corpus-tools.org/annis/aql.html). Annotations themsleves can also be constrained to certain layers, and regular expression patterns can be applied to filter annotation values.

Queries such as these will allow us to retrieve the large majority of data we require for the studies in the second part of this book, and I will refer back to these in some of the studies. The results from such queries can either be exported as tabular data (for example, containing all annotations of each of the matching nodes) or visualized in the ANNIS web interface using dedicated modules to display syntax trees, coreference annotations and more. Figure 3.12 shows several views of the same GUM document using different visualization modules (or 'visualizers') in ANNIS.

These will also be used to enable 'distant reading' of annotation patterns in some of the studies in the second part of this book (see Section 5.4), which will make use of the data models and corpus tools presented in this chapter.

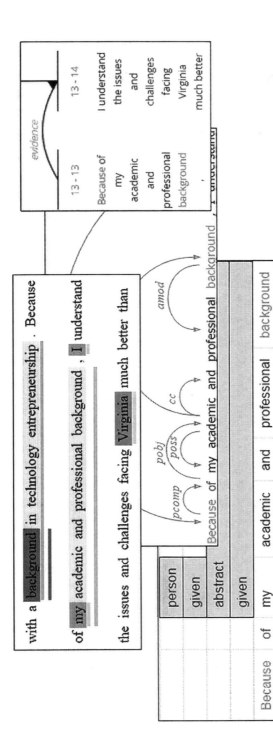

Figure 3.12 Multiple visualizations of the same corpus fragment from GUM. Clockwise from the top left: coreference, dependency syntax, discourse relations and entity annotations

Part II
Leveraging Multilayer Data

4 Probabilistic Syntax, Agreement and Information Structure

4.1 Introduction

Over a decade ago, Manning (2003) laid out a research agenda for theories of syntax that would be intrinsically probabilistic in nature. According to Manning, an empirically founded syntactic theory should be in a position to tell us not only which utterances are grammatical in a language, following the research program of generative grammar (Chomsky 1957: 13), but also what a speaker would choose to say, and with what likelihood, given the meaning they wished to express and the context in which they were making the utterance. He formalized this notion as in (21). For the converse notion – that language understanding was a function based on judging the likeliest meaning intended by a speaker given the form of the utterance and the surrounding context – Manning gives (22).[1]

(21) *p(form|meaning, context)*
(22) *p(meaning|form, context)*

Manning then proceeds to discuss several syntactic phenomena that can be modeled as a probabilistic function with multiple predictors, including argument linking as a passive or active utterance, given the discourse newness of the arguments (*the policeman scolded me* versus *I was scolded by a policeman*), the semantic role as agent/non-agent and the person feature's position on the person hierarchy (first > second > third person). This type of multifactorial view brings syntactic alternation phenomena closer to the domain of allophonic or allomorphic alternations in phonology and morphology, respectively. Although most competing syntactic constructions are not as predictable as allophones or allomorphs, using a wide range of categories that can be annotated in a multilayer corpus and a probabilistic view of syntax can sometimes

---

1. The third permutation not discussed by Manning, that of predicting the context given an utterance and knowledge of its meaning, is what we do when we overhear a sentence out of context that is insufficient for constructing much of the surrounding dialog with certainty.

bring the syntactic level of description quite close to having 'allostructions' (Cappelle 2006).[2]

Quite apart from the non-linguistic 'context' part of the equations provided earlier, the question of what constitutes a 'form' and a 'meaning' for probabilistic modeling is an open one. In this chapter and throughout the following ones, I will assume a constructivist approach in line with Goldberg's (2006) view of construction grammar (but cf. Kay and Fillmore 1999; Croft 2001, among many others, for similar ideas), which admits any configuration of lexically specified or schematic 'slots' as potential members in a hierarchy of constructions, which can become stored by means of entrenchment. The term 'construction' will therefore apply to all form–meaning pairings, including distributional and discourse-level meanings (e.g. choices signaling presence in a certain genre or a particular information structure, see below), and forms amounting to abstract argument structure constructions which specify a component of the meaning contributions of arguments. For example, the ditransitive construction imposes a recipient reading on certain arguments for verbs of giving or communication, even for novel verbs not lexicalized as ditransitive per se (e.g. *to MSN someone something*, see Barðdal 2008: 82–83). In some cases, annotation layers will correspond directly to the presence of such constructions, whereas in others, sequences of annotations can be used to identify them, potentially on multiple layers.

Questions such as the type of argument linking that is likely to be instantiated, given the surrounding factors, are a prime example of the kinds of linguistic facts that we can represent by working on multiple layers simultaneously. On the one hand, we want to make sure that the subset of features we are looking at is the best one for the task at hand. This means using model selection techniques; working with separate training, validation and testing sets; or using cross-validation and a variety of well-understood statistical and machine learning techniques which will figure prominently in the following chapters. On the other hand, we want relevant features that are reliably detectable beyond the purposes of a specific study (e.g. if we can agree on discourse newness for subjects of motion verbs, this does not yet mean that discourse newness is a reliable category in general, and we may prefer a general tag set that works for multiple studies to one that works slightly better but only for a very specific purpose).

A further concern is directionality of the predictors: state-of-the-art multifactorial models (Gries 2015; Levshina 2015: 253–394), which

---

2. This last term is preceded by a long tradition in structuralist linguistics treating the realization of syntactic patterns as tagmemes (Bloomfield 1933: 166) and their alternations in much the same way as allomorphy, e.g. as 'allotagms' (Barri 1977: 12) or 'allo-patterns' (Shisha-Halevy 1986: 73, and others).

Manning (2003: 330–336) also advocates, can help us to leverage correlations. Yet like most statistical procedures, they do not tell us about causation. For example, we may think that first person is a good predictor of oblique or passive subject argument linking for a given verb, but it is possible that we are missing other crucial facts: even if *I was sold a car* is more likely than *a car was sold to me*, we are possibly ignoring an interlocutive bias of the verb 'sell', which may be used disproportionally often with first-person arguments, or we may also disregard some important alternative variants with other competing verbs, such as *I bought a car* – this is a key problem in identifying the candidate variants of a Variationist variable (see Labov 2004). At the same time, much like earlier structuralist approaches (Bloomfield 1933: 145; de Saussure 1966: 116), many contemporary usage-based frameworks assume that the availability of a choice always implies some difference in meaning, that is, there is a principle of no synonymy (Goldberg 1995:67; see Uhrig 2015 for criticism). We will therefore often be interested both in what constrains a choice and what subtle differences in meaning a choice conveys.[3]

Although even a fully annotated corpus cannot tell us what variants to look at, having homogeneous annotations available for a dataset of running text means we can easily go back and retrieve values for alternatives that become apparent while working with the data (including by means of introspection or experimentation). The remainder of this chapter is dedicated to multilayer corpus studies of two topics involving such variation. The next section explores the relationship between active or passive voice, grammatical functions and information structure in influencing the choice of word orders as they appear in the GUM corpus (see Section 3.2). The goal in this study will not be to develop a concrete prediction engine for serializing word order (such a task is a central challenge of natural language generation and machine translation, involving substantially more complex features and architectures than those discussed here, see Ratnaparkhi 2000, Gatt and Krahmer 2018); instead, the focus will be on modeling the relative importance of the competing and potentially collinear cues assumed in previous studies. Section 4.3 then gives a larger scale modeling study, using data from the OntoNotes corpus (Hovy et al. 2006), which attempts to accurately predict an unusual agreement pattern in English referred to as notional agreement: use of plural pronouns to refer back to morphologically singular NPs. Section 4.4 ends with some conclusions and a discussion of desiderata for studies in Probabilistic Syntax.

3. I thank Hans Boas for commenting on this point.

4.2   Voice, Word Order and Information Structure

The relationship between semantic roles and their syntactic realization in argument structures has been a topic of acute interest and heated debate over the course of the last few decades in a range of fields, including syntactic theory, semantics and usage-based models of grammar (see e.g. Grimshaw 1990; Levin and Rappaport-Hovav 2005; Boas 2011). Multi-factorial studies of the past decade have shown that the choice of syntactic construction among competing alternatives is strongly predicted by using a wide array of variables (Gries 2002; Szmrecsanyi 2006; Bresnan et al. 2007). A sample of some of the factors found to be significantly predictive of syntactic alternation phenomena is given here:

- Phonological weight (in syllables/phonemes/stress; Gries 2002; Bresnan et al. 2007; Lohmann 2011 and others)
- Information structure (givenness, topicality, focus; Bresnan et al. 2007 and many others)
- Definiteness (in addition to, or as a proxy for givenness; Gries 2002; Bresnan et al. 2007)
- NP form: pronominal, common, proper noun (Bresnan et al. 2007; Lohmann 2011)
- Semantic classes (e.g. verb types such as 'communication verb'; Wulff 2006), aktionsart (achievement, state etc.; Deshors and Gries 2016), entity types (Spalek and Zeldes 2017)
- Morphological form (e.g. verb inflections, pluralization, person agreement; Lohmann 2011; Recasens et al. 2013)
- Animacy (binary, e.g. Gries 2002, or more complex hierarchies, e.g. Levshina 2016)
- Dialect/variety (Bresnan and Ford 2010; Deshors and Gries 2016)
- Genre and modality (Lohmann 2011; Levshina 2016)
- Negation, quantification (Recasens et al. 2013; Deshors and Gries 2016)
- Syntactic parallelism (same or similar construction in preceding discourse; Szmrecsanyi 2006; Bresnan et al. 2007)
- Other forms of priming (Gries 2005; Szmrecsanyi 2006)

Some of these factors are interrelated (pronouns are phonologically light, proper nouns are inherently definite) but can in some cases diverge (some nouns are shorter than some pronouns, some languages allow definite marking on proper nouns, etc.). It is part of the job of a multifactorial model used to predict the response variable to filter out those contributions that are significant given the other variables (all the while taking care not to overfit the data).

Multilayer corpus resources are the type of data best suited to performing studies of the sort mentioned earlier at scale. Although for some purposes it is enough to annotate a subset of examples in a table without resorting to complete running corpus annotation, the advantage of fully annotated data becomes especially clear when dealing with frequent constructional choices that play a role in almost every sentence. For example, the choice of active versus passive voice is ubiquitous: most sentences could hypothetically be expressed using either, but passives are comparatively rare. Characterizing their environments in a probabilistic model requires us to know the properties of essentially all sentences in a corpus. Additionally, if we want to look at more than just one construction at a time and also incorporate contextual factors, having naturally occurring running text annotated on as many levels as possible is invaluable. For example, studying the probabilistic interaction between word order and information structure requires fully annotated data, because any sequence of phrases in any sentence is a relevant datum. What's more, from a theoretical point of view we assume that speakers/hearers have access to precisely this kind of information (full context on all linguistic levels) as they construct and verbalize their discourse models.

The GUM data presented in Section 3.2 offers a good testing ground for the interactions between word order, information structure and voice, to which we turn next. Specifically, we would like to know which factors influence word order most and what happens when they pull in opposite directions. Information structure is known to be central to syntactic serialization, applying notions such as givenness, topicality and focus (see Krifka 2008 for discussion). Given information tends to occur before new information in English (Chafe 1976; Clark and Haviland 1977; Prince 1981) and cross-linguistically (Van Valin 1999; Büring 2010), with syntactic structure often accommodating this constraint. In English, subjects precede the verb and all subsequent arguments in most contexts so that a given referent is likely to be realized as a subject. At the same time, subjects usually also realize the agent role, but sometimes the agent is new, or even more unusually, the theme or patient may be given. This is one of the well-known factors contributing to passivization (cf. Halliday 1967), which exhibits a cross-linguistic complementarity with object fronting, that is, languages tend to prefer one of those two strategies in the presence of given patient arguments (Skopeteas and Fanselow 2010).

Weber and Müller (2004) demonstrate using corpus data for German that although canonical main clauses with SVO word order (the unmarked word order in German main clauses) do show the expected given-before-new pattern, fronted objects in OVS sentences do not indicate that the subject is more likely to be new. In fact, subjects were more likely than objects to be given, definite and pronominal in both word orders. Skopeteas and Fanselow (2010) use the QUIS questionnaire (Skopeteas et al. 2006) to elicit basic word orders in 12 languages under different given/new argument conditions and reach almost perfect consistency for elicited

English material, excluding contrastive contexts.[4] When the agent is given, 100% subject-first realization was observed, whereas for given patients, the agent was realized as non-first/non-subject 16.3% of the time. They classify English, together with French Canadian and other languages studied, as a passivizing, non-reordering language under these experimental conditions. However, such studies do not give us an idea of the prevalence of unexpected word order violations such as 'non-subject first', 'new before given', or 'long phrase before short phrase', or estimates of the relative importance of subject/agent givenness, passivization motivated by information structural constraints and length-based ordering in naturalistic data. In the following section we therefore begin by examining the distribution of grammatical function and voice before moving on to look at givenness and relative phrase length.

Grammatical Function and Voice

The relationship between givenness or information status, passive voice and syntactic function is easy to identify in data annotated for these categories. Following the annotation scheme in Dipper et al. (2007), the GUM corpus distinguishes three coarse types of information status, or 'givenness' (Chafe 1976; see Krifka 2008 for discussion). The label *new* is used for entities just introduced into the discourse, *giv* (given) for phrases denoting aforementioned entities and *acc* (accessible) for phrases denoting entities that have not been mentioned but are inferable from the situation (e.g. *pass the salt* when a saltshaker is visible at a meal) or from a previously mentioned phrase (i.e. bridging, for example, mention of a company licenses a definite first mention of *the CEO*; see Sections 3.2 and 5.4). These information status annotations can be cross-tabulated with grammatical functions covering subjects and objects from the dependency trees in GUM, as shown in Figure 4.1.

The figure plots the squared residuals for a contingency table of information status categories and the functions of nominal active subjects, active objects and passive subjects. In other words, each bar represents the value of one component of the chi-square statistic measuring the independence of the row and column variables. The area of each rectangle corresponds to the deviation of expected from observed values (O-E), and the base of each rectangle is the square root of the expectation, which can give us an idea about the amount of evidence that each rectangle is based on.

---

4. It should be noted, however, that it is not entirely uncontroversial to assume that the categories in question are comparable across languages, including the notions of subjecthood, arguments, voice, etc. (cf. Croft 2001), meaning that data comparing such tendencies across languages are always at risk of simplifying the facts.

subj_act   subj_pass   obj_act

Figure 4.1 Residuals for the association between voice and information status in GUM

The pairwise relationship and deviations overall are highly significant ($\chi^2 = 464.17$, df = 4, p < 2.2e–16, N = 7,149). It is immediately visible that passive subjects, though comparatively rare, cluster with active subjects, not objects: both contrast with objects by rarely being new. This is interesting because semantically, passive subjects occupy the same argument slots as corresponding active objects (usually a patient or theme role), so we would expect different entity-type biases in each column: active subjects are very often persons, which are very often given, whereas passive subjects less overwhelmingly represent persons.[5] Turning to objects, we find an unsurprising skew toward newness, but surprisingly, they are a little more likely to be 'accessible' than either active or passive subjects.

This information, interesting though it is, is still limited to the set of entities under examination: active and passive subjects/objects. Without data for the entire corpus, we cannot normalize our results against general expectations for information status and grammatical function. Are objects really very often new, or just more often than active subjects? Having a multilayer corpus with fully annotated running texts means we have the information to answer this question for the entire dataset, as shown in Figure 4.2 for 16,280 information status annotations. The bars for each function sum up to 100% of the occurrences of those functions in referring expressions in the corpus.

As the figure shows, objects are slightly less often given than 'other' function types, but the difference is slight (left group of bars). The more striking deviation by far is how given subjects are, and to a somewhat

5. We must keep in mind, however, that the verbs in each group do not necessarily correspond, i.e. we do not have the same set of verbs in the passive and active cases. For more on the special status of persons and other entity type effects, see the next section and Chapter 5.

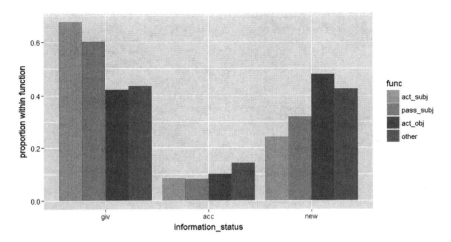

Figure 4.2 Proportion of information status groups for subjects, objects and other functions in GUM

lesser extent, passive subjects. The 'new' cluster of bars on the right is a mirror image of this result: Objects are new strikingly often, and passive subjects are somewhat less averse to newness than active subjects. Looking at the middle cluster, objects are actually closer to subjects in terms of likelihood to be accessible, with the largest proportion of accessible phrases in the 'other' category. In other words, phrases that are either predictable or inferable in context are used relatively rarely as core arguments in the corpus: Most such mentions are oblique. The largest group by far is prepositional phrases: About 40% of accessibles are prepositional, a subset of the 'other' category. Typical examples often contain generic or contextually recognizable locations as in (23)–(24).

(23) *In [the wild]*_{ACC}*, Formica fusca can encounter similar chemicals in aphids and dead ants.*

(24) *The city also expanded outward through rash development, particularly towards [the west]*_{ACC}

Both these examples can potentially be read as generic locations ('the wild', 'west'), though in the second one a bridging reading is also possible ('the west of the city').

The fact that objects can be given almost as often as the general population of non-subject phrases is, to some extent, not surprising. Although objects are less given than subjects, they are still integral to the main actors involved in the discourse, and are therefore prone to be repeated (even in the same function as object, for example, if an entity is the theme of multiple predicates). By contrast, the frequent newness of oblique nouns is especially evident in adjunct PPs, which may be mentioned once (new) and then never again. This is illustrated in the examples shown here, taken from GUM.

(25) *Columbia was lost tragically back on [February 1, 2003]*$_{\text{NEW}}$
(26) *Many of the neighborhoods are commercial centers and absolute heaven for [foodies]*$_{\text{NEW}}$

Some referents, such as places and times, are often mentioned circumstantially without being a topic for discussion. More salient entities, including humans, are also less likely to be given if they are functioning as modifiers, for example, here as a purpose or benefactive adjunct in (26) (not *heaven* in general but more specifically *heaven for foodies*). These results give a first glimpse of the distribution of individual phrases and their grammatical categories, but they also open up questions about the interactions between phrases: How are phrases ordered in a sentence? Do we get given objects simply because both arguments of a transitive clause have been introduced, and only one can be the subject? Are the phrases behind these numbers generally ordered by givenness (given before new)? What about other factors, such as phonological weight or phrase length? We turn to these in the next section.

Given Before New

The cross-linguistic principle of arranging given information before new has figured prominently in the discussion of the interplay between syntax and information structure. Clark and Haviland (1977) argued that given–new ordering was needed to promote "reasonably efficient communication" based on Gricean cooperativeness, because it allows speakers to attach pieces of new information to already established pieces of given information. In their account, this is accomplished using the following steps:

> At Step 1, the listener isolates the given and the new information in the current sentence. At Step 2, he searches memory for a direct antecedent, a structure containing propositions that match the given information precisely. Finally, at Step 3 the listener integrates the new information into the memory structure by attaching it to the antecedent found in Step 2.
>
> (Clark and Haviland 1977: 5)

This view corresponds fairly closely to the file card metaphor of File Change Semantics (Heim 1983), in which speakers manage a set of 'file cards' which are associated with discourse referents and then retrieve given files as required in order to update them with new information.

With this type of interpretive process in mind, the expectation that given information should precede new information can be cast as a violable pragmatic preference: Just like any cooperative maxim, communication efficiency through information ordering can be overridden, either due to competition with other known constraints or for reasons that we cannot (yet) identify. Some candidates for competing constraints include the processing factors surveyed at the beginning of this chapter, such as length in words/phonemes/syllables (some operationalization of phonological weight), or parallelism, but also conventional pressures, such as genre or text type effects. We may therefore begin by asking how often given–new ordering is observed, whether it is stronger/weaker than other effects (e.g. 'short before long' or 'subject first') and what is predictive of information status ordering violations. It is, however, clear from the outset that the expected preferences usually coincide: Especially in languages such as English, with SVO as the dominant word order, the first NP in most sentences is likely to be a given, short subject.

To find out how often given–new ordering is violated, we can search GUM for all ordered pairs of entity mentions $<e_1, e_2>$, such that the entities appear in order within the same sentence and have given or new information status (we omit the smaller 'accessible' class for simplicity). Thanks to the presence of sentence type annotations covering all tokens with their containing sentence span, this can be done using the AQL query in (27).

```
(27) s_type _i_  infstat=/giv|new/ .* infstat=/giv|new/ &
     #1 _i_ #3
```

This query stipulates that a span annotated with some s_type annotation includes (the operator _i_) a span annotated with the label 'infstat', having a value matching a regular expression matching 'giv' or 'new'. This span precedes (indirect precedence operator, .*) another span with the same annotation possibilities. Finally, we state that the s_type node, #1, also includes the third infstat node, #3 (see Section 3.5 on AQL).

The query in (27) effectively harnesses the information on multiple layers of information to retrieve about 33,000 pairings, which come from the cross-product of all possible ordered pairs of annotated entity spans contained within the same sentence span. Sentences containing only one entity (e.g. fragments such as headings consisting of a single NP) are excluded by the query, because it requires two entity NPs with information status annotations to be present. We can export the query results from ANNIS together with document metadata in order to get by-document and by-genre breakdowns. The results are cross-tabulated in Table 4.1.

The results for the entire corpus, in the last row, indicate that the given–new ordering constraint is more powerful than length-based ordering

Table 4.1 Percentages for violations of expected orderings in the GUM subcorpora

Sub-corpus	% violations			All three
	Giv-new	Short-long	Subj initial	
interview	17.75	27.55	27.36	3.97
news	21.18	35.73	32.96	1.99
voyage	20.35	32.70	33.06	1.75
whow	18.73	29.26	34.00	3.16
all	19.54	31.43	31.54	2.71

(short before long) or the preference for subject-first, when all phrases are considered. The latter inequality stems partly from the fact that evidence for given–new ordering is also provided by phrase pairs appearing after the verb, neither of which is the subject. Note also that the subject violations were counted only for sentences beginning with an entity term, and therefore imperatives and other types of non-nominal–first sentences were not counted. We also observe that the spread for given–new violations is the tightest (range 17.75%–21.18%, only 3.43 percent points), whereas other violation rates are more spread out (8.18 and 6.64 for the other two), which suggests that the given–new constraint is the most stable across genres. Violations of all three constraints at the same time are quite rare at 2.71% overall. These can be found in information structural environments which have been discussed in the literature, such as new frame-setters (see Jacobs 2001: 655–658; Krifka 2008: 268–269) and other fronted PPs in examples (28)–(29), taken from the GUM data.

(28) *In [a recently-accepted Evolution paper]*_{NEW} *Bos and colleagues describe ants appearing to self-medicate* (fronting a new, long, non-subject phrase as a locative frame setter)

(29) *Due to [its beautiful hand-painted tiling and magnificent public square]*_{NEW}, *it is considered to be one of the most beautiful cities in the world* (fronted causal phrase)

However, some arguable cases can also be found in the corpus in which new information is introduced while itself embedded within a given mention, as in the fronted appositional absolute clause in (30).

(30) *[An ancient town and capital of Persia from 1598 to 1722], [it] was long noted for its fine carpets*

In this example, the fronted non-subject phrase actually has identical reference with the short, given pronoun subject 'it', both of which refer to the city of Isfahan in Iran. This somewhat unusual configuration can probably be considered a specific construction in the sense of construction grammar, in that it has identifiable form (fronted nominal predicate without a verb, serving in apposition to the following clausal subject) and discourse functional meaning (both our ability to comprehend it as supplying background information about the subject and a genre-specific distribution which constrains its usage).[6]

Finally, comparing the different subcorpora in Table 4.1, we find that interviews exhibit the fewest violations in each category, which is unsurprising for the most conversational genre being examined. Conversational data are more subject to processing constraints and common ground management than other types, because interviewees must respond and verbalize more spontaneously, with fewer possibilities to plan and revise their utterances. At the same time, interviews have the highest rate of triple violations, suggesting that some otherwise rare constructions, and perhaps specifically fronted PPs representing long, new frame-setters, may be more frequent in this text type. To check whether this is the case, we would need additional annotations classifying such phrases, including a possible annotation layer for frame-setters and other types of topical information (see Dipper et al. 2007, for an annotation scheme which includes frame-setters).

The data we have gathered also allow us to construct multifactorial models to quantify and compare the influence of different variables on word order, while factoring out variation due to differences between individual documents. To construct such a model, we can look at the data from a different direction: We can 'forget' the order of each pair of phrases and attempt to predict what the order was based on the properties of the individual phrases. We can then use linear mixed-effects models to build a classifier of 'earliness', predicting which of two phrases will appear first. The features used for this model are chosen to correspond to the linguistic categories whose influence we wish to explore:

- Z-score scaled difference in phrase length
- Information status ordering (i.e. does the order obey given before new?)
- Function ordering (i.e. does the order obey subject before non-subject?)

---

6. The status of such configurations as constructions is probably less controversial in constructional approaches in the tradition of Berkeley or Goldbergian Construction Grammars, whereas some more formal approaches, such as Sign-Based Construction Grammar (Sag 2012) or Fluid Construction Grammar (Steels and de Beule 2006), might be content to allow the derivation of such patterns from more general apposition constructions. What we see here is a distinctive information structural property of this configuration, which can also argue for its status as a construction.

Phrase pairs are presented in a random order, meaning the original two phrases are assigned the labels A or B arbitrarily. The task of the model is therefore to choose 'A first' or 'B first'.

Because most phrases are non-subject and non-initial, we may expect length differences to be informative for more pairs than the other factors, which only help when one of the two phrases compared is either a subject or given. If neither is the subject, then the 'subject before non-subject' constraint is implicitly obeyed, and similarly if both phrases are given, new, etc. At the same time, length-based ordering may be unreliable (sometimes short phrases appear late), whereas an ordering based on grammatical function (especially 'subject first') is very consistent in English. The model computed from the data using the R package lme4 can tell us which factors are more significant when we look at all three layers of information at the same time:

```
Random effects:
 Groups    Name          Variance  Std.Dev.
 doc       (Intercept)   0.004704  0.06859
Number of obs: 33025, groups: doc, 76

Fixed effects:
                  Estimate  Std. Error  z value  Pr(>|z|)
(Intercept)       -0.23956     0.01610   -14.88   < 2e-16  ***
scale_len_diff    -0.10854     0.01197    -9.07   < 2e-16  ***
inf_vio=TRUE       0.07646     0.02848     2.68   0.00726  **
func_vio=TRUE      1.11474     0.03038    36.69   < 2e-16  ***
---
Signif. codes: 0 '***' 0.001 '**' 0.01 '*' 0.05 '.' 0.1 ' ' 1
```

All predictors are significant, even when allowing for different baselines per document (the 'doc' random effect), but the function violation predictor (subject should precede non-subject) receives the largest z-value and the large coefficient estimate. Interpreted as log-odds, the coefficient estimate of 1.11 for the function violation predictor gives an odds ratio of 3.04, meaning a pair exhibiting the features A:non-subj, B:subj should be three times as likely to be ordered <B,A> than the other way around. Information status, by contrast, gives a still significant but much weaker signal, given that we already know about length and subjecthood. Its coefficient estimate of 0.076 corresponds to an odds ratio of only 1.079, meaning only about 8% added likelihood of ordering to avoid the information status violation once we already know about subjecthood and length. We can also get an idea of the relationship between these coefficients and the strength of length-based ordering: A single standard deviation from the average length difference between two phrases is worth less than a tenth as much as a subject ordering violation, given that we know about subjecthood and information status.

These results converge with what we know about English word order: SVO is very important even once we know everything else; length and givenness are also significant, but to a much lesser extent, and in that order. The regression model can quantify and relativize the effects in an interpretable way, as well as factor out variation based on tendencies of individual documents or authors. However, as a practical predictive model it falls rather short: If we measure the success of the model in terms of classification accuracy, it only predicts the correct ordering 59.01% of the time. Because the pair orderings were randomized, this is an improvement of only about 9% over a 50–50 baseline, which is a very modest improvement. The reasons for this performance are twofold: First, the predictors are very impoverished, because much more is involved in determining actual word order than subjecthood, information status and length. Second, the regression model is linear, meaning it cannot take complex interactions into account (it's possible that some predictors have rather different effects in specific constellations). Although it is conceivable to add some interactions to a linear model, if the phenomenon being predicted is highly non-linear, other types of models or machine learning approaches will have more classification success (though often with a cost of lower interpretability, see Karpathy et al. 2016 for discussion and Section 6.4 on neural models, which are the current state of the art for serializing output in natural language generation). In the next section we turn to more powerful models for the accurate prediction of a complex alternation that is highly non-linear.

4.3 Predicting Alternating Agreement Patterns

Some alternation phenomena are highly unpredictable, so much so that they create the appearance of a totally free alternation. However, as noted in Section 4.1, many usage-based approaches to variation subsume a principle of no synonymy (e.g. Goldberg 1995: 67), suggesting that no alternation is completely free. An example of a phenomenon which is very difficult to pin down is notional agreement: the appearance of grammatical agreement patterns that do not match a noun's morphological category, based on notional or semantic categories. In this section I will focus on plural agreement with singular nouns instead of singular agreement, as in (31)–(32), taken from Quirk et al. (1985: 316).

(31) [*The government*] *has voted and* [*it*] *has announced the decision*
(32) [*The government*] *have voted and* [*they*] *have announced the decision*

These examples contain two kinds of variable agreement: between the subject NP and its verb and between that NP and a subsequent pronoun. Although notional agreement for subject–verb pairs has been studied extensively (Dixon 1977; Nathan 1981; Sparks 1984; Reid 1991; Sobin 1997; Bock et al. 2001; den Dikken 2001; Levin 2001; Sauerland 2003; Pearson 2011), including using POS tagged corpus data in different varieties of English (e.g. Depraetere 2003; Martinez-Insua and Palacios-Martinez 2003; Annala 2008), notional agreement in pronominal anaphora has remained almost completely unstudied, in part due to the difficulty of obtaining a large set of unrestricted examples for quantitative study. The goal in this section will therefore be twofold: On the one hand, we wish to concretely model the factors contributing to the occurrence of notional agreement in particular (see also Zeldes 2018a). On the other hand, we wish to find out more generally if a high-level alternation of this type, spanning aspects of syntax, morphology and semantics, is addressable using a multilayer approach.

It is tempting to postulate that the same underlying phenomenon is responsible for both kinds of agreement seen earlier and to suggest that an NP with a morphologically singular head is designated as a plural by the speaker at the point of utterance. Some theoretical approaches (den Dikken 2001; Sauerland 2003) have suggested that notional agreement implies the presence of a kind of null pronoun head within an NP such as 'the government' earlier, which confers a plural agreement pattern for that NP. However, using corpus data, it is not difficult to find cases with mixed agreement, such as (33)–(34), suggesting first that notional agreement in anaphora can be distinct from subject–verb agreement and that the agreement pattern chosen is renegotiated as discourse progresses.

(33) *[CNN]* **is** *my wire service; [they]*'**re** *on top of everything.* (OntoNotes)
(34) *[one hospital in Ramallah]* **tells** *us [they] have treated seven people* (OntoNotes)

Both of these examples were found using ANNIS in the OntoNotes corpus, introduced in Section 1.4. Because OntoNotes contains gold-standard syntactic parses and coreference annotation, we can use the corpus to study notional agreement in anaphora on multiple layers and see just how unpredictable this type of incongruent agreement is.

Types of Agreement

In order to find cases of plural pronouns referring back to singular heads, we can use the OntoNotes coreference annotation, encoded in ANNIS as a pointing relation between two span annotations (cf. Section 2.4).

However, OntoNotes annotates mentions of discourse referents as flat spans of tokens, which are co-indexed based on referring to the same entity, as shown in the XML excerpt in (35) for the example in (34).

(35) `<COREF  ID="133"  TYPE="IDENT">one   hospital   in`
`<COREF ID="176" TYPE="IDENT">Ramallah</COREF></COREF>`
`tells  . . .`

To establish the agreement mismatch, information from the POS tagging layer of the corpus is needed, as the PTB tag set used in OntoNotes fortunately distinguishes singular (NN) from plural (NNS) nouns (and, for present-tense verbs, also distinguishes third-person singular: *tells* is tagged VBZ). However, this information is not yet sufficient: The flat span annotation does not immediately tell us which noun within the span with ID 133 is actually the subject of the verb *tells*, nor more generally what the number feature of the entire phrase is; for example, the head could have been *Ramallah*, another noun inside the span which also happens to be singular, but a proper noun (tagged NNP). There is thus no token annotation establishing the head of the phrase.

To get the needed information we enrich the corpus in two ways. We first add dependency information by automatically converting the gold constituent trees available in OntoNotes into dependency trees using Stanford CoreNLP (Manning et al. 2014). This layer is merged to the data using SaltNPepper (see Section 3.4), representing the dependencies as annotated pointing relations between tokens. Next, we use a Pepper module which applies the head-finding strategy presented in Section 3.2 (see Figure 3.3 there) to find the head token of the span by looking for a token which has an incoming dependency relation whose source is outside the span – this token will be the head of the span.[7] The POS tag of this token will determine the singular or plural number assigned to the entity mention. Finally, we add to each token an annotation indicating its running token number (position in the document), and we add a metadatum to the document indicating its total token count.[8] Querying the resulting data in ANNIS can now be accomplished using an AQL query as in (36).

(36) `pos=/PRP\$?/ _=_ entity ->coref entity ->head pos=/NNP?/`
(a query for a personal pronoun, covering the same text as an entity span, which points with a 'coref' relation to an entity span, which points to a singular noun as 'head')

---

7. The module implementing this procedure is freely available for download as a Pepper plugin at https://github.com/korpling/pepperModules-HeadMarkerModule.
8. Code for these steps is available at https://github.com/korpling/pepperModules-CounterModule.

We can then divide the pronouns into normal singular ones (*I, it, she* . . .) and potentially notionally agreeing plural ones (*ours, they, them* . . .). Second-person pronouns are ambiguous and therefore omitted (*you* could be singular or plural). The complete dataset without second-person cases is then filtered to include all plural pronouns referring back to a singular, but also all normal cases of singular pronoun agreement if and only if the nouns involved are also attested in notional agreement. This allows us to focus on cases of ambiguity, because we want to see whether we can predict the behavior of nouns which exhibit both patterns.

The criteria presented here result in a dataset of 4,940 anaphor–antecedent pairs. Manual filtering revealed 67 erroneous types, for which all tokens were removed in singular and plural agreement attestation, resulting in 3,488 anaphor-antecedent pairs, of which 1,209 exhibited plural agreement (34.6%). Among the plural cases, three coarse-grained types can be distinguished. The most frequent type involves the 'group' nouns discussed by Quirk et al. earlier, as in (37). These are sometimes called 'committee nouns' after the frequent example of 'committee', or 'pluringulars' in den Dikken's (2001) terminology.

(37) [. . .] *the problem that* [*the Yemeni government faces*]$_i$ *is* [*they*]$_i$ *don't actively control the countryside*

For such nouns, a different semantic construal as a monolithic or distributed set has been assumed to play a role in singular versus plural mention. I will refer to these cases as Type I. Type I cases are also possible outside of third-person reference, such as when an individual is speaking for a notional group. For example, in OntoNotes, cases such as (38) are annotated as coreferent.

(38) *Bear Stearns stepped out of line in the view of* [*the SEC*]$_i$ . . . [*we*]$_i$*'re deadly serious about bringing reform into the marketplace*

Here the speaker is using the plural 'we' to refer to his entire organization, the SEC, which is mentioned explicitly in the preceding context, resulting in the coreference annotation in OntoNotes. Although it is debatable whether the underlying grammatical and psycholinguistic phenomenon is the same as in third-person plural reference to an organization, there are similarities (the SEC is a 'mass' of persons, cf. Sauerland 2003), and for the practical goal of building a classifier to recognize exceptional agreement (plural -> singular), these cases will be included later.

The second type is headed by 'bleached' or 'transparent' quantity nouns, which are morphologically singular but semantically function as modifiers to the plural PPs they govern. Frequent Type II items include 'a number' and 'a majority', as shown in (39)–(40).

(39) [*A large number of cadres and workers of the textile industry*] have already realized the seriousness of the difficulties [*they*] face

(40) [*a majority of OPEC's 13 members*] **have** reached [*their*] output limits.

These are distinct from Type I, because although in both cases we see plural pronouns referring back to singular nouns, the motivation for these cases is different: Here the pronoun simply agrees with what is construed as the semantic head. Although 'the Yemeni government' is semantically a kind of government no matter whether it is understood as atomic or as a collection of individuals, we would not normally say that 'a large number of workers' is primarily a kind of 'number'. Semantically, it can be seen as a phrase denoting workers, despite being syntactically headed by the quantity noun. The unpredictability of these cases comes because we cannot assume that a certain item, such as 'number' or 'majority', will always be associated with a plural reading. As a borderline case, we can consider a 'a collection of stamps', which may be considered a Type II case if referred back to in the plural, because a 'collection' is also a kind of quantity (albeit more likely to be referred back to in the singular than 'number'). This type is also compatible with first-person reference ('a majority of us is/are . . .'), but pronominal reference is then usually plural.

Types I and II can usually be distinguished intuitively, but some cases are difficult, as in (41)–(42), taken from the Corpus of Contemporary American English (COCA, Davies 2008–). In both examples the head 'third' is a quantity, but it seems to be less 'bleached' in (42), where it is still referential enough to agree with the verb.

(41) [*a third of Americans*] **are** no different than they were in 1968 (COCA)

(42) [*a third of cases*] **is** enough to make it correct? (COCA)

Predicting these correctly in context will therefore be challenging.

The third class of cases, Type III, is rather different and results from gender-neutral or 'generic' (sometimes called epicene) pronoun agreement (see Huddleston and Pullum 2002: 493–494; Curzan 2003). The construction is shown in (43).

(43) *I'll go and talk to* [*the person here*]$_i$ *cause* [*they*]$_i$ *get cheap tickets* (OntoNotes)

Although clearly distinct from the other two types, I will attempt to include these cases in the model developed later for several reasons. From a practical point of view, if we want to be able to apply a classifier to unrestricted natural language data (for a given phrase in context, predict which pronoun will be used), then hiding these cases from the classifier will lead to errors. Such a classifier could be useful in natural language processing for applications such as automatic coreference resolution (see more in Chapter 5), but also in natural language generation for deciding the pronoun that a computer system should use, or in the development of theoretical computational models for the generation of referring expressions (see van Deemter 2016). Second, there are actual confusing cases in which it is difficult or even impossible to distinguish Type III with certainty, as in (44)–(45) (both taken from OntoNotes).

(44) [*The enemy*] *attacked several times, and each time* [*they*] **were** *repelled*

(45) [*a publisher*] **is** *interested in my personal ad book* . . . *I looked* [*them*] *up*

It may seem unlikely that 'they' would be used in (44) to present a gender-neutral 'enemy', but we cannot rule out such a reading, much less expect an automatic classifier to do so. Even more so, in (45) we could be using 'a publisher' to mean a 'publishing house' (potential Type I case), or the actual person in charge of such a company, which is being referred to in a gender-neutral way (Type III). We will therefore attempt to induce a classifier for plural-to-singular agreement which is trained on all of these cases, and which will hopefully be robust enough to handle unrestricted unseen data.

Individual Layers

In order to select the relevant features for a predictive multifactorial model, we can examine how individual annotation layers correlate with the target variable. Broadly speaking, previous literature suggests at least three families of features that are relevant for predicting the agreement type:

1. Processing factors, which relate to salience of the nominal referents, distance between nominal and pronominal mention and other information structural properties which may promote morphologically strict (i.e. singular) or loose (notional, plural) agreement.
2. Conventional factors, involving either specific words or constructions, or conventions related to genre or text type (e.g. agreement is more strict in newspaper articles) and modality (characteristics of spoken language, which may exhibit more notional agreement, cf. Quirk et al. 1985: 758).
3. Formal factors, including morphosyntactic and semantic classes of words, such as animacy, or subjecthood or categories that promote distributive readings for group nouns (e.g. predicates such as *consist of*, or *quarrel*, see Depraetere 2003; Pearson 2011).

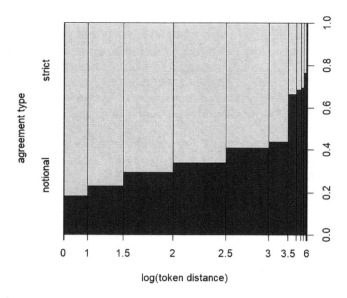

Figure 4.3 Proportion of notional agreement with growing log-distance between anaphor and antecedent

Causes can be hard to tease apart, because, for example, the issue of spoken vs. written language is intertwined with processing issues, as spoken language is subject to more immediate processing pressures than written language.

Looking at processing issues first, we can ask whether speakers (or writers) use notional agreement because in some sense they forget how they expressed themselves with growing distance. If this is the case, we would expect to see a correlation between the distance separating a noun and its pronoun and the likelihood of notional agreement. Figure 4.3 shows that this is in fact very clearly the case: There is a perfectly monotonic rise in notional agreement likelihood with growing distance in tokens, shown in the figure in log-scale. The breadth of each column in the spine plot corresponds to the amount of data it is based on, with log token distances of over 3.5 (about 33 tokens) being very rare. Even before truly rare distances are reached, the rate of notional agreement doubles from the minimal ~20% to just over 40%.

In addition to surface distance, psycholinguistic literature on notional agreement (see Bock and Eberhard 1993; Eberhard et al. 2005; Wagers et al. 2009; Staub 2009) has suggested that prominence or level of activation is relevant for retaining strict agreement. Although distance is likely to correlate with any measure of 'activation' (cf. Szmrecsanyi 2006; Chiarcos 2009), we may also consider repeated mention as a sign of prominence or activity level by checking whether the antecedent is itself given (the

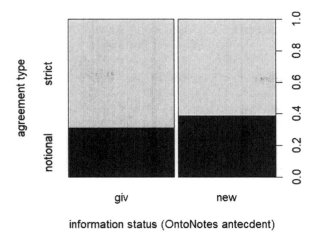

Figure 4.4 Proportion of notional agreement for new and given entities, using a previous antecedent as a proxy for givenness

anaphor is always given by definition). Although OntoNotes does not have an explicit layer of information status annotation, we can test the effect of previous mention by using the coreference annotation layer, equating given status with the presence of an earlier antecedent appearing before the nominal mention that we are examining. The effect is not strong, but significant ($p < 0.00001$, $\chi^2 = 23.185$, $\phi = 0.08$), and can be recognized in Figure 4.4.

A further possible processing factor is fatigue: If at least some cases of notional agreement are seen as a form of disfluency or inattention (see e.g. Osborne 2013),[9] we might expect to see higher rates of plural-to-singular agreement in later portions of a conversation, or even in written texts. There are several problems in testing this possibility. First, document lengths vary considerably across the corpus, meaning it is difficult to compare short documents (in which we expect less fatigue) and long ones. Second, there is a problematic confound for written texts in certain genres: We may expect especially newspaper texts to be subject to late changes by an editor, who may change notional to strict agreement, and may also experience fatigue effects (more editing early in the text). Because OntoNotes contains both spoken and written data, we can examine a possible fatigue effect for written, spoken and all documents separately to check for the latter issue. To preempt the issue of differing document

9. My intention here is not to classify notional agreement as a disfluency in the sense of ungrammaticality, for which fatigue may more readily be assumed to play a role, but rather to suggest that processing load may play a role in the recoverability of the exact agreement category of an antecedent, creating a pattern of more local grammaticality, in line with psycholinguistic literature on number attraction (Bock et al. 2001; Wagers et al. 2009, etc.).

lengths, we can also examine a subset of long documents, defined heuristically as documents with above-median length, and see whether we find different results. Figure 4.5 plots the positions of notionally and strictly agreeing anaphors based on the percentile position of the anaphor token out of the total document length (i.e. an anaphor in the middle of the document is in the 50th percentile).

All panels in Figure 4.5 show the same effect: a slight spike in strict agreement density in the first quarter of documents, covering both modalities. The somewhat higher density of notional agreement late in the documents is not much more extreme in long documents, suggesting that if there is a 'careful speech' effect early in a document, it dissipates quickly even in shorter documents.

Figure 4.5 lumps together all types of spoken and written language, but OntoNotes contains rather different text types within each of these categories: Spoken data includes unscripted telephone conversations, broadcast news and broadcast conversations, whereas written data contains newswire material, web data and text from the Bible, as well as sections of text translated into English from Arabic and Chinese. The importance of different genres and text types in shaping the choice of words has been demonstrated repeatedly (Biber 1988; Gries 2006; Biber and Conrad 2009), and we should therefore consider how different subcorpora within OntoNotes might differ in their behavior. Whereas spoken data are generally expected to show more notional agreement (Quirk et al. 1985: 758; Watson 2010), phone conversations are probably closer to the prototype of spoken English than broadcast news. Similarly, it can be expected that a highly conservative text such as the Bible will show stricter morphological agreement, and more generally that translations, including translations of modern texts, will be carefully redacted, leading to less notional agreement than less restricted language from the Web.

We can begin by confirming that spoken language exhibits more notional agreement, as shown in Table 4.2 (see Watson 2010 for similar results using the COCA corpus).

Notional agreement is more than 150% likelier in the spoken data (present in about 47% of cases, compared to only 28% in written data).

Next, we can compare the different subtypes within each modality. Figure 4.6 gives an association plot for construction choice and text type (again, raised bars signify positive deviations, and lowered bars the opposite).

In line with the expectations noted earlier, the Bible is the strictest text type, followed closely by translations and newswire. Web data clusters with spoken language in showing notional agreement above expected levels, although broadcast language turns out to have even higher rates than telephone conversations. It is important to note that these correlations do not tell us whether the effect is a result of processing constraints or perhaps rather conventionality effects: If using notional agreement

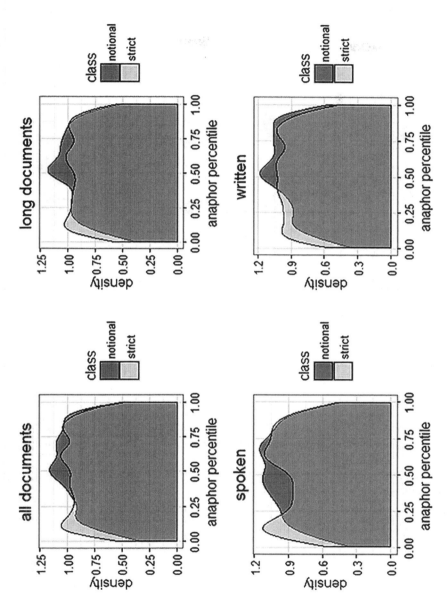

Figure 4.5 Strict versus notional agreement as a function of anaphor position in the document for all documents, documents with higher than median length, all spoken and all written documents

Table 4.2 Strict and notional agreement in written and spoken data from OntoNotes

	Notional	*Strict*	*Total*
spoken	593 (47%)	668 (53%)	1261
written	616 (28%)	1611 (72%)	2227
total	1209	2279	3488

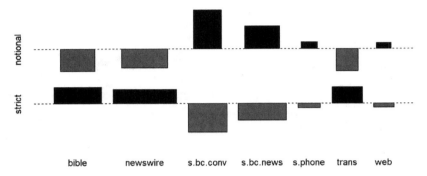

Figure 4.6 Association plot of chi-square residuals for agreement type by genre

is conventional to broadcast news language (at least for some lexical items), then this may be unrelated to the processing constraints imposed on a newscaster, or a studio guest, or a speaker on the phone. What is clear is that text types differ substantially and that allowing a potential classifier to know about text type will therefore likely be useful. Because most of the main expectations noted earlier turn out to be reasonable when looking at the data, we can expect the variables and intuitions in question to generalize to unseen data.

Moving on to grammatical factors, we can now look at the behavior of specific syntactic functions and semantic classes of antecedent nouns and the predicates governing them and their anaphors. Previous studies have indicated the importance of characteristics of the antecedent NP (e.g. reference to persons or groups of persons, see den Dikken 2001) and governing verbs for both the antecedent and the anaphor (distributive predicates or ones conferring human-like properties, such as verbs of saying, see Depraetere 2003 for an overview). Looking at grammatical functions of the anaphor and antecedent, we find that for anaphors, being a grammatical subject favors notional agreement, whereas being a possessive pronoun favors strict agreement (Figure 4.7). For the antecedent, the opposite holds: Subjects favor strict agreement, whereas possessive and other functions favor notional agreement.

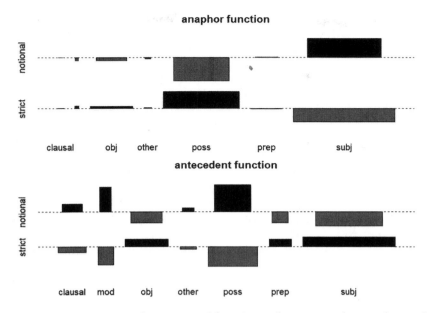

Figure 4.7 Association of grammatical function and agreement for anaphor and antecedent NPs

Needless to say, grammatical function alone cannot function as a strong predictor of the agreement pattern chosen, as virtually all functions are found in both patterns, often with the same lexemes. However, the associations we find and especially the complementary picture of the role of subjecthood for anaphors versus antecedents seem to fit with the idea that stronger persistence in memory may be responsible for the higher proportion of antecedent subjects that show strict agreement. If the representation of the antecedent is more accessible, then its literal ostensible morphological form may be stronger in memory and can exert more influence on pronoun choice. Conversely, when the anaphor is a subject, the position at which it is uttered may have more influence on the chosen realization due to the prominence of the subject position, and if it is in a 'notional' environment, then it can promote less strict agreement. The following examples show the typical cases in which a subject anaphor to a possessive antecedent is notional (46) and a possessive anaphor referring back to a subject antecedent is not (47).

(46) *Regarding [the company's] competition for the third license to operate cell phones in the Kingdom, he said that [they] have an alliance with the Turkish Turkcell Company*

(47) *[The Clinton administration] is clear on [its] view on the Milosevic move*

Without an experimental study, it is hard to say whether minimally changing the grammatical functions would push speakers toward the other pattern (i.e. does the following version promote notional agreement: "The Clinton administration's statement makes it clear how they view/it views the Milosevic move"?), but taken together with other factors in context, the trend observed in Figure 4.7 suggests that these functions are relevant.

A likely co-variate of this tendency is whether a subject anaphor is governed by a verb which promotes notional agreement, because more 'personifying' verbs (e.g. certain kinds of communication verbs, as in 'the committee . . . they/it say/says') or distributive verbs (e.g. 'it/they disbanded', cf. Depraetere 2003) can influence or coerce a mass or collective reading, depending on the entity type in question (an organization, a geopolitical entity, etc.). In order to study the semantic effect of predicate and entity types, we must enrich the OntoNotes data with further layers of information. Because OntoNotes only contains Named Entity Recognition tags, many of the NPs we are interested in, such as common noun NPs and pronouns, are not annotated for entity type. We therefore use the automatic non-named entity recognizer xrenner (Zeldes and Zhang 2016, see Section 3.2), bearing in mind the potential for annotation errors. To classify governing predicates we use VerbNet classes (Kipper et al. 2006), which give rough classes based on semantics and alternation behaviors in English, such as ALLOW for verbs like {*allow, permit*, . . .} or HELP, {*aid, assist*, . . .}, etc. Because some verb classes are small or rare, potentially leading to very sparsely attested feature values, classes attested fewer than 60 times are collapsed into a class OTHER (for example, VerbNet class 22.2, AMALGAMATE). Verbs attested in multiple classes are always given the majority class; for example, the verb *say* appears both in VerbNet class 37.7, SAY and class 78, INDICATE, but was always classified as the more common SAY. Finally, some similar classes were collapsed in order to avoid replacement by OTHER, such as LONG + WANT + WISH, which were fused into a class DESIRE. Nominal governors (e.g. for possessive NPs, whose governor is the possessor NP) were classified based on their entity class as assigned by xrenner, using the entity classes from Section 3.2. Table 4.3 gives an example of tendencies for the baselines of classes governing the anaphor, sorted by their deviation from the mean notional proportion (approximately 34.6%).[10]

We can see a connection between typically 'human-agent' classes at the top of the table and notional agreement. This includes desideratives, possession and communication verbs that typically take an addressee (the TELL class). Interestingly, there is a contrast with the less notional SAY class

---

10. These are attestations with any grammatical function, although we can certainly expect different tendencies for subjects and objects of the same verb; the multifactorial model to be constructed in the next section will take into account such interactions between verb class and grammatical function, as well as other variable interactions.

Table 4.3 Agreement preference deviations for verb classes governing the anaphor

Class	% notional	Deviation from Ø
OWN (*have, possess..*)	48.55%	+13.95%
TELL (*inform, update..*)	47.83%	+13.23%
GET (*receive, attain..*)	43.79%	+9.19%
DESIRE (*want, wish..*)	42.78%	+8.18%
. . .		
COGNITION (*consider, comprehend..*)	37.37%	+2.77%
SAY (*declare, proclaim..*)	35.90%	+1.30%
TRANSFER (*give, put..*)	35.06%	+0.46%
MOTION (*go, run..*)	34.86%	+0.26%
. . .		
FIT (*serve, hold..*)	33.33%	−1.27%
BUILD (*make, formulate..*)	31.48%	−3.12%
EXIST (*be, become..*)	25.26%	−9.34%
CONTIGUOUS_LOCATION (*meet, touch..*)	10.29%	−24.31%

in the middle of the table. To gain an intuition regarding this difference, we can consider some examples from OntoNotes:

(48) [*The U.S. Navy*]$_i$ *is revising the timeline* (. . .) [*It*]$_i$ *says the explosion happened* (. . .)

(49) [*the Bush administration*]$_i$ (. . .) *Nevertheless* [*they*]$_i$ *told us* (. . .)

It is possible that cases with an addressee are more personified to some extent, perhaps more so with a first-person addressee as in the case of the speaker in (49). Again, this is relevant primarily for the subject argument, and as we will see later, it can be important to know both the verb class and the grammatical function filled by the anaphor or antecedent.

Much as semantic classes for governing predicates can influence the choice of construction, so can entity types both affect the general proportion of each variant and give rise to special combinations which favor a particular realization. Figure 4.8 visualizes these preferences as an interaction plot of chi-square residuals associated with the antecedent's entity class in each agreement pattern. Lines sloping top-right to bottom-left correspond to entity types preferring strict agreement (OBJECT, PLACE, PERSON), whereas top-left to bottom-right lines correspond to types preferring notional agreement (QUANTITY, TIME, ORGANIZATION).

Although we have seen that 'personification' may lead to notional agreement (e.g. in conjunction with communication verbs), the PERSON

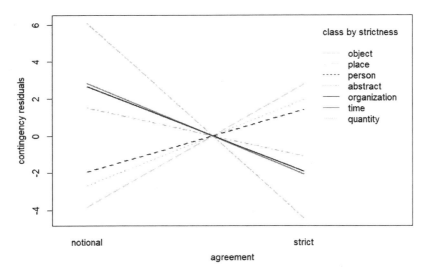

Figure 4.8 Interaction plot of chi-square residuals for antecedent entity and agreement type

class actually favors strict agreement. This is, however, not actually surprising if we consider the examples discussed for the personification effect earlier, such as 'administration' in (49). Lexemes of this kind are actually categorized as ORGANIZATION by xrenner, and therefore do in fact belong to a class that favors notional agreement above expectation. The most common NP head noun classified as PERSON is *family*, and together with other similar non-orgnization PERSON nouns causes the preference for strict agreement. A second reason for the preference for strict agreement for PERSON comes from singular cases of nouns with a potential for Type III agreement (recall that any noun attested in both patterns is included in the data). For example, the common non-generic '$baby_i$ . . . her_i/his_i' takes strict agreement, and is attested less often in the epicene pattern '$baby_i$ . . . $they_i$'. Other types, such as QUANTITY and TIME, are less surprising to see with notional agreement, because they include common cases such as '*a third of . . . they*' (cf. examples (41)-(42)) and counted time units in Type II phrases such as '*a couple of (minutes/hours) . . .*'.

A Multifactorial Predictive Model

With the knowledge accumulated about individual features so far, we can now attempt to construct a multifactorial model predicting which variant will be chosen in practice. To build and evaluate the model, we divide the complete dataset at random into 90% training material and 10% test data. Based on the total of around 3490 anaphor–antecedent pairs collected from OntoNotes, the test set amounts to 349 cases, stratified to include approximately the same proportions of genres, as well as notional vs. strict agreement cases: about 65% strict agreement and 35% notional. This is important in order to ensure we can test the classifier using data that has a natural distribution, similar to our training instances, which will also generalize to unseen cases from similar sources in a practical application (e.g. for coreference resolution or natural language generation).

In Section 4.2, we used linear mixed effects models to classify alternating word orders and information status conditions, based on very simple features. For a complex, 'high-level' alternation such as notional agreement, which involves interactions between multiple semantic classes (anaphor, antecedent, governing lexemes), grammatical functions, genre, distance, givenness and more, we cannot achieve usable levels of accuracy using linear models without assuming a large number of interactions. In fact, using logistic regression without interaction terms, we can reach approximately 74% accuracy on unseen data, an improvement of only 9% over the majority baseline of 65%. Although it is certainly possible to improve this number by assuming a number of interactions, allowing n-way interactions between all predictors mentioned earlier, many of which are categorical variables with dozens of levels, would result in an explosion of coefficients. In order to achieve better performance while avoiding overfitting, we will take a machine learning approach using a variant of the Random Forest algorithm, which has been gaining popularity in corpus linguistics studies due to its ability to recognize meaningful interactions and choose optimal models without overfitting the data (see Levshina 2015; Deshors and Gries 2016).

The algorithm trains multiple decision trees on randomized parts of the training data and polls them to classify unseen instances. Polling the trees reveals which outcome a majority of trained classifiers in the forest ensemble predict, and checking the proportions with which their predictions were true under similar circumstances during training gives an estimate of their certainty. Figure 4.9 shows an example tree from the ensemble, which splits the data into different bins at each step, based on the portion of the training data that it has seen.

The tree begins at the top by checking whether the anaphor should refer to first or third person (>1, on the right).[11] If the anaphor is a third-person pronoun, information status is checked: New mentions go on the far right, and given ones are classified further based on whether the anaphor and antecedent are more or less than 16 tokens apart. Each tree receives a random subset of the available features, enabling different trees

---

11. In the following, features of the anaphor are prefixed with n_, and features of the antecedent with t_. Thus, n_person is the person of the anaphor, and t_infstat is the information status of the antecedent.

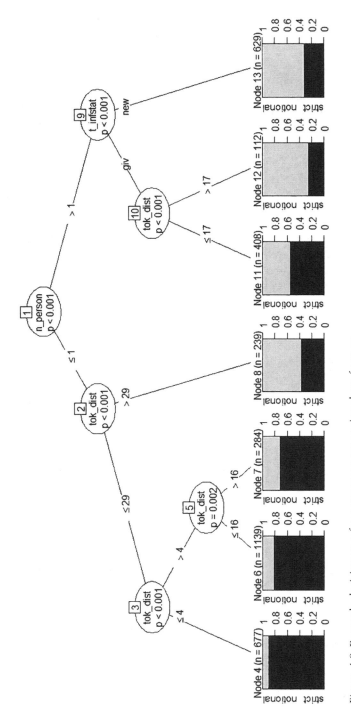

Figure 4.9 Example decision tree for agreement type using three features

to remain robust in cases where a feature that would otherwise be crucial is not available or not as informative as in the training data. The tree is constructed with the goal of maximizing each split's purity, culminating in the leaves at the bottom of the figure. The branch on the far left has the highest purity, containing almost only 'strict' cases. The degree of purity, measured in units of the Gini index, can then be used to assess the quality of the feature responsible for the split (see below).[12]

For the current task, we use the Extra Trees variant of the Random Forest algorithm (Geurts et al. 2006), which introduces randomness into the selection of the optimal branch splits at each depth level of the tree and often leads to globally superior performance for the ensemble. Using a grid search with fivefold cross-validation on the training data, the optimal parameters for the Extra Trees classifier were found, leading to the use of 300 trees limited to the default number of features, which is set to the square root of the number of features, rounded up. The best performance in cross-validation on the training set was achieved using the 20 features outlined in Figure 4.10, meaning that each tree receives five features to work with at random, thereby reducing the chance of overfitting the training data. After training on the entire training set, the classifier achieves a classification accuracy of 86.81% in predicting the correct form for the unseen test data using these features, an absolute improvement of over 21% above the majority baseline of always guessing 'strict'. Figure 4.10 gives the relative feature importances, with error bars indicating the standard deviation from the average importance across all trees in the ensemble.

Evaluating the importance of features can be done in multiple ways: For some practical applications, for example, it might be more interesting to know the reduction in accuracy caused by dropping each individual feature. However, if two features are both individually useful but to some extent mutually redundant, accuracy will not decrease substantially by dropping just one feature. In the context of understanding the correlation of the linguistic variables with notional agreement, it is therefore more interesting to ask which features did most trees rank as most useful, given that they were exposed to those features. Here we use the average Gini index of purity achieved at all splits using each respective feature, evaluated across all 300 trees in the ensemble. A Gini index of 0 means complete homogeneity (a 50–50 split on both sides of a junction), whereas 1 would mean perfect separation based on that feature. In addition to

12. Note that although it is possible to get p-values for individual decision tree junctions, as in Figure 4.9, by treating each split decision as a binomial variable, this is not a feasible evaluation metric for the ensemble, for two reasons: First, it is not possible to aggregate p-values from multiple trees in a sensible way, and second, the alpha error from a massive amount of repeated tests would be compounded, greatly inflating values to the point where adjusting the required threshold (e.g. using a Bonferroni adjustment) would become unfeasable.

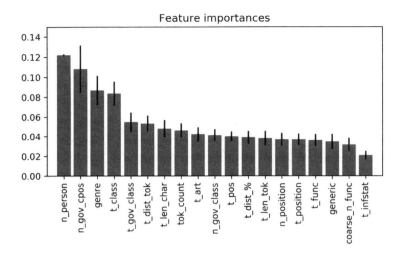

Figure 4.10 Variable importances for the notional agreement classifier

features discussed earlier, a feature 'generic' was introduced for phrases headed by words such as 'anyone', 'someone', 'somebody', etc., and a feature 't_art', distinguishing explicit demonstratives and definite and indefinite articles on the antecedent, as well as bare noun status or presence of quantifiers. These are ranked together with other features in Figure 4.10.

Although the 'person' feature is probably not very useful in isolation, it is clearly the most important one in trees using it, because plural reference to nouns also seen as singulars is almost entirely restricted to organizations (cf. example (38)), meaning that this feature is pivotal when coupled with the entity class. Observations that are good candidates for Type III epicene agreement (e.g. antecedent heads such as 'person' or generics such as 'somebody') will virtually never be realized as plural if we know that the referent is now speaking in the first person.[13] The second most important feature is the coarse[14] part of speech of the anaphor's governing token, probably in conjunction with the governor's class. The coarse category allows the classifier to know whether the pronoun in question is the subject or object of a verb, or the adjunct or possessor of a noun, etc., which, taken together with grammatical function and verb or noun class,

13. Hypothetically it is conceivable to have a generic such as "*if [somebody]*₁ *thinks 'this will not affect [us]*₁'", using 'us' as a true epicene anaphor for 'somebody', but the potential for ambiguity is high ('us' could be that somebody together with others). Such examples are not present in our dataset.
14. The PTB tag set distinguishes third-person singular and other present-tense verb forms with the tags VBZ and VBP. In order to withhold information potentially revealing the number of the anaphor, which we are trying to predict, we do not expose the classifier to the exact POS tag, but use a coarser version without this information.

can approximate its semantic role. Genre may appear as a surprise in third place, but given the different styles and levels of strictness found in different genres (see Figure 4.6), as well as the absence of Type III agreement in certain genres (notably the Bible), it turns out to be quite important. Next comes the antecedent noun's entity class, which is important for reasons discussed earlier (e.g. ORGANIZATION vs. PERSON, etc., for Types I and III, and also the QUANTITY class for Type II).

From the fifth rank onwards, we see a drop in average purity index, although it should be noted that taking any one of the subsequent predictors away results in a decrease in classification accuracy of about 1%. Information structural and processing properties are clearly less decisive and populate this part of the plot, including length and position effects, givenness and article type. It should also be noted that using the antecedent article's type (t_art) is a stronger signal than information status alone. However, information status is not completely redundant, and in fact removing it as a predictor degrades prediction accuracy by about 1.2%. Grammatical functions were tested in two variants: coarse labels as used in Figure 4.7 (e.g. 'subj', 'clausal') and all available labels in the Stanford basic label set (de Marneffe and Manning 2013, distinguishing active 'nsubj' and passive 'nsubjpass', different types of clauses, etc.). Based on cross-validation in the training data, the classifier achieves optimal performance using coarse labels for the anaphor's function but fine-grained ones for the antecedent. This may be related to the different functions that are attested for each NP (for example, the apposition label 'appos' is attested for the antecedent but ruled out for pronominal anaphors) and their distribution (for example, nominal antecedents are very often prepositional objects, but anaphors rarely are, whereas anaphors are often possessives, but antecedents much less so). This underscores the importance of tag sets and transformations of tag sets in modeling complex alternation phenomena, especially with machine learning tools which allow us to model relatively large inventories of feature values.

To get an idea of the classification quality of the model as a whole, we can examine the confusion matrix in Table 4.4. The current classifier predicts 'notional' incorrectly only 7 out of 349 times, while making an overly 'conservative' decision in favor of 'strict' in only 39 cases.

Table 4.4 Confusion matrix for the classifier's predictions on unseen test data

		Actual	
		Strict	*Notional*
pred	*strict*	222	39
	notional	7	81

A manual inspection of errors reveals that only six false 'strict' cases belong to Type III, which suggests that the classifier does not suffer from modeling this type together with the more frequent types. Looking at errors qualitatively also shows that misclassifications are not necessarily unacceptable productions, as shown in (50)–(51).

(50) [*Comsat Video, which distributes pay-per-view programs to hotel rooms*], *plans to add Nuggets games to* [*their*] *offerings* (OntoNotes, WSJ_1461)

(51) *With the February 1987 U.N. accords "relating to Afghanistan,"* [*the Soviet Union*] *got everything* [*it*] *needed to consolidate permanent control.* (OntoNotes, WSJ_2052)

In both these cases, which the classifier misclassifies, it is relatively easy to imagine the alternative pronoun being used. 'Comsat Video', in particular, is quite possible to realize later as a singular in 'its offerings', and although the Soviet Union might seem odd to pluralize, it is not difficult to find similar corpus examples in the plural, such as (52).

(52) [. . .] *it was a significant threat to* [*Russia*]$_i$ *and not surprisingly* [*they*]$_i$ *responded by beefing up their offensive capacity* (GUM corpus)[15]

Despite not quite reaching into the 90% accuracy decile, the classifier therefore seems to be fairly reasonable, at least within the domains it has been trained on. For the remaining ~13% accuracy we must either look for more or better features, or accept some level of residual inter- and intra-personal variation which we do not have the power to explain.

4.4   Interim Conclusion

In this chapter we have explored some of the ways in which data from very many layers of information at once can help us to model even high-level, complex and rather unpredictable alternation phenomena. Having access to information structural annotations for an entire corpus of running text meant that we could compare the relative influence of grammatical function, passive or active voice, phrase length and information structure on word order in ways which go beyond specific targeted studies of individual constructions. This type of study puts multifactorial work using such predictors in a broad language system context, because the results allow us to ask, for example, not only whether phrase length affects a

---

15. This example admittedly, and perhaps significantly, comes not from a written text, but from a spoken interview. The interviewee is incidentally Noam Chomsky, so that the speaker is not only verifiable as a native speaker but also a linguist.

word order phenomenon such as particle placement (Gries 2002) or alternations such as the dative alternation (Bresnan et al. 2007), but also to what extent the effect holds for all phrases and whether it is weaker or stronger than otherwise in specific settings.

Using regression models, it is possible to quantify effects in terms of their significance, but also to relativize effect sizes – for example, although information status has a general influence on word order, it only adds about 8% in odds ratio for the ordering it favors, provided that we also know about subjecthood and phrase lengths. This is understandable if we consider that much of the literature on information structure examines asymmetrical situations in which there are often only two arguments, of which one is given and one is new, or also infrequent but strongly marked contrastive contexts. In the running corpus analysis, most sentences have annotations for more than two phrases, and often the model is attempting to explain the ordering of a pair of phrases in which either both are new or both are given and no strong contrast reading is involved. As a result, length differences are a better cue to rely on, at least until we can add more complex and reliable information structural annotations (see Cook and Bildhauer 2011; Lüdeling et al. 2016). Using mixed-effects models also allows us to factor out individual variation by modeling per-document baselines as a random effect. Inter- and even intra-speaker variation is a factor that is often lost in multifactorial work not taking such random effects into account (see Gries 2015).

In Section 4.3, we looked at a broad range of annotatable categories for which we can assume a high degree of interactions. The phenomenon of notional agreement can be considered not only complex, but also unpredictable, and for many sentences multiple options seem to be valid. From a methodological standpoint, factors such as genre conventions and processing constraints complicate the issue by introducing competing tendencies that would require a vast amount of interaction coefficients, for example, one for each unique combination of grammatical function, part of speech and semantic class for the anaphor and the antecedent, resulting in an explosion of feature values. At the same time, linear models are at risk of overfitting the training data, especially for sparse combinations. The decision tree-based ensemble method used here makes it possible to navigate these factors by exposing different parts of the ensemble to different data subsets and features, reducing spurious reliance on very specific combinations, and making the classifier robust for unseen data. The relatively high accuracy of the classifier on unseen data suggests that this is a promising approximation of the highly interactive nature of notional agreement, which is notoriously hard to pin down (see e.g. Sauerland 2003; Depraetere 2003). Nevertheless, the results of the analysis may become less transparent by moving away from clear significance values, as well as introducing randomness into the classifier's training process and a lack of readily interpretable coefficients or log-odds (though Gini indices provide some insights). The issue of interpretability will become even more substantial when even less transparent methods are used, such as neural networks (see Section 6.4).

As a final note, it is important to recall that the corpora used in this chapter were not constructed specifically with the aim of studying active versus passive voice, or to predict notional agreement in particular. These possibilities fall out naturally from the annotations available in a richly annotated corpus. The relative independence of the various layers means that they provide at least partly orthogonal signals for multifactorial models of probabilistic syntactic phenomena. Although such phenomena are not as predictable as allomorphy and allophony in their respective domains, multilayer corpora allow us to leverage separate annotation layers to give a similar treatment to 'allostructions' and bring the tools employed in this chapter to bear on the environments conditioning their distribution.

5 Entity Models and Referentiality

5.1 Introduction

One of the key tasks in modeling the contents of a running text or conversation is the construction of discourse models representing all referential entities that occupy the mental space shared between speakers and listeners, or writers and readers. Formal theoretical work on such models in semantics has concentrated on the term 'common ground' (Stalnaker 1974; Krifka 2008), which starts out from a model of "information that is mutually known to be shared [between speakers] and that is continuously modified in communication" that can subsume both information pertaining to truth conditional knowledge and "communicative interests and goals of the participants" (Krifka 2008: 245–246). Cognitive approaches have discussed very similar concepts, such as coordination of 'intersubjectivity' (Traugott 1999; Verhagen 2005) in a constant mutual tracking process that speakers employ to update a mental model of their interlocutors. Many aspects of these theoretical frameworks have been implemented in computational approaches to discourse processing (see Stede 2012: 40–51 for an overview), for which multilayer corpus data are invaluable.

Whatever framework we use, it is clear that some pieces of information must be included in any operationalized model, such as the set of discourse referents introduced as the text progresses. This is essential to establishing notions such as identity of reference across referring expressions and the coding of ontological types of entities such as people and places, which are essential for communication. A simple operationalized model associating referring expressions with different types of discourse referents across sentences could look like the analysis in Figure 5.1. The analysis in the figure, created using an entity and coreference resolution system (xrenner, Zeldes and Zhang 2016), models underlying data structures to identify and represent some ontological categories, such as mentions of people, places or organizations, and marks co-referring expressions using boxes styled in the same shade (e.g. *Jane, she, she* or *Antarctica, there*).

Building an operationalization for a mental model of a particular discourse similar to the one in Figure 5.1 is, on the one hand, very

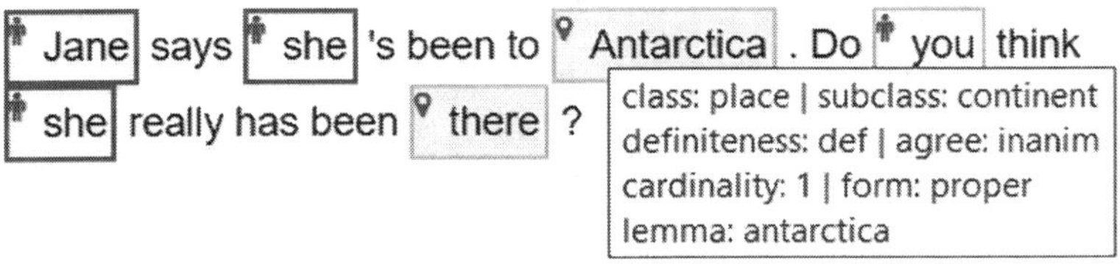

Jane says she 's been to Antarctica . Do you think she really has been there ?

class: place | subclass: continent
definiteness: def | agree: inanim
cardinality: 1 | form: proper
lemma: antarctica

Figure 5.1 A rough analysis of entity mentions in a discourse fragment, created automatically using xrenner. An info box supplies some features for the referring expression *Antarctica*

challenging, but, on the other hand, very rewarding: On a theoretical level, mental models of entities in discourse underlie many levels of linguistic abstraction, including argument and event structure (see Levin and Rappaport-Hovav 2005), bound and discourse anaphora (Chomsky 1981; Ariel 1990; Pollard and Sag 1992) and a multitude of aspects of information structure (Féry and Ishihara 2016). On a practical level, having access to such a model and an ability to extract it reliably from textual data are key capabilities in enabling advanced corpus analysis at more semantic levels, and for downstream natural language processing tasks in general. Relevant tasks include coreference resolution (using rule-based approaches, e.g. Lee et al. 2013, or machine learning, Durrett and Klein 2013; Lee et al. 2017, or both, Clark and Manning 2015), knowledge and entailment extraction (Dagan et al. 2013; Roth et al. 2014), automatic summarization (e.g. entity sets, see Boguraev and Kennedy 1999: 103; Hovy 2005 for an overview), and more.

What does a mental model of language data contain? At a minimum, we expect that speakers retain a list of discourse referents under discussion (cf. Discourse Representation Theory [DRT], which postulates a 'universe' of discourse referents relevant to each discourse representation structure, Kamp and Reyle 1993: 63). Psycholinguistic evidence (Pulvermüller 1999) as well as theoretical accounts from cognitive science (Barsalou 1999) have suggested that people do much more: They track entities in discourse and can not only identify and associate distinct referring expressions with the same entity, but also to some extent predict the likelihood that an entity will be mentioned again later on. Centering Theory (Grosz et al. 1995, see below) in particular suggested that hearers track mentions of entities that act as 'centers' linking previous and subsequent mentions, while psycholinguistic experiments (see Kehler and Rohde 2013 for an overview) have shown that specific linguistic means used to refer to entities or insert them into the common ground in discourse can be predicted and manipulated using linguistic cues, such as grammatical function, definiteness and more. Such cues can help to maintain and coordinate the awareness of co-conversants' corresponding discourse models.

Fragments of such models can be embedded in argument structures that correspond to conventional meaningful scripts or 'frames' with which we are familiar (see Gawron 2011 for an overview of frame semantics; Boas 2009 on frames as cross-linguistic generalizations). These can be a series of actions that typically appear in sequence (e.g. going to a restaurant, ordering food, eating the food, paying the bill, see Schank and Abelson 1977), in which each action or frame has typical participants, and these participants may be shared across multiple frames (the same person is the agent in the entire restaurant scenario earlier, but a waiter may be involved in only the second and fourth actions). Prototypical sequences of frames sharing some of the same entities as arguments can coalesce to form frequent 'narrative schemas' (Chambers and Jurafsky 2009), which can also feed into our ability to process past discourse and prepare for the following utterances.

At each point, entities from the existing discourse model are selected, and these contrast with other possible referents which are potentially available for discussion at every point with varying probabilities (see Spalek and Zeldes 2017). For example, in the following cliché discourse, familiar from jokes, a protagonist is introduced using a typical sequence and embedded into predictable frames[1]:

(53) *A man walks into a bar. He hasn't had a drink for 10 years, so he asks the bartender . . .*

Linguistic entities involve symbolic encodings of meaning components that have semantic interpretations beyond pure extensionality (e.g. the setting invoked by a man walking into a bar who has not had a drink in ten years, with implications and expectations beyond a set of possible denotations). In each sentence, syntactic arguments are mapped onto entities in the developing discourse model, so that *he* can be resolved to the same entity as *a man*. Later the *bartender* comes into play as a possible antecedent, complicating the interpretation of pronouns such as 'he', and so on. At the same time, hearers/readers are compelled to construct a meaningful discourse out of the sequence of linguistic input, such as establishing certain coherence relationships: It is relevant that the man has not had a drink for ten years, because, presumably, he has walked into the bar with the intention of ordering one. Although this is not stated explicitly by any overt linguistic means, we can deduce that in most cases, such discourse relations apply (cf. DRT, Kamp and Reyle 1993, and Segmented

---

1. This particular pattern, which we can term the 'man walks into a bar' construction, has received attention before, see Smith (1990: 92–93) on its tense, Timmis (2015: 97) on comprehensibility for ELT and Ritchie (2004: 89, 115–121) for prototypical examples in the context of joke analysis. For the related cataphoric 'this man walks into a bar' see Gernsbacher and Jescheniak (1995).

DRT, Asher and Lascarides 2003, see Section 6.1). In fact, some segments of the text offer such information more directly, as in the connector *so*, which leads us to believe that the bartender is being asked for something *because* the man has not had a drink in ten years, or at least that this fact is somehow pertinent.

Discourse relations of this sort will be explored in Chapter 6; but first we must begin by considering who or what the relevant entities in the discourse model are, for which we may later examine more or less coherent chains of events. After all, if we theorize that speakers maintain a representation of common-ground entities which facilitates their recognition and manages expectations about their mentions, then we must have a way of operationalizing these representations. We can then evaluate the quality of our model by considering how well it can exploit some of the same cues we postulate for speakers and hearers in tasks such as recognizing novel mentions or predicting the likelihood of further mentions. The annotation and evaluation of such models will be the focus of the main research questions for this chapter, which include: What cues can speakers use to construct their mental models? Can we build operationalized computational models of these cues? How are new entities introduced into discourse? What features are helpful in prioritizing and predicting which expressions hearers are supposed to recognize already, or which ones are likely to be mentioned again? And are there linguistic conventions that call for different signals, for example, in different text types or genres?

In order to empirically investigate and make use of the patterns introducing discourse referents and allowing their resolution, we require suitable annotation schemes to encode the different relevant levels of structure in the discourse. Surveying and reusing existing standards for this purpose is key to the comparability of findings and allows us to benefit from computational tools (cf. Stede and Huang 2012). With those at hand, we can examine correlations across annotation layers and extract predictive cues. As in the previous chapter, my focus will be on exploiting richly annotated running discourse, rather than isolated sentences, using a multilayer corpus approach, specifically by leveraging data in the GUM corpus introduced in Section 3.2.

5.2 Annotating Entities

The study of discourse referents pre-supposes our ability to recognize and categorize referential mentions. Usually, referential NPs are the target of entity annotation schemes, such as 'a man' in the 'man walks into a bar' construction, which refers to a specific man in context. Such units can then be annotated further for their entity type (e.g. 'person'), their definiteness ('indefinite'), information status in the discourse (e.g. 'discourse-new') and so on.[2] If we intend to talk about entity models for corpus data, it is fairly clear that such NPs need to be included in whatever list of mentions we are annotating.

However, not all referenceable entities in a text are referred to via NPs (Artstein and Poesio 2006), and not all NPs represent referenceable entities (Dipper et al. 2007: 152–153). The former case is most often evident when a pronominal antecedent refers to more than just what is denoted by an NP (in English especially using *that*). For example, in (54), which is taken from the TRAINS corpus (Gross et al. 1993), a common non-NP antecedent reading has been pointed out by Artstein and Poesio (2006: 61) as a reference to a whole plan of action, rather than an NP constituent of the larger clause. Similarly in the GUM corpus introduced in Section 3.2, we often find circumstantial and evaluation clauses of previous statements summing those up with a pronoun as their attachment marker (see Chapter 6), as in (55), which is especially typical in the spoken parts of the corpus.

(54) *[the shortest route would be back through Dansville again] [that]'ll take 4 hours* (TRAINS, Artstein and Poesio 2006: 62)
(55) *[I am going to Las Vegas and Los Angeles next month, Italy in November]* . . . *[That]'s as of now.* (GUM, GUM_interview_ brotherhood)

If *that* in (54) is taken to refer to the entire plan of going through Dansville, then the proposition about it being the shortest route may be seen as a discourse referent in itself. Similarly, if what is true in (55) as of now is that the speaker is going to a variety of places, then that entire proposition is a referenceable (albeit abstract) entity in the discourse, and may merit a place in our representation of the text's entity model.

Conversely, idiomatic NPs in phrases such as *on the other hand* are not normally considered referential at all, except under very constructed or meta-linguistic circumstances.[3] Some annotation schemes do not mark up NPs of this kind at all (e.g. OntoNotes, Hovy et al. 2006, see below, RefLex, Baumann and Riester 2012), whereas others give them a specific category, such as 'idiom' (e.g. Dipper et al. 2007 for the case noted earlier). Such cases are by no means very common, but they are not negligible either, forcing us to reconsider a simplistic approach equating discourse referents with syntactic NPs. There has also been substantial work showing the

---

2. Next to categorical labels of information status, one could also consider annotating gradient variables such as a numerical estimate of salience in context (cf. Chiarcos 2009).
3. There is also a range of more or less 'weakly referential' expressions, which may not be felicitous to refer back to but do correspond to actual entities in the world, e.g. *John is in jail.* #*It is a big building* (see Aguilar-Guevara et al. 2014 for further discussion; on use and omission of articles in such constructions, see also Himmelmann 1998).

drastic influence that entity and utterance border definitions can have on theoretical findings (most exhaustively for referentiality in the framework of Centering Theory, see Poesio et al. 2004). For example, defining the annotation regions in word tokens for mention borders (also called 'mark-ables', i.e. areas that can be marked up with annotations) to include long relative clauses elaborating on a core NP can radically increase the average mention length. At the same time, such increases only affect a subset of mentions (those with relative clauses), so that the variance we see across different mentions of similar entity types rises substantially. In practice, what we get out of studying the interrelations between layers of information will, as always, depend on what we put in, meaning we will have to take care to be as explicit as possible, and to match what we annotate with what we want to model and predict in unseen data.

Beyond the more typical explicit nominal mentions, a variety of 'corner cases' have been studied that are more or less frequent in different languages.[4] For example, VP ellipsis anaphora as in (56) (see Sag and Hankamer 1984; Heim 1997) and other event anaphora as in (57) require us to extend the pool of annotatable antecedents to phrases headed by verbs, as well as contend with zero anaphors, which may or may not be anchored to 'empty category' tokens (see Section 2.2).

(56) *The children asked to be [**squirted with the hose**], so they were [Ø]* (squirted with the hose; from Sag and Hankamer 1984)[5]

(57) *we [**count every day how many ants died**]. [**This**] gives us the data* . . . (GUM, GUM_interview_ants)[6]

---

4. Although the focus here is on English, many of the same issues apply to other languages, and in some cases with much higher frequency. The non-'pro drop' nature of English in particular, which is typologically speaking rare (Dryer 2013), means that for many other languages there is a much greater focus on 'elliptical' phenomena relating to the absence of overt arguments, and especially subjects (for theoretical discussion see Ariel 1990; Speas 2006, among many others; for computational approaches see Iida and Poesio 2011; Chen and Ng 2013).

5. Some restrictions are said to apply to possible anaphoric interpretations. Compare, for example, a continuation: 'so we did', which Sag and Hankamer mark as ungrammatical. However, it is in fact possible to find counterexamples in corpora, such as the following, taken from the spoken portion of Corpus of Contemporary American English (COCA, Davies 2008–):

   My wife and I met in a professional setting, and she sent me a note, which told me, hey, she was open to be called. And so I did. [call—AZ] (text ID 233898)
   [I]t 's something that has to be taken very seriously. And we do. [take it seriously—AZ] (text ID 249218)

   These types of sentences seem to be rare, but not ruled out – more detailed corpus studies will to be needed to discover whether certain conditions in particular license the occurrence of patterns like these.

6. This case can be annotated in several different ways, taking the whole first sentence, its VP or just the lexical verb as the antecedent (for more on the latter option, see below).

Other phenomena are less problematic from a data modeling perspective but require annotation schemes that are more refined than simply pointing out coreferentiality: for example, so-called 'vague' or 'sense anaphora', as well as 'one' anaphora as in (58), which require us to resolve their antecedent before determining anything about them ontologically (see Bresnan 1971; Payne et al. 2013; Recasens et al. 2016). 'One' anaphora are particularly challenging, because there are many types of entities that could be referred to via 'one' (persons, things, abstractions, but also events and more), and many possible relation types, for example, partitive (*three birds . . . the big one*), new instantiation (*Asian restaurants . . . an Italian one*) and many others.[7]

(58) *Yes, he wanted to marry with [a queen], but not [the one of Scotland]* (from Payne et al. 2013)

For each type of phenomenon, if we assume that the bracketed spans of text in the examples are possible loci for discourse referent status, then our annotation scheme must be capable of accommodating them. In (56) this could mean representing something like the position marked by Ø as a markable, whereas in (57) we would need to accept VPs or whole clauses as at least potential loci for markables to be drawn.

Often we will want to know something about the semantic or ontological types of mentions (people, places, things), but for many questions, morphosyntactic features such as pronominality, definiteness, number, gender and others will be relevant. In some cases, annotations of spans will be done directly using appropriate labels for each entity type, whereas in other cases we may opt to use more general labels and distinguish relational subtypes by labeling the edges between nodes (cf. Section 2.4) – for example, we can annotate an anaphor as pronominal, or annotate the connection to its antecedent as a case of pronominal anaphora. In this chapter I will assume that the multilayer corpus architecture gives us the possibility to annotate edges, which allows us more freedom; for example, we can annotate multiple, distinct types of annotations emanating from the same node. The remainder of this section will discuss node labels for entity types, and the next will outline edge labeling strategies.

Multiple schemes exist for the ontological categorization of entities, often motivated or inspired by applications in Named Entity Recognition (NER). The currently most widely used set of labels for English (and to a large extent Chinese and Arabic as well) is the OntoNotes scheme (Weischedel et al. 2012) with 21 entity types such as PERSON or LOCATION, which was introduced and contrasted with the GUM scheme

---

7. For a survey and analysis of subtypes which could merit distinct annotations, see the categories of 'one' anaphora in Payne et al. (2013).

in Section 3.2 (Table 3.3). As we will see in Section 5.4, different entity types exhibit rather different behavior in terms of referentiality and mention patterns: We tend to speak about people, events, abstracts and inanimate objects rather differently, and these patterns co-vary with many other variables, such as register, genre, speech act, and more (see Biber and Conrad 2009).

Annotation schemes that encode an 'event' category typically allow for sentential or verbal markables, though their extent may differ: in OntoNotes, only the verb corresponding to an event is marked up, and only in the presence of a definite anaphoric expression (pronoun or definite NP) as in (59). This makes it easier for automatic tools evaluated against OntoNotes to recover the correct target span, which is always only the lexical verb itself, excluding any possible auxiliaries. In other corpora, including GUM, the span including the verbal antecedent can have an arbitrary extension based on meaning, and any type of reference to the event will be annotated, regardless of definiteness, as in (60).

(59) *The IRS warnings stem from a 1984 law that [requires] anyone who receives more than $10,000 in cash . . . Delegates passed a resolution in 1985 condemning [the IRS reporting requirement]* (OntoNotes)

(60) *more details about how [the papers came to be on a road] . . . However, when [a government document has been found on the streets], the government then says . . .* (GUM)

The latter strategy is interesting for investigating exactly how much propositional content is actually being referred to in subsequent mentions of events expressed as verbal predicates, but makes the job of automated tools attempting to reproduce this decision substantially more complex. Whereas in the former case, the goal is just to match an NP headed by a nominalization like *requirement* with the verb *requires*, the latter case requires reasoning recognizing that the subject of the verb is included in the subsequent mention, because *papers* also refers to the same thing as *a government document* in context. As we will see later, mention border definitions play a substantial role in models predicting referentiality, so that decisions made at this stage carry over into subsequent analyses.

Finally, we must keep in mind that mentions can be, and often are, nested, so that we cannot run analyses that assume that each token in a mention belongs to exactly one semantic type. Figure 5.2 uses the multitiered grid view from Section 2.1 to give a fairly deeply stacked, but in many ways not unusual, example of fourfold entity nesting in GUM: Each of the entities involved can have different discourse status and function, and may or may not have been introduced already, or be destined for subsequent mention.

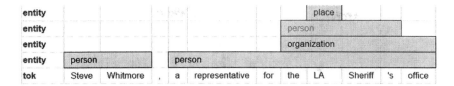

entity							place		
entity						person			
entity						organization			
entity	person		person						
tok	Steve	Whitmore	,	a	representative	for	the	LA	Sheriff	's	office

Figure 5.2 Nested mention spans for a person, containing an organization, containing a person, containing a place. Recursive-tiered grid view using ANNIS (Krause and Zeldes 2016)

5.3 Annotating Coreference Relations

Once mention types and borders have been defined, the much more complex issue of annotating referentiality relations can be approached. On a most general level, we can define the basic task of coreference annotation as a type of relational annotation indicating the source or sources of information that allow us to identify the discourse referent denoted by a certain linguistic expression. This can be contrasted with schemes which annotate pure information status on mention nodes as span annotations, marking certain mentions as discourse-given or discourse-new, but without indicating the source of information via a link or co-index (see Dipper et al. 2007: 150–161, for example; for an overview see Kübler and Zinsmeister 2015: 118–134; Lüdeling et al. 2016). Although many types of information serve to identify denotations of expressions, the focus in coreference annotation has been on the 'identity' relation, which indicates that two expressions refer to the same entity in the world. This category is especially central to anaphora resolution.

For example, the OntoNotes guidelines (Weischedel et al. 2012: 20) frame the purpose of OntoNotes' coreference annotation as follows:

> The goal of OntoNotes coreference annotation and modeling is to fill in the coreference portion of the shallow semantic understanding of the text that OntoNotes is targeting. For example, in "She had a good suggestion and it was unanimously accepted", we mark a case of IDENT coreference (identical reference) between "a good suggestion" and "it", which then allows correct interpretation of the subject argument of the "accepted" predicate.

This view is focused on information extraction or argument structure retrieval[8] as a goal for coreference annotation. Other projects have taken

---

8. These can be thought of as tasks concerned with understanding 'who did what to whom'. Related tasks also include shallow semantic parsing or semantic role labeling (see Gildea and Jurafsky 2002; Foland and Martin 2015), which benefit from coreference resolution.

a more theoretical and relatively open view of coreference, with the aim of building a better understanding of the phenomena involved. An example of such a project is the ARRAU corpus (Poesio and Artstein 2008: 1170):

> The primary goal of our annotation effort was to develop methods for marking ambiguous anaphoric expressions, and expressions which refer to abstract entities such as events, actions and plans. We conducted a series of experiments to test the feasibility of annotating these phenomena, and then annotated texts from a variety of genres. In addition, we annotated information that we knew could be annotated reliably from previous efforts, including information about agreement features and bridging relations.

The strategy of concurrently annotating comparatively reliable categories with high inter-annotator agreement is more typical in projects with relatively open-ended target phenomena of this kind (see also Lüdeling et al. 2016), because the hope is that these will facilitate recognition of trickier categories.

Although it is often assumed that coreference resolution is a well-defined task, when we look at specific examples, it is not always clear that unambiguous coreference resolution is possible. As Poesio and Artstein (2005) point out, in the following example from TRAINS, the anaphor *that* could conceivably refer to either *the boxcar at Elmira* or *a bad wheel*, or the entire proposition, and there may be no way to resolve this ambiguity (though it would certainly be possible to annotate such ambiguities explicitly in a multilayer architecture).

(61) *it turns out that **the boxcar at Elmira** has **a bad wheel** and they're . . gonna start fixing **that** at midnight* (TRAINS)

In many cases, the type of coreference relation we see is much less explicit than the identity (or near-identity) relation in (61), where 'that' and either the 'wheel' or 'boxcar' are virtually the same. More subtle relations are generally discussed under the heading of 'bridging' (see Asher and Lascarides 1998; sometimes also called 'associative anaphora', see Le Pesant 1996), that is, relations that connect the identifiability or inferability of some mention's denotation based on a mention which does not refer to exactly the same entity in the world. The most prominently discussed relation has been the meronymic, or part–whole relation, as in (62), but as we can see in (63), what parts something might have can be hard to list exhaustively or predict (both examples from the Wall Street Journal section of OntoNotes, which leaves these unannotated).

(62) *The parishioners of [St. Michael and All Angels] stop to chat at [the church door]* (bridging from 'door' to the church, because doors are a predictable part of St. Michael's; note the expression 'church door')

(63) *Mexico's President Salinas said [the country's] recession had ended and [the economy] was growing again* ('economy' is a non-physical but accessible part of Mexico)

In (62), the identity of 'the economy' requires reference to Mexico to resolve which economy is meant, and this can be seen as a part–whole relationship similar to the church and door example in (63) (Mexico has an economy, or in other words the economy is 'part of' Mexico).[9] The use of definiteness without previous mention is often taken as a signal for either such bridging relations, or some other type of situational or generic accessibility (e.g. 'pass **the** salt', available in the situation, or '**the** sun', a unique, always accessible referent, see Dipper et al. 2007: 150–161; Baumann and Riester 2012 and Kübler and Zinsmeister 2015: 134–140 for a comparison with some further annotation schemes).

A further complication arises when we consider variability in our perceptions of what constitutes coreference to begin with: Some theoretical approaches separate bound anaphora (Reinhart 1986) as a purely syntactic phenomenon, or perhaps just reflexive pronouns, co-referring expletives and more. All of these may be annotated normally, or using special categories, or simply be ignored. As an example, consider the following cases: In (64) we see the OntoNotes treatment of nested coreferent mention. OntoNotes mention borders encompass relative clauses, but coreference between pronouns inside a relative clause and their antecedent in the main clause is only carried out if there is a subsequent mention, as in (65); in (64), we find no coreference annotation at all, because OntoNotes regards the entire NP with the relative clause as a single mention. Single mentions (or 'singletons') receive no annotation according to the OntoNotes guidelines (see Zeldes and Zhang 2016 for discussion of these and some other problematic cases, as well as their consequences).

(64) *He has in tow [**his prescient girlfriend**, whose sassy retorts mark [**her**] . .]* (not annotated in OntoNotes, due to nesting)

(65) *[**The American administration** who planned carefully for this event through experts in media and public relations, and [**its**] tools] . . such an opposite result, which along with the destructive consequences have caught [**them**] by surprise* (all annotated, due to subsequent mention)

---

9. There are many subtypes often subsumed under bridging, such as inferable and non-inferable relations. Compare these examples from Baumann and Riester (2012):

I walked into my hotel room. The chandeliers sparked brightly (chandeliers fairly expected in hotel room)
John was murdered yesterday. The Japanese kitchen knife lay nearby (specific weapon rather unexpected)

For more discussion see Poesio and Vieira (1998); on cases that can be interpreted as elliptical, see Pesant (1996); for related corpus annotations see Björkelund et al. (2014).

Such design decisions have their justification in reasons pertaining to the envisioned research questions and applications planned by the corpus designers; however, if we are interested in modeling properties of mentions that are subsequently referred to as opposed to ones that are not, we need to use maximally inclusive data, including annotations for singleton mentions that are never referred to again, and comprehensive links between those that are.

In order to consider as many cases as possible and benefit from concurrent and often less controversial annotation layers, such as part-of-speech and syntactic analysis, we will be using the GUM data for the remainder of this chapter, which includes coreference annotation, including markup of singletons, event anaphora and bridging (see Zeldes 2017a; Zeldes and Zhang 2016). After presenting the structure of GUM's coreference annotation layer, we will look at the behavior of discourse referents across layers.

5.4   Discourse Referents and Information Status: A Multilayer Study

In addition to the syntactic layers explored in the previous chapter, GUM contains coreference annotations of both definite and indefinite expressions, including bridging as discussed in the previous section and cataphora annotation for pronouns which are resolved in a subsequent mention. These include 'true' cataphora, where a pronoun precedes a nominal mention as in (66), and so-called 'empty' pronoun cataphora, a correlate of a postponed clausal subject which is left unannotated in some corpora, notably OntoNotes (67)[10]:

(66) *In [**her**] opening remarks for attendees, [**Waters**] pointed out those features to attendees* (GUM)

(67) *[**it**] may be helpful [**to focus your efforts on opening your reserve parachute**]* (GUM)

The breakdown of annotation types contained in the corpus is given in Table 5.1. As we can see from the table, there are fewer markables than nominals (nouns and pronouns), despite the fact that not all markables are nominal. This suggests that a substantial number of nominals are non-referring expressions.

With the data at hand, we can now consider the distribution of markables representing referential entities: How can we model the multiple

---

10. Some schemes, such as the UCREL Discourse Annotation Scheme (Garside et al. 1997), have even distinguished more than just edges pointing backwards (anaphora) vs. forwards (cataphora), but also ambiguous and 'meta' coreference links, e.g. for expressions such as 'this chapter' (anchored to the beginning of the chapter containing it? Or the chapter up to this point? Or the end?).

Table 5.1 Breakdown of coreference annotation in GUM (version 3)

	Total	Ø per document
documents	76	—
tokens	64,005	842.17
nominals	20,017	263.38
markables	16,281	214.22
coreference relations	8,969	118.01
—of which cataphora	90	1.18
—of which bridging	964	12.68

factors that speakers leverage in order to follow entities through a discourse? What makes us choose pronominal or nominal realizations for a specific term? What signals coreference in a lexical NP?

From a theoretical perspective, many accounts have considered a competition between multiple factors used in resolution (Hobbs 1979, 1990; Ariel 1990; Bosch and Umbach 2007; Bosch et al. 2007; Kehler et al. 2007; Kehler and Rohde 2013). These factors include grammatical relations (especially subjecthood), head form (pronominal, common or proper noun head), definiteness and information status (Krifka 2008) and measures of salience and topic continuity (Givón 1983; Chiarcos 2009). A multilayer corpus gives us the necessary testing grounds for examining the interplay of these factors and others in natural running discourse.

As a case study, we will concentrate on the characteristics of full lexical NPs (non-pronouns) which have antecedents in the text. The issue of identifying co-referring lexical NPs is of considerable theoretical and practical importance: On the one hand, we would like to know how speakers come to interpret a sequence of propositions as involving the same individuals in the world; without lexical coreference, quite apart from the question of pronoun resolution, we can hardly make sense of any sequence of sentences. Theoretical frameworks such as Centering Theory (Grosz et al. 1995) postulate that speakers track the likelihood of subsequent mention for referents in each utterance as potential 'Forward-Looking Centers', even before subsequent mention occurs. On the other hand, for computers faced with the practical task of coreference resolution, it is also not obvious for a given lexical NP whether antecedents should be looked for or not. Whereas a phrase such as '*her*' is automatically expected to have an antecedent in the text, a phrase such as '*the president*' may or may not be resolvable to a particular person mentioned elsewhere in the text. It is therefore interesting to ask what are the characteristics of a lexical NP that increase the likelihood of antecedents or subsequent mentions being present. Because GUM equally contains singleton and coreferent mention annotations, the corpus allows us to gather several sources of information for this purpose.

Previous approaches have generally used definiteness, proper noun status and grammatical function to predict further mentions (e.g. Ritz 2010; Recasens et al. 2013). Intuitively, lexical NPs that do have an antecedent should be definite, though proper nouns, which are, by nature, definite, may or may not signal previous mention. Entity type can also be related: People are likely candidates for subsequent mentions in a text, whereas dates are not as likely to be discussed repeatedly. Entity types, such as those portrayed in Figure 5.1 at the beginning of this chapter, are frequently used by coreference resolution systems to match properties with antecedent candidates (Lee et al. 2013; Zeldes and Zhang 2016). Grammatical function, especially in the context of chains of co-referring subjects in a narrative chain, may also be relevant, though it should be noted that recurring lexical NP subjects are perhaps less likely, because we would expect them to be replaced by a pronoun before long. Recasens et al. (2013) used additional factors such as the length of each referent (longer phrases contain more information and suggest entities not previously discussed), number (plural number may be less specific and somewhat less prone to coreference in context) and higher-level features at the syntax–semantics interface, such as presence of a negation or modal scope over a mention, both of which make subsequent mention less likely.[11]

Position in the sentence as a proxy for information structure (see Chapter 5), as well as position in the text, may also have an influence, as most referents are expected to be introduced early in the text (see Baayen's 2001: 6–7 study of articles across *Alice in Wonderland*), whereas given referents are typically used early in the sentence (see Féry 2006). Finally, it is possible that the different genres in the corpus correlate with different patterns of coreference. Whether this is the case and to what extent is a matter that has not yet been studied in depth, but is possible to inspect in a corpus covering several genres (see also Zeldes and Simonson 2016).

Genres and Coreference

We begin by considering the genre question: Is there a different pattern to coreferentiality in lexical NPs across the genres in GUM? Version 3 of the corpus contains texts from four rather different sources: interviews and news texts (both from Wikimedia), travel guides from Wikivoyage (abbreviated 'voyage' below) and how-to guides from wikiHow (abbreviated 'whow'; see Zeldes 2017a for more details). Because these sections of the corpus have rather different communicative purposes and conventions (we can treat these, respectively, as predominantly conversational,

---

11. The goal for Recasens et al. was specifically to identify singleton phrases, i.e. phrases that *do not* have an antecedent or subsequent mention in the text, and find a confident model for rejecting unlikely anaphors/antecedents, focusing on precision rather than recall.

narrative, informative and instructional), we might expect different patterns of entity introductions and subsequent mentions.

Figure 5.3 shows the distribution of the types of coreference discussed in the previous section as they break down by genre.[12] Bar width corresponds to the amount of data supporting each type of coreference. The differences between genres are in part rather pronounced: non-lexical identity types in particular are rather heterogeneous (i.e. 'ana', 'cata' and 'bridge'). The lexical identity types (connections of two lexical NPs, designating an identity relation), which include appositions and other types of lexical coreference, are distributed fairly evenly, with the most visible deviation being appositions in news texts. This is due to the higher likelihood of constructions introducing entities with an apposition on first mention in news texts, as in (68) and date appositions which are annotated in GUM, as in (69):

(68) [*Major general Fuad Basya*], [*spokesman for the Indonesian military*], *said . .*
(69) [*Monday*], [*May 18, 2015*]. *On Friday, fishermen rescued . . .*

For the remaining coreference types, we can see that the voyage and news texts cluster together in dispreferring anaphora, whereas how-to guides exhibit more bridging than other genres. For comparison, in voyage texts appositions are more prevalent than bridging, but the opposite is true for how-to texts. This is likely to be due at least in part to different communicative functions and in part to conventions: how-to guides are technical and contain many implied connections or part–whole relationships, whereas travel guides often supply additional information about place names using appositions. Data for cataphora ('cata') is very sparse, as represented by the thin bar size, and should be interpreted with caution.

It is also interesting to consider when we get higher proportions of 'none' cases. Whereas pronouns are almost always coreferent with some previous mention, lexical NPs may or may not be mentioned again, and we can explore this contrast by considering the categories 'coref' versus 'none'. The association plot in Figure 5.4 shows that news and how-to texts cluster together for these lexical NPs, with less 'coref' than 'none' in both. The area of the rectangles in the plot gives the difference between observed and expected frequencies in each category based on an expectation of independence between the two variables (above expectation for the raised rectangles, or below for the lowered ones). The width of each rectangle gives the squared root of the expected frequency, which is calculated based on the frequency of each category, and can therefore be seen as

---

12. We keep in mind that mentions with no antecedent (the type 'none') and bridging are included; some of the types discussed in Section 3 remain to be studied in this corpus, notably sense anaphora and weakly referential NPs.

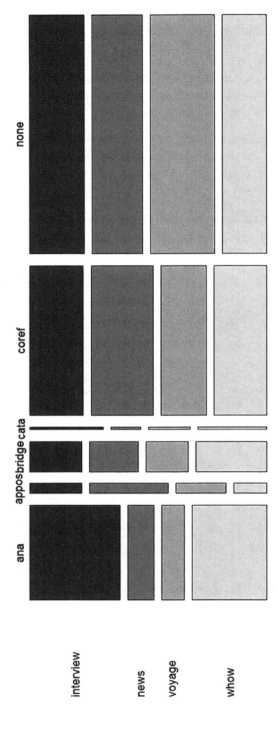

Figure 5.3 Coreference type proportions across genres. Bar widths represent the relative amount of data they are based on

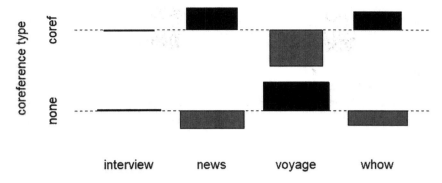

Figure 5.4 Association of lexical coreference with genre

a measure of that category estimate's reliability (in this case all categories are well attested, and all rectangles are similarly wide).

From inspection of the texts the effect seems to be related to the narrower thematic focus of news and how-to guides, both of which concentrate more on one topic (news-worthy event or topic of instruction), whereas the voyage and interview texts switch topics more frequently, leading to more, and shorter, lexical coreference chains. Voyage texts also frequently list places to see or things to do, which may only garner one mention before shifting to another topic, as exemplified in (70). In this example from a travel guide to Athens, all mentions except for 'the Olympic Games' are non-coreferring, giving new information as part of the guide which does not become topical.

(70) . . . [the restoration of [the picturesque neoclassical [Thissio] and [Pláka] districts]]. [The ancient Olympic Games] took place in [Olympia] from [776 BC] to [394 AD]. .

This kind of more 'disjointed' or less coherent discourse structure leads to islands of mentions, rather than long homogeneous chains, though both exist side-by-side to some extent. For example, Athens is discussed throughout the text containing (70). The differences that distinguish texts in this respect are not categorical but rather quantitative, and can only be recognized at a distance, when an overall picture of documents is composed across layers of information.

Visualizing Coreference Patterns

Before we turn to modeling interactions of multiple factors which may be more difficult to interpret intuitively, it is worth considering what of the earlier discussion can be observed with the naked eye using more global visualization techniques. Accompanying quantitative analysis with visualization can be very useful to get a sense of the meaningful patterns behind numbers,[13] as advocated also in some recent digital humanities work under the heading of 'distant reading' (cf. Moretti 2013). Although 'distant reading' has sometimes been criticized as vulnerable to a false sense of objectivity (e.g. Ross 2014), more holistic visualization can, when used cautiously and with explicit operationalization next to validated statistical tests, provide support for conclusions which are otherwise mathematically sound but harder to grasp and accept as plausible. In this section I would therefore like to take a look at the referentiality structure of texts as a set of high-level organic constructions.[14]

Now that we have seen how features of individual discourse referent mentions can be annotated, we can look for larger configurations in our data. The focus here is on patterns of mention clusters: ways in which novel entities are introduced; how they are referred to subsequently; and typical properties of certain positions in a chain, such as second, third or last mention, in interplay with other layers describing the textual environment. At the beginning of this chapter I considered the example of a typical joke opening starting with *a man walks into a bar. . . .* This type of opening is also the beginning of a typical chain in terms of definiteness and pronominalization, often unfolding over three mentions in the narrative present, which can look like this (cf. Smith 1990: 92–93; Ritchie 2004: 89, 115–121; Gernsbacher and Jescheniak 1995):

A Man . . . the Man . . . He . . .

These and other types of chains recur in GUM to varying degrees in different genres. For example, in introductions to interviews we can find patterns such as *[Full Name] . . . [Last Name] . . . [pronoun]*. We can easily find examples of such transitions in our corpus data, two of which are visualized next as larger patterns with intervening context marked by ellipses. Note in (72) the interweaving of this pattern with two other genre-appropriate ones: the apposition (*Sarvis, nominee*) and the prefixed professional title (*Attorney Robert Sarvis*, an instance of a title construction *[Profession] [Full Name]*).

13. Cf. Baayen (2008: viii), who points out that visualizations "generally provide far more insight into the data than the long lists of statistics that depend on often questionable simplifying assumptions".
14. I will be taking a broad and relatively agnostic view of the theoretical status of such recurring constructions here, but much of this type of data can feed in to construction grammar approaches (e.g. Goldberg 2006), which assume that arbitrarily shaped, and potentially large, constellations can become conventionalized and acquire unpredictable, language-specific meaning. See Chapter 1 for a brief overview of the relevant ideas, and see the conclusion of this book for some discussion.

(71) [*Jack Herrick*]. . [*Herrick*] *explains what wikiHow is, why* [*he*] *decided to create it* . .

(72) [*Attorney Robert Sarvis*], [*the Libertarian Party's nominee*] . . [*Sarvis*] *has garnered double digits* . . *The latest Newsmax / Zogby poll from late September placed* [*him*]. .

This type of chain works well if no other human discourse referents are mentioned, which is typically the case in the introduction to an interview.[15] However, it is not hard to show that the issue is more related to salience than ambiguity, because even human referents with a different gender can disrupt the preference for such patterns, as we can see in the following example from a news text.[16]

(73) . . . [[*Paris's*] *father*], [*Albert Jaquier*], *committed suicide after* [*he*] *lost* [*his*] *fortune to Scientology.* [**Paris**] *claims that* [*she*] . . .

Here a naïve expectation might be that there is no need to repeat the boldface name *Paris* in the second sentence, because she is the most recently mentioned female, but clearly, the shift in subject leads to a preference for lexical re-mention, fitting the type of model suggested by Centering Theory.

The effects of text-wide properties, including but not limited to genre, on typical referentiality patterns can also be visualized by considering the 'tiling pattern' that a coreference graph creates in a delexicalized representation of documents, in which all specific words have been made unrecognizable. Figure 5.5 shows such patterns for coreferent mentions in four documents from two different genres in GUM, in which the actual word forms have been blurred.

The figure shows spans of text referring to the same entity highlighted in the same color, allowing us a kind of 'distant reading'. Even without being able to read the actual words, it is evident that the impression of similarity is greater within, rather than across, genres, and this offers an intuitive view of what less easily interpretable statistics will also reveal later. Cross-referencing these patterns with the underlying texts shows some more typical recurring constructions.

A relatively trivial example is the appearance of the 'date block' in news texts, usually in the second utterance, containing an apposition of the form

---

15. In fact, in cases involving multiple referents, some languages have pronouns to distinguish whether a transition is staying with the previous topic/subject or shifting to a non-subject, e.g. German demonstrative *der* 'that one' as opposed to *er* 'he'. These pronouns have been characterized as avoiding 'perspectival centers' (see Bosch and Umbach 2007; Hinterwimmer and Bosch 2016).

16. The interviews in GUM contained no such examples of intervening referents in the introduction.

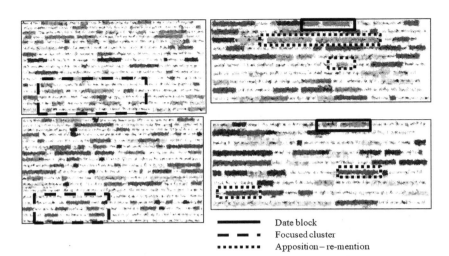

Figure 5.5 Blurred coreference patterns in four GUM documents. Left: how-to guides (*How to Grow Basil, How to Wash Overalls*); Right: news articles (*Over 900 Asylum Seekers Rescued, Scientology Defector Arrested*, the article containing (73))

'[Saturday], [October 9, 2010]' (in the black boxes on the right hand side panels of Figure 5.5). The tendency to appositions is, as we have seen, generally more pronounced in news texts, and, with the exception of the *date* entity type, these are typically mentioned again later, indicating that apposition is a cue that a discourse referent will be revisited later. The following examples correspond to the dotted boxes on the right panels of the figure:

(74) [*Major general Fuad Basya*], [*spokesman for the Indonesian military*] . . [*Basya*] *also believes* . .

(75) [*its elite group*] [*the Sea Org*] . . [*the Sea Org*] *requires members* . .

The how-to texts on the left, by contrast, have much shorter mentions, without appositions, and with a few very repetitive ones corresponding to the focus of the current instructions, often as an object to an imperative. We can think of these as 'focused clusters' of mentions, dedicated to one subtopic, or in this case, subtask (marked with a dashed box in the left panels of Figure 5.5). Here is just some of the red highlighted cluster in the bottom-left panel.

(76) *It's ready to provide the right environment for* [*the basil seeds*] *to germinate. 4 Plant* [*the seeds*]. *Drop* [*one to two seeds*] *into each container. Cover* [*them*] *lightly with soil* . . .

As we can see, the short mentions are not only due to pronominalization, but also to the ease of identifiability of salient entities in the guide (e.g. seeds) and the style, which decouples descriptions into separate utterances for each step. News texts, by contrast, are rife with non-restrictive adjectival and prepositional modification, which lengthens even subsequent mentions atypically:

(77) [*the Scientology organization*] . . . [*the organization founded by science fiction writer L. Ron Hubbard*]

In this example, even though we are looking at the tenth mention of Scientology in the article, there is still room for new modifiers,[17] which give elaborating information bundled together with the mention itself, rather than as a separate predication.

A Multifactorial Model

Beyond intuitive impressions from visualizations and data from individual layers of information that we have examined, we would like to know what we can learn by looking across annotation layers. Given the specific subset of phenomena we are examining and the way in which we have chosen to annotate them (recall the different options in Sections 5.2–5.3), is there a significant covariation between genre and coreference likelihood? If so, how much of the variation in coreference proportions is genre responsible for? What happens on other annotation layers at the same time? To explore these questions, we can use some of the modeling techniques introduced in Chapter 2.

A simple linear model will attempt to find associations above and beyond chance between the presence of coreference and the different genres in the corpus: A correlation can always be due to chance, but the significance (p-value) given to each of the variants that we are looking at will tell us how likely it is to see such a correlation if we were randomly shuffling entity mentions and genre labels. We therefore begin by running a simple linear model of coreferentiality, that is, modeling the likelihood that some (non-pronominal) NP has an

---

17. Outside of news texts, this tendency has been noted to be rare (Fox 1993), and some coreference resolution systems explicitly make the assumption that subsequent mentions will not, or are highly unlikely to, add new modifiers in subsequent mentions (Lee et al. 2013: 891). In fact, allowing new modifiers and diagnosing which lexical items are likely to be added and in which contexts can increase recall in coreference resolution without hurting precision (see Zeldes and Zhang 2016). There is also some experimental evidence that speakers may 'overspecify' in entity mentions depending on their sense of information shared with or privileged from the addressee (Heller et al. 2009).

antecedent, as a function of genre in the statistics software R, which
is summarized here:

```
Coefficients:
             Estimate   Std. Error   t value   Pr(>|t|)
(Intercept)  0.380582   0.008922     42.659    < 2e-16    ***
genrenews    0.058975   0.012500      4.718    2.41e-06   ***
genrevoyage  -0.063329  0.012440     -5.091    3.62e-07   ***
genrewhow    0.042343   0.013137      3.223    0.00127    **
---
Signif. codes:  0 '***' 0.001 '**' 0.01 '*' 0.05 '.' 0.1 ' ' 1

Residual standard error: 0.4851 on 11681 degrees of freedom
Multiple R-squared: 0.009754, Adjusted R-squared: 0.0095
```

The model shows that, with *interview* as the reference level (or 'intercept'), both *voyage* and *news* differ very significantly. The *voyage* travel
guides are showing less coreference than expected, as shown by the
negative estimate, whereas *news* texts have a positive estimate.[18] The
estimate for how-to guides (*whow*) is also significant and positive, suggesting that it clusters with *news* in promoting more coreference than
the other genres.

However, even if the distribution of coreferentiality across genre is not
coincidental, how predictive is genre really? To check, we look at the r^2
value, which, much like the correlation metric for a standard trend line,
tells us how much of the variance between data points can be ascribed to
the predictor that we are looking at. The adjusted[19] r^2 value shows us that
only very little of the variance in coreference proportions is explained by
genre (about 0.0095, or just over 0.9%). This is not surprising: If we were
to try to predict the proportion of coreference in a document based solely
on being told that it's a news article rather than an interview, we would
not get very far. Still, differences are pronounced enough for a significant
result. What is it about the genres that makes them differ significantly?
To answer this question, we turn next to examining more fine-grained
factors, which co-vary with genre as well.

Examining each genre separately gives us some insights about the way
that different text types with different communicative purposes tend to

---

18. The exact numerical meaning of the coefficient for binary prediction (coreference or
    non-coreference) can be interpreted as the log-odds ratio, i.e. the exponent of the ratio
    between the quotients of coreference to non-coreference in the genre being compared
    vs. the baseline. For more details see Gries (2013: 178–190), Baayen (2008: 214–227).
19. Adjustment of r^2 is a standard strategy to penalize models with very many predictors by
    adjusting for the expected amelioration of fit as predictors are added (see Gries 2013:
    265); in the case of this very simple model, very little adjustment is required.

behave, but what we still cannot see is what happens when we consider multiple factors at once. Although it is possible that, for example, how-to guides are very 'on topic' or focused on few discourse referents, it is possible that this observation could be explained better by considering the fact that how-to guides tend to contain many imperatives, which leave subjects unexpressed and reduce the number of possible mentions of overt subjects. To test hypotheses like these, we can examine individual annotation layers and their influence on mention behavior. The linear model shown next uses the sentence type annotations from Section 3.2 (see Table 3.2 there) to test the relationship between lexical coreference likelihood and the environment within a question, imperative, fragment, etc.

	Estimate	Std. Error	t-score	p-value	
(Intercept)	0.386033	0.005203	74.189	< 2e-16	***
frag	-0.072700	0.018504	-3.929	8.59e-05	***
ger	0.035019	0.064624	0.542	0.587900	
imp	0.069935	0.016078	4.350	1.37e-05	***
inf	-0.283469	0.078046	-3.632	0.000282	***
other	0.019196	0.028284	0.679	0.497352	
q	-0.010093	0.042489	-0.238	0.812231	
sub	-0.004694	0.022512	-0.209	0.834819	
wh	0.103900	0.040179	2.586	0.009724	**

The model shows that imperatives favor coreferentiality (significant positive estimate), as do wh-questions and declaratives (the intercept level), but fragments and infinitive clauses do the opposite, all other things being equal. We can postulate several reasons why this may be: Imperatives, at least in the texts in question, are likely involved in instructional sentences regarding the manipulation of some object in a how-to guide (cf. (76) earlier), or a destination to visit or sight to see in a travel guide (e.g. *have a look at this statue*), which can subsequently be elaborated on. Similarly, wh-questions typically set up a discussion of the thing or person being asked after (see Zeldes and Simonson 2016 for more discussion of coreferentiality and sentence types).

Taken individually, such factors seem to have an effect – but some of these potential cues may be redundant with others, and some are very interdependent. For example, it is likely that imperatives are short, so perhaps sentence length is a better predictor of their behavior; but then we might expect fragments, which are also short, to behave similarly. Even worse, although imperatives in our corpus seem to favor lexical coreference, they are also concentrated in how-to guides, meaning that genre and sentence type are tightly linked, and perhaps so is sentence length. A multifactorial approach building on multilayer data can address complex interactions like these: By feeding these and other predictors to a joint regression model, we can discover which effects remain surprising, above and beyond chance, given everything that we know about our texts. We will therefore try to find out what a model predicting lexical coreference likelihood might look like when our information is pooled together.

Before proceeding to include all of the factors mentioned earlier in our model, three caveats must be kept in mind:

1. There is a high risk of overfitting the model to the data on account of the large amount of categories in some of the factors. This is especially true for annotation layers with larger tag sets, such as parts of speech, grammatical functions or even sentence types: If the unique combinations of these layers lead to very sparse data, we risk building a model that memorizes the effect of each combination on a case-by-case basis.

2. Our model construction in this case proceeds post hoc, after the data have been seen. This is true in the first instance because we have already discussed several of the main constituent factors, but also in the second instance whenever we are analyzing data that we have already annotated: Inevitably, the data will have been inspected in detail over the course of annotation, meaning some of our conclusions can be seen as post hoc.

3. Some of the variation across the corpus will inevitably be tied to specific documents. This is intuitive when doing close reading of documents: Some interviewers or interviewees repeat themselves unusually often; some writers have a proclivity towards pronouns, others towards lexical mention, etc. Separating this 'random' variation from systematic effects is an important challenge.

The first issue can be dealt with by only considering the most powerful and intuitively plausible levels, such as not looking at all grammatical functions, but just, for example, subjecthood, which is known to be closely related to salience and coreference next to and in combination with other factors (cf. Kehler and Rohde 2013 for experimental studies, Recasens et al. 2013 for corpus data). The second issue is more difficult: The optimism of the fitted model must be tested by cross-validation, but as far as the choice of selected factors is concerned, validation against further data completely unseen during development is desirable. In most cases, the factors will have been used before in previous studies, giving some independent merit to their selection. Finally, the third issue can be addressed using mixed-effects models: By assuming that some factors, such as the identity of the document or writer, may interfere with our measurements, we can calibrate our model to include a corresponding random effect. This random effect will allow us to assign a divergent 'baseline' coreference likelihood to each separate document before assessing the influence of other factors above and beyond this baseline (see Baayen 2008: 263–327 for an overview).[20]

A linear mixed-effects model containing these factors is shown next, including the sentence types discussed earlier and the position of the head token in terms of percentage of document length (i.e. whether this entity appears right at the beginning or 0%, in the middle at 50% or the end at 100% of document length, cf. Section 4.3). We also include several interactions which are significant: between subjecthood and proper noun status and subjecthood and markable length (being long is an indication of newness, but less so for subjects); position in document and definiteness and length (these have a different influence depending on position in the document); and proper noun status and length (some names are long, but this does not have the same consequences as long common noun markables). We also include a random effect for the document in question. The model is constructed using the lme4 package in R.

```
Random effects:
 Groups Name            Variance  Std.Dev.
 docname (Intercept)    0.1011    0.318
Number of obs: 11684, groups: docname, 76
```

```
Fixed effects:
                  Estimate    Std. Error  z value  Pr(>|z|)
(Intercept)       -0.7360098  0.1067687   -6.893   5.44e-12  ***
entity=event       0.5111625  0.0850816    6.008   1.88e-09  ***
entity=object      0.5852341  0.0759730    7.703   1.33e-14  ***
entity=           0.6488685  0.0925285    7.013   2.34e-12  ***
organization
entity=person      0.4786488  0.0737879    6.487   8.77e-11  ***
entity=place       0.8208560  0.0732719   11.203   < 2e-16   ***
entity=plant       1.9137469  0.2012406    9.510   < 2e-16   ***
entity=substance   1.3943939  0.1206680   11.556   < 2e-16   ***
entity=time       -0.7024715  0.1153651   -6.089   1.14e-09  ***
doc_position       0.4964794  0.0729353    6.807   9.96e-12  ***
is_proper          0.4485828  0.0599157    7.487   7.05e-14  ***
is_subject         0.4937535  0.0935510    5.278   1.31e-07  ***
is_plural         -0.4941868  0.0543606   -9.091   < 2e-16   ***
is_indefinite     -0.7320243  0.0529747  -13.818   < 2e-16   ***
s_type=frag       -0.2883714  0.0913747   -3.156   0.001600  **
s_type=ger         0.2213110  0.2932114    0.755   0.450379
s_type=imp         0.0473887  0.0923620    0.513   0.607898
```

20. This family of statistical models distinguishes itself in being able to factor out meaningful correlations and residual variation, but has only begun to see extensive use in corpus studies in recent years; it has been called the 'most underused statistical method in corpus linguistics' by Gries (2015).

```
s_type=inf        -1.8835935  0.5511043  -3.418 0.000631 ***
s_type=other      -0.0232205  0.1320312  -0.176 0.860395
s_type=q           0.1935358  0.2018476   0.959 0.337649
s_type=sub        -0.1266944  0.1088701  -1.164 0.244537
s_type=wh          0.4278370  0.1848107   2.315 0.020613 *
genre=news         0.1831669  0.1191836   1.537 0.124331
genre=voyage      -0.4004167  0.1252400  -3.197 0.001388 **
genre=whow         0.1306459  0.1276824   1.023 0.306209
markable_length    0.0003153  0.0458852   0.007 0.994518
proper*length     -0.2147709  0.0685991  -3.131 0.001743 **
subj*length       -0.7282191  0.0992601  -7.336 2.19e-13 ***
position*length   -0.6704422  0.0890234  -7.531 5.03e-14 ***
subj*indef        -0.4521711  0.1210514  -3.735 0.000187 ***
---
Signif. codes:  0 '***' 0.001 '**' 0.01 '*' 0.05 '.' 0.1 ' ' 1
```

The model compares the values for each variable to a reference level, the intercept, which is arbitrarily set by an alphabetic criterion to be the entity type *abstract*, the sentence type *declarative* and the genre *interview* (cf. the simpler model using genre only at the beginning of this section, in which the genre *interview* was taken as the reference level for comparison). Negative estimates and z-scores for a variable suggest that it is correlated with a lack of antecedent compared to the reference level, proportional to the estimate's magnitude and with a degree of certainty expressed by the t-value. For example, among the entity types, all types are more likely to have an antecedent than abstracts (positive values), except for mentions of *time* (e.g. referents like '1990', 'last year' or 'Monday'), which are the least likely to have previous mentions. All of these effects have very low p-values, meaning that they are highly unlikely to be coincidental. The most likely to be rementioned are plants, which is, however, likely an artifact of two of the wikiHow articles on growing basil and cacti, respectively, which contain almost all references to plants in the corpus. Persons, by contrast, are not very likely to have an antecedent, though more so than abstracts and times: This is because a person mentioned by a lexical NP and not a pronoun is often discourse-new. If the person has already been mentioned, pronominal reference is usually more expected. Proper nouns behave similarly to persons in this respect: Both have antecedents more often than not, but the effect is modest.

The strongest effects we can observe are for indefiniteness and mention length, though for the latter the interactions with other factors drive its significance. The coefficients for interactions with length are especially notable if we consider that the estimate for the coefficient is multiplied by the actual length to derive a prediction. In other words, indefinites and long mentions are both significant signals of a novel: first mention. Long mentions are especially indicative of novelty in interaction with subjecthood: Whereas subjects at large usually have antecedents (positive coefficient), the interaction with length can tip the scales in the opposite direction more powerfully than for non-subjects. There is also some influence from some of the sentence types: wh-questions usually involve given information being asked something new about, as in (78), whereas utterances headed by an infinitive, which are most often headings or captions, are likely novel and inherently without overt subjects, as in (79)–(80). These effects survive from the sentence type-based model, whereas an independent effect for imperatives, for example, does not.

(78) [*The Spitfire Tournament in Canada*] *was a really good tournament actually. It was a tournament that I wish we'd actually gone back to more often. Who plays in* [**that one**]$_{GIV}$?

(79) *How to Grow* [**Basil**]$_{NEW}$ (Main heading of article)

(80) *why not make* [**the word Birds**]$_{NEW}$ *'Vogelaviatiolaps'* [. . .]? (discussion on inventing a constructed language)

Another important point is the modest influence of genre, with only 'voyage' disfavoring coreference compared to the intercept. The addition of the random effect for document may have detracted some of the variance explained by the genres, because the documents fall into genres themselves. However, if the baseline for all or most documents in some genre is higher than in others, the model will assign the significance to the fixed genre effect, and we can see that this is the case for the travel guides. In fact, the random effect for the document is responsible for a rather small amount of variance compared with the fixed effects' influence. We can therefore conclude that the other fixed predictors in the model largely obviate or subsume the genre effect.

The latter conclusion may seem surprising given the significant effect that we found for all genres in the last section. But in fact, what the previous model does is, in many respects, break down what it is to be in a certain genre into multiple constituents, at least in so far as likelihood of subsequent mention is concerned. This is not so surprising: Proportions of sentence types, entity types, verbosity in terms of mention length and so on are themselves covariates of register (see Biber 2009; Biber and Conrad 2009). Questions are characteristic of interviews; just as imperatives dominate how-to guides, so those predictors may suffice to model baselines in those documents. Plants are almost never discussed in news texts, but a little more in travel guides, and somewhat coincidentally very often in our how-to guides.[21] The added insight of the model, however, is that in cases where variables cross-classify across genres, our effects

---

21. Whether or not these facts belong in a linguistic analysis or are simply 'facts about the world' is hard to tease apart and essentially impossible to draw a general hard-and-fast line for. From a usage-based perspective, the attempt to do so may also be theoretically undesirable, see Chapter 1.

might be better explained by referring to factors like mention length, even if these are correlated with genre themselves.

In terms of predictive power, a model with the previously noted factors but without genre correctly classifies 70.54% of the data on average, with a standard deviation of 1.3%. This result is based on a tenfold cross-validation trained on non-overlapping, randomly divided 90% slices of the data and checked against the remaining 10% in each case. This is a modest, but substantial, improvement over a majority baseline of 61.1% (assuming referents never have an antecedent, the more common option). Despite the small size of the corpus, it seems that the model, which is based on 11,684 individual referents out of the 16,281 annotated in the corpus in version 3 (including anaphors etc.), is quite stable and not substantially overfitted: All of the effects, including the interactions, remain significant in all slices, suggesting that the factors used here are truly relevant for the phenomenon in question across genres.

Although a classification accuracy of 70% is not nearly sufficient for independent application, it should be kept in mind that it is rather unrealistic to expect an accurate prediction of the presence of an antecedent based solely on the properties of the referent itself (i.e. without actually looking for an antecedent in previous text), and the evaluation is quite stringent in not considering pronouns at all, which are 'the easy cases' for this task.[22] Seen in this light, the results of the model are actually quite good and fall in line with ideas from Centering Theory positing that, at least to some extent, speakers can already rank 'Forward Looking Centers' and 'Backward Looking Centers' (potential referents) based on subsequent mention likelihood.

As a multilayer corpus analysis tool, this model is a starting point for considering the properties of a typical coreferring, non-pronominal NP in empirical English data like GUM. A coreferential lexical referring

---

22. We can easily add pronouns to the data included in the model. This would raise accuracy to 88.26%, and makes the effect of infinitive sentence type insignificant (possibly because these virtually never contain pronouns and are drowned out by the pronoun data), whereas length effects become stronger (because pronouns are short). These results are better than the 72.2% precision reported in Recasens et al. (2013), though we have some predictors they did not have, including gold entity and sentence types, and our data contains substantial amounts of 'easy' first- and second-person pronouns in the interviews. In any event, I believe that mixing evaluation on pronouns and nominals obscures the theoretical issue (which is admittedly not Recasens et al.'s main interest, as their paper is primarily concerned with improving English coreference resolution in practice).

expression is more likely than not (cf. the positives coefficient estimates in the final model, which predict coreference):

- Definite.
- A person or concrete object, a substance or plant[23] but rarely a time, and infrequently a place.
- Quite likely headed by a proper noun.
- Often the subject of the sentence.
- Usually not plural.
- More likely to be part of a wh-question than a non-coreferring counterpart.
- Short.
- Later in the text (measured as percentile position in document).
- If it is somewhat long, being subject or proper noun is less important; increased length later in the document is also an indication against coreference.

Knowing these features almost removes the significance of an independent effect for genre. The features also coincide in large part with the features used deterministically by Lee et al. (2013) to predict coreference, and also with those use to predict given status by Ritz (2010) (specifically grammatical function, proper noun inclusion and definiteness), but some of them are novel (sentence type, interactions of length with other factors, position in the text), as is the stochastic approach relating them together in a mixed-effects model classifying coreferentiality and the findings regarding their distribution across several genres.

5.5 Interim Conclusion

In this chapter we have seen the multifaceted nature of referentiality in the context of discourse entity models representing running texts. Very many factors interact in the way that discourse is structured: how entities are introduced, mentioned and discussed. As we saw in the first part of this chapter, the definitions which we employ in delineating entity boundaries, the labels we choose to annotate entity mentions with and the ways of connecting certain types, or even which connections we choose to include, all influence the results we will get regarding the interaction between levels.

At the same time, we have seen repeatedly that interesting correlations across layers exist at every turn: semantic and morphosyntactic categories

---

23. The latter is clearly due to two documents dealing with the cultivation of basil and cacti, and can therefore be expected not to generalize well; however, given the similarity of these two documents, we could think of this as a genre-specific effect, coming from the horticultural subdomain of how-to guides, which are likely to contain other similar texts.

such as definiteness, pronominality, sentence type and length have a strong connection to the types of entity mentions we see. Functional aspects such as utterance type and communicative intent are also significant and coalesce together with formal properties to form part of what we label as genres. Disentangling these factors too much and examining them in isolation may obscure their overlap and interdependencies, whereas lumping them all together and looking at macro-categories such as genre without peeking into what constitutes them can make us lose sight of recurring effects that cross-classify across text and genre borders.

Throughout the last section we saw that multifactorial methods can help us to navigate between the multitude of relevant predictors to get models that are at once powerful in their predictive and explanatory capabilities and also generalizable and operationalizable in ways that allow them to be applied to further data. Many of the predictors that we have used can be annotated automatically or semi-automatically, meaning that we can test these models and find pivotal differences compared to other text types by collecting more data and using computational tools. However, for some types of annotation, this is not yet feasible, and considerable effort is required to collect and analyze such layers of information. In the next chapter we will explore one of the more contentious types of annotation, for which automatic approaches are not yet very successful, and on which inter-annotator agreement is somewhat lower than for entity and coreference annotation: the area of discourse organization, and more specifically, functional discourse relations between clauses and utterances.

6   Discourse Organization

In the previous chapters, we mainly looked at properties of sentences and entity mention phrases, without dealing with the relationships between sentences and clauses, which structure the text. This chapter goes 'up' one level in integrating signals from phrases, clauses and sentences to examine discourse structure, both in terms of microstructure in arranging cohesive entity mention chains and recognizing discourse functions, and in macrostructure, which can be explored quantitatively and visualized using distant reading techniques. The following section presents in more detail some of the notions of discourse annotation that were introduced in Section 3.2, as well as different data models which can be used to represent them. The remaining sections then present a series of studies focusing on multilayer data containing discourse parses in Rhetorical Structure Theory (RST, Mann and Thompson 1988): an overview of genre variation as it is reflected in discourse parses (Section 6.2), a predictive multifactorial model of referential accessibility in discourse, based on parse tree topology (Section 6.3) and an analysis of neural models of attention to discourse relation signaling (Section 6.4).

6.1   Discourse Annotation

Theoretical Frameworks

As we saw in Section 3.2, discourse relations can be added to a corpus like GUM in order to explore relationships above the sentence level between richly annotated propositions. In choosing the annotation scheme to work with for discourse relations in GUM, several frameworks were considered: Rhetorical Structure Theory (RST, Mann and Thompson 1988), Segmented Discourse Representation Theory (SDRT, Asher 1993) and the more recent Penn Discourse Treebank's annotation scheme (PDTB, Prasad et al. 2008), all of which have been implemented in annotated corpora. What these frameworks have in common is expressing a type of graph, with discourse segments (often sentences or clauses) realized as nodes, and discourse relations between these realized as edges, representing categories such as 'causality' or 'circumstance' that are often signaled by conjunctions or prepositions, such as 'because' or 'while'. Although RST was ultimately chosen for annotations in GUM, it is worth briefly discussing the alternatives, all of which have been put to use in the context of multilayer corpora.

Key differences between the three frameworks include not only the inventories of relations and segmentation guidelines that have been adopted in corpora annotated using them, but also in structural, graph-topological aspects, mirroring the discussion in Chapter 2. For example, whereas SDRT and RST enforce a complete document graph, in which each utterance (and often smaller units) is a node in the graph, PDTB only connects units with explicit connectives (e.g. a word such as 'because') or adjacent units within the same paragraph. As a result, PDTB's annotation graph structure is a set of subgraphs which may or may not be interconnected. The following abridged example from PDTB illustrates these points (roman numerals denote paragraphs, sentence numbers are given in square brackets, explicit connectives are in bold).

I. [1] *Kemper Inc. cut off four big Wall Street firms.*
II. [2] *The move is the biggest salvo yet in the renewed outcry against program trading.*
III. [3] *The Kemper Corp. unit and other critics complain that program trading causes wild swings in stock prices.*
   [4] *Over the past nine months, several firms have attacked program trading as a major market evil.*
   . . .
IV. [5] *Kemper* **also** *blasted the Big Board for ignoring the interests of individual and institutional holders.*

The relations annotated in PDTB for this example are labeled as:

• conn|Expansion.Conjunction(1,5) (signaled by 'also')
• specifically|Expansion.Restatement(3,4) (no connector, items in same paragraph)

Relation names are hierarchical and can mention an explicit connective (conn) or an implicit one, such as 'specifically', before the vertical pipe '|'. The hierarchical relation name is separated by dots, for example, 'Conjunction' is a subtype of 'Expansion'. In this example, sentence [1] has a discourse relation connected with [5], because [5] refers back to [1] explicitly, using the connective 'also'. Units [3] and [4] are implicitly connected, because it is easy to imagine that [4] is an expansion of [3] which could have been marked overtly, for example, with a connective such as 'specifically'. The relationship is therefore annotated with this implicit connective as 'specifically|Expansion.Restatement'. Unit [2] has no relations with other sentences, because it has no neighboring units within its paragraph and no explicit connectives marking a relation to it. Note, however, that from an unrestricted discourse analysis perspective, [2] could equally be considered to be an expansion of [1], notwithstanding the PDTB annotation guidelines which only allow implicit relations for adjacent units within the same paragraph.

In SDRT and RST, by contrast, each and every unit has at least one relation or 'function', but the frameworks differ in a number of assumptions: RST's document model is either a strict tree of units (as shown in Figure 6.1) or, in some corpora, a non-projective tree, allowing for crossing edges. Each unit is only allowed to have one outgoing relation, and there is no structure sharing (multiple parentage). In all RST corpora, two different kinds of relations are distinguished: satellite–nucleus relations, which are asymmetric, with the nucleus node being more prominent or indispensable for the text, and multinuclear relations, which coordinate multiple nodes with the same degree of prominence (see Taboada and Mann 2006: 426–427). Nodes in the tree can be simple clauses, in which case they are called Elementary Discourse Units (EDUs), or they can be complex groups of nodes, spanning multiple EDUs. For example in Figure 6.1, the nucleus in the EDU [9] is being expanded upon with a satellite using the *cause* relation to explain the cause of a stampede that is being reported on. Unit

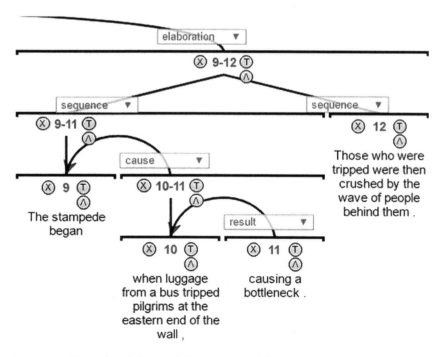

Figure 6.1 Part of an RST graph for a news article in GUM

[12], by contrast, is placed in a coordinating multinuclear relation called 'sequence' with the block of nodes spanning [9–11]: the stampede first began and then people were injured, a progression signaled, among other things, by the word 'then' in unit [12].

Unlike RST, SDRT allows multiple relations per node, including between the same two nodes, as illustrated in (81) (Asher and Lascarides 2003: 236).

(81)   π1: Did you buy the apartment?
   π2: Yes, but we rented it out.
   • Contrast(π1, π2), Narration(π1, π2)

As a result, SDRT's data model is a directed acyclic graph (DAG, cf. Section 2.4), rather than a tree (cf. Section 2.4). This results in substantially more complex graphs and a more challenging computational task for automatic parsers (see Afantenos et al. 2010, 2015; Perret et al. 2016), because we cannot assume that every segment has exactly one function and one parent node. Additionally, if we are interested in measuring the distance between units in various settings, as we will be in Section 6.2, multiple parentage substantially complicates the possible ways of operationalizing any graph-topological metrics based on paths along edges.

In many ways, the insights of the main frameworks for discourse parsing are complementary and do not really replace each other completely. One possibility is to annotate in multiple frameworks, merge the data (cf. Section 3.4) and see what we can learn from the interactions between layers. This is, of course, very labor intensive, but in fact, parts of the same underlying Penn Treebank data have been annotated in both PDTB and in the largest annotated RST corpus, the RST Discourse Treebank (RST-DT, Carlson et al. 2003). This approach may become more feasible for new datasets as entry-level automatic discourse parsing becomes more accurate (see earlier for SDRT parsing, Surdeanu et al. 2015 and Braud et al. 2016, 2017 for RST parsing and Lin et al. 2014; Wang and Lan 2015 for PDTB-style parsing). On the other hand, Stede (2008) points out that the goals of a 'single tree' (or DAG) annotation mode in general conflates multiple levels of information (in his view: referential structure, thematic structure, conjunctive relations and intentional structure). He proposes a multilayer approach ('MLA', or Multi-Level Annotation) within the area of discourse parsing, which decomposes discourse annotations into several, less complex subtasks.

In this chapter the focus will be on a standard 'ground truth' approach using RST, which assumes that the gold-standard discourse analysis in our corpus is somehow 'correct', without questioning it further. However, it should be recognized outright that there is reason to believe that some ambiguity may be inherent in the subjective part of discourse annotation, that is, that some disagreements will always persist, even among expert annotators (see Das et al. 2017). In such cases, a multilayer approach could give additional cues for ambiguous cases. In Section 6.4 we will also look briefly at some of the conflicting cues for different relations in the same unit, but first we will discuss different ways in which even a single ground-truth relation can be represented.

Data Structures for RST

The evaluation of RST graphs is complicated by the fact that tree paths between nodes are influenced by the existence of further nodes in the tree. If we wish to measure the graph path distance between two nodes, for example, the answer may vary depending on whether or not one of those nodes is a member of a larger group. To illustrate this, we can consider the examples in Figure 6.2.

In both fragments, units [2] and [3] are connected by a 'result' relation, indicating that the nucleus "I'll make sure to arrive late" has an expansion "That will make Bob angry", which is taken as a satellite specifying a result. However, if we evaluate the distance between [2] and [3] as expressed on the left by counting edges between the units, we arrive at a Rhetorical Distance (RD) of 2, because on the left, [2] is grouped with a conditional [1] under the node labeled [1–2]. The intervening non-terminal node creates a further path component which does not exist on the right, where [2] and [3] are connected directly, and RD(2,3) = 1. For a variety of research questions, this situation is problematic, because it seems counterintuitive to suggest that [2] is farther from [3] on the left simply because [2] is modified by an additional conditional.

A further problem in distinguishing these two structures is that if [2] is then made into a 'background' satellite of another unit [4], then the function of [2] would be immediately clear on the right: It would simply be 'background'. But on the left, because RST represents a tree structure without multiple parents, the combined group [1–2] would have to be the source of a 'background' relation connecting to the next unit. As a result, we could say what the function of [1–2] is, but not exactly what the function of [2] is. In the theoretical literature on RST, it was suggested

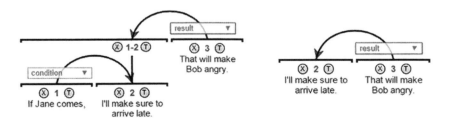

Figure 6.2 Nested and unnested units in a 'result' relation

relatively early that if a relation holds between any non-terminal nodes in a tree, then that relation also holds between the head EDUs of those nodes. In Marcu (1996: 1070), this is called the Compositionality Criterion for Discourse Trees (hence CCDT): "spans can be joined in a larger span by a given rhetorical relation if and only if that relation holds also between the most salient units of those spans" (see Zhang and Liu 2016 for an empirical study of this claim, largely supporting the idea).

Based on the CCDT assumption, a number of dependency-like formalisms have been developed for RST, completely eliminating non-terminal nodes in the graph and connecting mononuclear relations by joining the head EDUs of the nucleus unit and the dependent satellite node's head directly (see Hayashi et al. 2016 for an overview). The main complication in dependency conversion for RST is the handling of multinuclear relations, which cannot be trivially reduced to dependencies: Both the outgoing function of the entire multinuclear node (or 'multinuc') and the internal relation (e.g. *contrast*, *sequence*, etc.) must be represented. Two distinct solutions have been suggested for the problem, detailed in Hirao et al. (2013) and Li et al. (2014). The main difference, shown in Figure 6.3, is in whether the first node in the multinuc is seen as the parent of the other members (Li et al.), or as a sibling (Hirao et al.).

Although a sibling solution may seem reasonable, because multinuclear child nodes are in some sense coordinate, Hirao et al.'s representation has two disadvantages: It loses the relation type inside the multinuc (the *contrast* relation is lost in the example), and it leads to added non-projectivity in the tree (see Hayashi et al. 2016 for discussion). In this chapter we will therefore use the Li et al. representation whenever we require a dependency structure. It should be noted, however, that the Li et al. solution is not entirely natural either and in some sense arbitrary: There is no real reason why the leftmost unit acts as a 'head' for the multinuclear daughter nodes.[1] In many ways, this decision is similar to the handling of coordination in syntactic dependency trees, in which the function of a coordination is marked on the first head token (e.g. as a subject or object), and subsequent conjuncts are marked by a relation such as 'conj'. The idea is then that the actual function of further conjuncts can be read from the function of their head (the first conjunct). Another way of thinking of this representation is to regard the 'contrast' relation in Figure 6.3 on the right as a 'bi-directional' relationship, although when taken literally, that option would break the assumption of an acyclic graph.

1. Maite Taboada (p.c.) has suggested that a counterargument to this position would be to posit that if we do not have any obvious cues for either unit subordinating the other, then it is reasonable to assume an interpretation in linear order, in which the second unit is more of an expansion to the first than the other way around; this would be similar to the asymmetry presupposed by the Right Frontier Constraint in SDRT (see Polanyi 1988; Asher 1993), which suggests that a newly introduced discourse unit attaches either to the preceding discourse unit or to one that dominates it directly or indirectly.

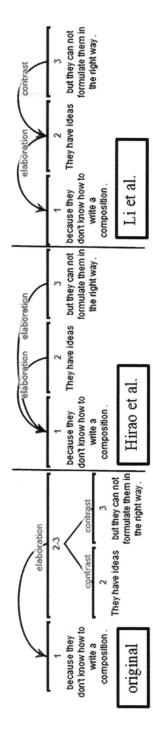

Figure 6.3 Dependency representations for an original RST fragment with a multinuclear node

Adding the (directed) dependency representation to the GUM data amounts to introducing a set of spans connected via new pointing relations: Because RST dependencies do not imply coverage (in both dependency representations earlier, unit [2] does not contain unit [1], or vice versa), we do not need hierarchical nodes or dominance relations (see Section 2.4). Data can be converted from hierarchical RST trees automatically,[2] and because the underlying tokenization remains the same as for other layers, the results can be merged via Pepper (see Section 3.4).

With the RST dependency representation at hand, we can now look at properties of the RST layer itself, such as distances between parent and child nodes (while ignoring nesting spans, for the reasons discussed earlier). And because the layers are merged into one corpus, we can also look at interactions between discourse parses, other layers of annotation and metadata. In the next section we begin by looking at the properties of discourse parses across different text types in the GUM subcorpora.

6.2   Text Type Variation

One of the central questions of discourse modeling in general, and RST in particular, is 'how do discourse functions interact with text type variation?' (see Eggins and Martin 1997; Taboada and Lavid 2003; Gruber and Huemer 2008; Taboada 2011; Matthiessen and Teruya 2015, among many others). As a result, most recent RST corpora in a variety of languages include a range of genres and topics with an aim to cover variation in discourse structures across genres and other text type categories (e.g. da Cunha 2011 for Spanish, Toldova et al. 2017 for Russian, as well as GUM). It seems clear that the distinct communicative functions of different types of text will have reflexes in the likelihoods of specific relations, but it is also conceivable that the graph topology of data from different genres or registers will have unique or typical signatures, as well as recurring macroscopic 'chunks'. To begin with a simple example, we may consider two basic properties of discourse annotation graphs: directionality and distance. Using the dependency representation detailed in the previous section, Figure 6.4 gives boxplots of the average distance in discourse units between an RST head unit and its dependent in each sub-corpus of GUM, with head-first relations showing positive numbers, and head-last negative. Due to the highly spread-out nature of the distribution (most relations are adjacent, i.e. distance 1, but there are many outliers), the numerical axis has been scaled to an inverse hyperbolic sinus.[3]

---

2. Code for automatically converting RST data to the Li et al. representation is freely available at https://github.com/amir-zeldes/rst2dep.
3. Inverse hyperbolic sinus (asinh) scaling is similar to log scaling in making differences between large numbers appear smaller, but is well defined for the entire axis, including negative values. True axis labels have been retained, so that '–20' literally means a distance of –20, i.e. the dependent precedes the head by 20 units.

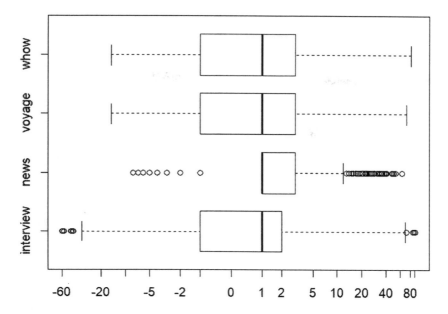

Figure 6.4 RST head-dependent distances by genre (inverse hyperbolic sinus-scaled)

The figure reveals some striking imbalances between news, interviews and the other two genres: travel guides ('voyage') and how-to guides ('whow'). News texts are the most unique in having a strong preference for positive distances (head-first) and relatively short distances in general. This corresponds to a style of cascading expansions, in which important information (the nucleus) is stated first and then expanded sequentially (see below for the typical appearance of this structure). Interviews, by contrast, have the broadest range of distances, which is spread out to such an extent that only very extreme values are labeled as outliers, based on distances of more than 1.5 times the interquartile range away from the median. On the positive distance end, this suggests that interviews feature more recapitulations or returns to points mentioned substantially earlier than other genres; this would be consistent with digressions followed by a distant back-reference in the discourse graph. On the negative distance side, it means that interviews also favor long-distance 'set up' units, for example, supplying background information many discourse units before the unit that it supports. Finally the remaining two genres occupy a middle ground in somewhat preferring the more common head-first direction but still covering a broad range of values. Differences between the two genres cannot be discerned on the basis of distance and dependency direction alone.

To interpret these results, we examine some typical shapes for RST constituent graphs in two genres: news versus how-to guides.[4] Figure 6.5 gives intentionally miniaturized views of the analyses so that global patterns can be observed in a more distant reading mode (cf. Section 5.4). Although details cannot be recognized, the clear 'staircase' shape of a typical news article can be seen in the fragments on the left: Expansions to the left are almost always a single heading (labeled as a *preparation* for its section) or a very brief *background* unit. More often than not, *background* will branch out to the right, after a nuclear statement, and even more often, *elaboration* satellites are used to give further details on the right of a previous segment (see below for more on specific relations). Looking at the images on the right, we see a 'flatter' image: Although right-hand-side branching is still more common, there is more branching to the left, and depth is also lower – whereas the 'staircases' on the left have a large nesting depth of constant right branching, the how-to texts exhibit a more 'siloed' appearance of breaking the text up into small subsections with a smaller nesting structure. Multinuclear splits, and especially multipronged sequences of nodes, are more common on the right. These observations all relate to the communicative function of news texts versus how-to guides. News language narrates events, gives background needed to understand them and elaborates and analyzes these narratives, quoting relevant people and giving evidence after reporting events. How-to guides are typically broken into a sequence of sections and subsections with multiple steps and minimal explanations required for each step, quickly moving on to the next part in a set of instructions.

To see the specific RST relations which distinguish all four genres, we can consider the relative proportions that they occupy across texts. There are several important caveats when doing this: First, we must keep in mind that the annotation scheme used in GUM is, like all discourse annotation frameworks, idiosyncratic to some extent. The relations that we can observe only cover those that are defined in the scheme, and this subjective selection naturally limits our scope; it is hoped that largely adhering to commonly used relation definitions (see Section 3.2) will increase the relevance of the results (cf. Knott 1996 on selection criteria and an evaluation of commonly used inventories of relations). A second important caveat concerns the interpretation of the distribution: Although the quantities extracted from the corpus are 'objective', to the

---

4. Similar observations could be made about the RST dependency representation as well; however, it would be much less suited to distant reading due to the clutter caused by all nodes and edges occupying the same horizontal axis without depth. This underscores the importance of considering different representations for different purposes, but also motivates potential future work on visualizing RST dependencies in more readable ways.

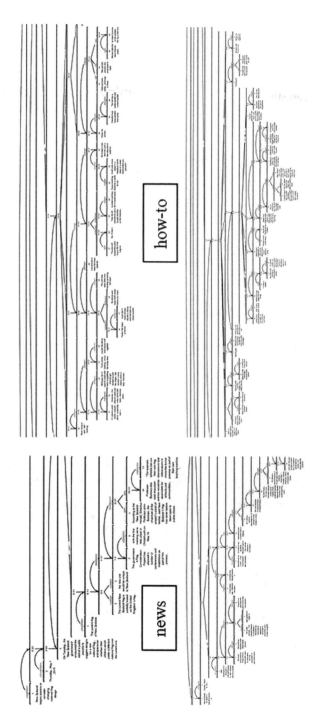

Figure 6.5 Distant views of two RST analyses in each one of two genres

extent that the annotation scheme is believed to be consistent within the annotated data, our interpretation of why certain relations are frequent in certain genres is in the first instance subjective, although it is based on both commonsense reasoning and annotation experience through contact with the corpus documents. We must therefore be cautious in accepting explanations as exhaustive, because they are, at best, high-level generalizations that do not apply to all cases, but mostly to prominent subsets of cases.

If we take the sum total usages of each relation in the entire corpus as 100%, regardless of whether that relation is more or less common in total, we can plot the relative proportion within those 100% which each genre occupies. Figure 6.6 gives such a plot, which again reveals stark contrasts between genres with respect to most relations. The data are normalized to the number of EDUs in each sub-corpus to account for different dataset sizes.

Some of the imbalances are fairly trivial: For example, the *solutionhood* relation, which is used to connect questions and answers in dialog, is used almost exclusively in interviews; its other use, to indicate a solution to a problem raised in a monologue, is found primarily in how-to guides, and rarely in other genres. A typical example is shown in (82).

(82) *If your plants show signs of mold growth . . they may be too close together. [Weed out the smaller plants to give the larger ones more space.]*solutionhood

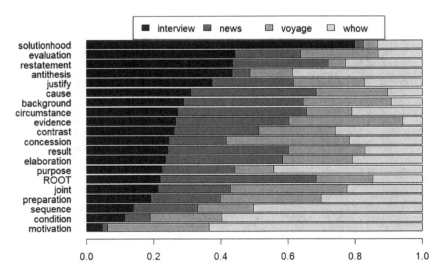

Figure 6.6 Proportional distribution of relations across genres in GUM

The distribution of other relations is less trivial but understandable as well: Subjective *evaluation* satellites are most common in interviews, followed by travel guides, which often evaluate travel destinations, restaurants, etc. Contrastive relations such as *contrast* (a symmetric, multinuclear contrastivity without preference to one alternative) and *antithesis* (presenting an alternative with the aim of favoring the other option) are most common in interviews, indicating a more subjective and polemic discursive point of view. Interestingly, the same cannot be said of the *concession* relation, which concedes the possible value of an opposing idea; it is common in all genres but news. This means that suggesting viable alternatives to a main idea is also a feature in how-to and travel guides but less so in news narrative, which is often largely one-sided.

Looking at subject matter relations, which provide information without attempting to influence the reader's state of mind (Mann and Thompson 1988, see also Knott and Sanders 1998; van der Vliet and Redeker 2014), we see that *elaboration* occurs about equally in all subcorpora, whereas *circumstance* modifiers are rarer only in travel guides. This is likely because *circumstance* typically sets the stage for understanding concurrent activities by supplying spatio-temporal information, which is relevant for how-to guides (concurrent states) and narrative text (either conversational in interviews or in third-person news language) but less so in the informational language of travel guides. Conditions, by contrast, are rare in all genres compared to how-to guides, which frequently need to give contingency plans for different results at each step. In narrative texts, conditionals are mainly used for hypotheticals, because a past narrative is already determined; unsurprisingly, voyage texts are more similar to how-to guides here, because they also suggest contingencies for a prospective tourist's behavior, as shown in (83)–(84).

(83) [*if you haven't pre-organised transport,*]$_{condition}$ *you will have to walk* (from a Wikivoyage travel guide the Chatham islands)

(84) [*If they get upset,*]$_{condition}$ *gauge their anger.* (wikiHow, 'How to detect arrogant people')

We can continue to examine more presentational relations which attempt to influence the reader's state of mind. The prototypical presentational relation, *motivation*, is characterized by trying to convince the reader to do something, and is again found in how-to and travel guides, but much less in interview texts, and almost not at all in news, which is often meant to be impartial. *Justification* and *evidence*, by contrast, are not common in how-to guides despite their perhaps expected relationship with instructional modes of communication: Although a how-to guide tells readers what to do, it pre-supposes the expert status of the author to some extent. As a result, information can be presented directly, with less supporting material needed for it to be accepted. Examples (85)–(86)

contrast the matter-of-fact expertise of wikiHow writing with an interviewee justifying himself.

(85) *I am the only candidate . . who embodies both physically and philosophically the growing diversity of the commonwealth. [(I am mixed-race (half-Chinese) and in an interracial marriage.)]*$_{justify}$

(86) *Simply put, confidence is sexy. This is more true for real-life situations than it is online, but this mantra has some truth in the world of IM flirting as well.*

In (85) a politician interviewed about his candidacy is not unexpectedly justifying his position in a statement about himself, whereas in (86), from a how-to guide on flirting, the writer is under less pressure to justify general statements such as 'confidence is sexy', the less so because the writer is taking the position of an expert.

This qualitative analysis of the quantitative distribution of relations across genres should be taken with a grain of salt, due to the highly varied nature of the actual instances leading to the categories examined here. However, although it is clearly less detailed, the distant view of the genres being analyzed here does allow us to see some discourse structure features of the different circumstances that surround the production of different types of text. In the next section, we will continue by examining what discourse graph topology is predictive of in the behavior of other annotation layers and how the layers can be combined to shed light on the topic of Domains of Referential Accessibility, that is, what parts of the discourse graph can and typically do refer to what other parts.

6.3 Referential Accessibility in Discourse

In the decade following the publication of Mann and Thompson's (1988) original proposal for RST, one line of research examined the idea that RST graphs also constrained the referential potential of expressions in terms of the accessibility granted to entity mentions from one segment to 'view' (i.e. refer back to) mentions in other segments. Probably the most well-known formulation of this constraint is Veins Theory (Cristea et al. 1998), although a very similar idea goes back at least to Polanyi (1988: 616), who suggested that a 'stack' of discourse units determined which discourse referents were available for pronominalization, and similar ideas have been expressed in SDRT (Asher and Lascarides 2003). Because it is formulated in terms of RST trees, the Veins Theory proposal is easiest to discuss here, using the example shown in Figure 6.7.

According to Veins Theory, the antecedent for a discourse referent mention is expected to occur only within the Domain of Referential Accessibility (DRA) of its segment. That domain is expected to extend from an EDU to all of its preceding satellites, but also to satellites along its 'vein',

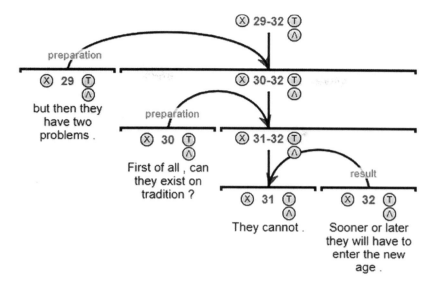

Figure 6.7 RST fragment illustrating DRAs: [29] and [30] are accessible from [31], but not from [32]

that is, the trunk of nodes that head the constituents above it, regardless of distance. The relationship is thus akin to c-command in constituent syntax trees (Reinhart 1976). In the case of Figure 6.7, the vein definition means that [31], the local head of the subgraph, can access discourse referents in [30] and [29], because they are satellites along the main trunk of dominance expressed by the vertical lines above [31]. By contrast, [32] does not have access to [30] and [29], because they are dependents of nodes in the trunk emanating from [31] and are not connected to any node dominating [32] vertically. The expected consequence for referring expressions is that whereas a pronoun in [31], such as 'they', can refer back to NPs in [29–30], no pronoun in [32] can refer back to anything except within [31] (its own nucleus). As a result, the noun 'tradition' in [30] is not a possible antecedent for a hypothetical anaphor 'it' in [32]. If we measure distance along the lines described in Section 6.1 (not counting the vertical edges), we note that the distance in terms of number of edges between [32] and [30] is the same as between [31] and [29] (RD = 2), but the path from [32] to [30] also goes against the direction of the arrow between [30] and [31], unlike the path from [31] to [29]. I will refer to the latter type of path (always in the direction of the arrows) as a 'direct parentage' path, and the former type as 'non-direct'; this distinction will become important later.

Initial work on DRAs was very optimistic about their potential in aiding the solution of practical tasks, such as coreference resolution. Based on small-scale evaluations of five texts in three languages and later 30 newspaper articles (Cristea et al. 1998, 1999), initial results indicated that at least for pronominal anaphora, back-reference generally did adhere to the predictions of Veins Theory. There were also some suggestions that the theory may hold to some extent for other types of coreference, such as lexical coreference (e.g. by Cristea et al. 1999 for lexical coreference in general, but also similarly in earlier literature for demonstratives, such as discourse deictic *this/that*, Webber 1991). For bridging too (see Chapter 5), which also relies on conceptual access to an antecedent; it is not unreasonable to suggest that DRAs may be relevant (see Zeldes 2017b in more detail).

However, later work by Tetreault and Allen (2003) using the much larger RST Discourse Treebank (Carlson et al. 2003) cast doubts on the reliability of DRAs and suggested in the context of the coreference resolution task that their "results indicate that incorporating discourse structure does not improve performance, and in most cases can actually hurt performance" (Tetreault and Allen 2003: 7). Subsequent papers on the topic focused on different operationalizations of the theory and comparisons of the relative strength of RST graph distances and surface distances in predicting anaphoricity (see Chiarcos and Krasavina 2008).

Surprisingly, little attention has been paid to the idea that multiple predictors working together could define a more powerful concept of DRAs, including both rhetorical and surface distance, but also incorporating other layers of information that can enable us to predict the scope of referential accessibility more accurately. In particular, the original formulation of Veins Theory explicitly disregards RST function labels, meaning that veins consist of purely unlabeled paths. However, there are commonsense reasons to believe that coreference within an RST *restatement* is rather likely, whereas in *purpose* satellites, which often consist of a to-infinitive (or 'in order to' + infinitive), we may be less likely to see entity mentions coreferring with mentions in the nucleus of the relation.[5] Another intuitive confound using the same relations as an example is EDU length: *purpose* EDUs are usually shorter than *restatement* EDUs (on average, about 11 versus 14 tokens in GUM), meaning there are more opportunities for coreferential mentions in restatements. At the same time, it is possible that these predictors interact, for example, that restatements might promote coreference more than *purpose* EDUs, even at the same length in tokens, but that very short restatements might have a particularly high (or low) coreference likelihood. Looking at some examples from GUM, we may guess that the former is the case: Short restatements are very likely to be anaphoric, but short-purpose EDUs less so. The satellites marked in

5. In fact, work on specific relations has shown clear tendencies in choosing anaphoric discourse connectives for specific functions, see e.g. Stede and Grishina (2016) on causal connectives implying event anaphora, such as *therefore*.

(87)–(88) are both six tokens long, but (87) has room for two anaphors (a subject demonstrative and an embedded subject pronoun), whereas the *purpose* clause in (88) has no overt nominal referents at all.[6]

(87) . . . *Last year in my section at the stadium I had a banner that read We Know'. [That's all it said.]*_{RESTATEMENT}

(88) *Your setup needs to be both realistic and exaggerated [in order to be funny —]*_{PURPOSE} . . .

Given even these few examples of confounds and interactions, it can be expected that a multifactorial model taking different variables into account is likely to give a much more accurate picture of the relationship between the discourse graph and Domains of Referential Accessibility. Because of the highly interacting nature of the variables in question and the large number of feature values (e.g. 20 distinct RST relations in GUM), the model developed in this section to account for referential accessibility will again take advantage of Random Forests, rather than a linear model (cf. Section 4.3; see also Zeldes 2017b for some details on linear models for referential accessibility). Before constructing the model, we must consider several questions:

1. How can we operationalize accessibility (i.e. what variable are we trying to predict)?
2. Which phenomena do we include? Should the model be restricted to anaphora, or also lexical coreference, or perhaps also bridging?
3. How do individual predictors behave and what can they show us?

There are two main ways of answering the first question: On the one hand, we may be interested in a variable close to the original formulation of Veins Theory, and more specifically its Conjecture C1: "References from a given unit are possible only in its domain of accessibility" (Cristea et al. 1998: 282). This can be operationalized as a binary prediction *whether* there is any coreferent pair between an ordered pair of EDUs (anaphor in the late EDU, antecedent in the early EDU; we will ignore cataphora for this study). On the other hand, we could be interested to know the *degree* of coreferentiality between two EDUs, operationalized as the number of pairs of coreferent mentions between them. Second, we can choose to look only at pronominal anaphora, or also at lexical coreference, and perhaps even bridging, because all of these signal different

---

6. Paul Portner (p.c.) has suggested to me that the typical infinitive subject control in English *purpose* clauses, interpreted as a null pronoun PRO in generative grammar, may contribute to sparseness of anaphora in this relation. If the GUM annotation scheme included empty PRO referents as tokens (much like the Penn Treebank's constituent parses), we would indeed see more coreferentiality in such clauses.

aspects of discourse accessibility versus encapsulation. For anaphora and lexical coreference, we may also consider separate probabilities for an EDU to contain the exact (i.e. most recent) antecedent of a referring expression, or only some coreferent mention (even if it is not the most recent one); for bridging, this distinction is not relevant, because bridging does not usually form natural chains (a subsequent mention of a bridged entity is a case of normal lexical coreference, and bridging again to a third entity is a rare phenomenon).

All of these parameters are exposed through the annotation layers in GUM, meaning we can extract all possible ordered pairs of EDUs <edu1, edu2> which appear in text order in the same document, and collect the count of coreferent entities, as well as the Rhetorical Distance (RD) metric based on the structures detailed in Section 6.1. Varying the values of the parameters noted earlier, we can then explore the effects of individual layers of annotation and their interplay with the discourse (sub-)graph, and in particular the effects of RD and its contribution above and beyond surface distance, which is likely to be related to referential accessibility. Figure 6.8 plots the correlation between EDU distance (bottom) or RD (top) and direct coreference (right) or indirect coreference (left), including both anaphora and lexical coreference. The plots contain around 170,000 pairs of EDUs, which are all possible ordered pairs in each document in GUM.

In all panels, we can see that the individual correlations of RD and surface distance are fairly weak. Although there is a vaguely diagonal shape in the left column of panels, the Pearson's correlation values

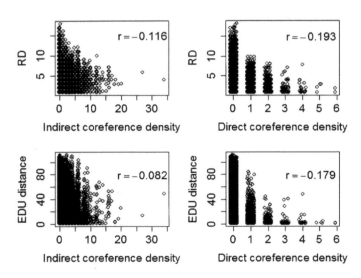

Figure 6.8 Coreference density as a function of EDU distance and RD

overlaid on the plot attest to a negligible effect for indirect coreference density, despite all being significant at p < 0.001 due to the large amount of data. Direct antecedents on the right are much sparser, with the overwhelming majority of EDU pairs unsurprisingly not containing an immediate antecedent (density = 0). A slightly higher density and better correlation with RD than surface distance can be seen on the right, where the bars for RD = 1 and RD = 2 in the top-right panel are slightly more dense, and the absolute correlation coefficient value is a little larger.

Because these data also include lexical coreference, it is possible to suggest that a stronger effect could be observed for anaphora only. To test this, we plot the distribution of anaphor–antecedent density as a function of EDU distance and RD in the graph. We also compare this density with bridging, which requires referential 'access' to resolve, but is a lexical phenomenon. As we have already seen, the vast majority of possible pairs show no links at all; Figure 6.9 therefore shows only pairs exhibiting an immediate antecedent link, with different shades for direct and indirect RST parentage types, and circle size representing the amount of shared anaphor–antecedent mention pairs between a pair of EDUs. Pronominal anaphora is displayed on the right, with bridging for comparison on the left.

In terms of the effect of distance, we observe that $RD = ED = 1$ in the largest number of cases: 40.5% of EDU pairs, covering 42.5% of mention-pair cases for anaphora, and somewhat less for bridging, at 30.2% of EDU pairs, covering 32.1% of bridging mention cases. This is not surprising, because anaphora is usually a 'close range' phenomenon, whereas bridging, which is less ambiguous, can occur at greater distances. The mean EDU distance for bridging is 5.27 (comparable to average immediate antecedent distance in lexical coreference: 5.23) compared to 2.55 for anaphora. The difference in RD is less striking, with a mean of 2.45 for bridging compared to 2.21 for anaphora. These differences are not large, but significant at p < 0.001, as well as differing significantly from the slightly higher baseline of immediate lexical coreference, at mean RD = 2.62.

Because Veins Theory doesn't make any predictions with regard to distance (as long as two units are connected by a 'vein'; but see Chiarcos and Krasavina 2008 for the influence of different operationalizations), we should consider how often we see indirect parentage in the two panels, because these are the cases that violate the Veins Theory constraint on DRAs in RST constituent trees. The shading makes it clear that indirect parentage is not rare: In fact, despite the fact that pronominal anaphora is semantically more underspecified than bridging (the potential for ambiguity would normally be considered higher in anaphora), only 43.2% of anaphora cases exhibit direct ancestry in line with the expectation based on Veins Theory. The percentage for bridging is actually a little higher at 45.7% of EDU pairs containing bridging. Both of these numbers are

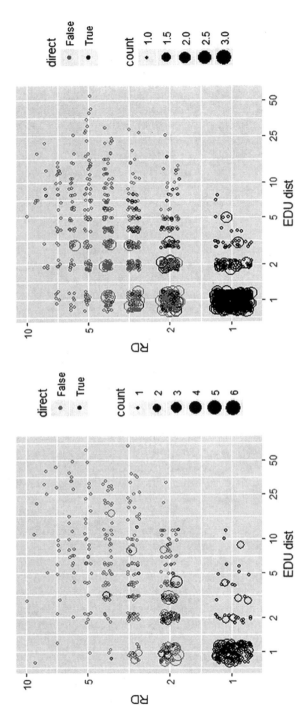

Figure 6.9 RD versus EDU distance for bridging (left) and pronominal anaphora (right). Each circle is one pair of EDUs sharing a mention, with circle size corresponding to the amount of shared mentions, and shading indicating direct or indirect parentage in the RST graph

rather low: The majority of cases do not obey the generalization in Cristea et al. (1998).

Although these initial results largely confirm Tetreault and Allen's (2003) conclusion that discourse graph structure is in fact not a potent predictor of reference domains by itself, the question remains whether there is truly no reality to the intuition behind Veins Theory, which seemed to be confirmed in anecdotal examples such as the one in Figure 6.7. Thinking about the issue from a multifactorial perspective, it becomes clear that evaluating Veins Theory using only direct parentage, or even quantitatively using distance metrics, opens the door to rather many confounds on other layers of information. Perhaps most crucially, we can imagine that long EDUs are a priori much more likely to share entity mentions with other EDUs, simply because they will contain more nouns and pronouns. Moreover, and importantly for the area of discourse relations, we have already raised doubts about the nature of the function or relation an EDU realizes being truly irrelevant for Conjecture C1, meaning that relation type should probably also be fed to a multifactorial model attempting to account for Domains of Referential Accessibility. Other relevant factors include the sentence type containing the EDU (e.g. imperative, question, etc., cf. Section 3.2), and possibly genre. If these predictors can be combined to reach a high level of accuracy in operationalizing DRAs, they could form an important cue for tasks such as coreference resolution, and possibly help us in understanding the relationship between discourse structure and referential accessibility. In the following, I will concentrate on the most helpful model for coreference resolution, which seeks to quantify the likelihood of lexical or pronominal coreference, whether as a direct antecedent or otherwise.

Because of the likelihood of noise and strong interactions between predictors, we will return to the Extra Trees algorithm from Section 4.3. To evaluate the model, a randomized test set of 10% of EDU pairs (~17K) is created, which is stratified by degree of coreference: The 10% and 90% partitions each have the same proportions of no coreferent mentions, single pair, two pairs, etc. Unlike in the case of notional agreement in Section 4.3, this time we have a choice of modeling either the binary prediction task (some coreference or none) or using regression analysis and attempting to predict the exact degree of coreferentiality (number of coreferent mention pairs). We therefore construct both a binary classifier for the presence of coreference (yes/no) and a numerical regressor, using the Extra Trees ensemble. The best features and hyperparameters are selected using fivefold cross-validation on the training set, resulting in the selection ranked in Figure 6.10. To get an idea of how well the classifier is doing compared to naïve distance-based metrics, we also train baseline classifiers and regressors on RD and EDU distance only. The results evaluated on the unseen test set are shown in Table 6.1.

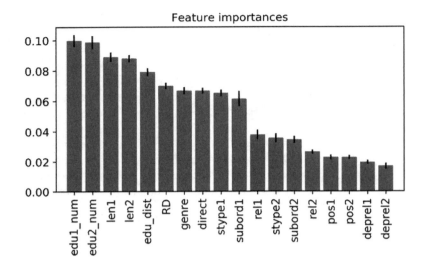

Figure 6.10 Feature importances for the Extra Trees binary classifier (predicting coreference: yes/no)

Table 6.1 Performance for the Extra Trees classifier and regressor, next to distance-based baselines. The classifier is evaluated on accuracy (% correct) and the regressor using the root-mean-square error (RMSE), that is, deviation from the correct number of coreferent mention pairs

Features	RMSE (regressor)	Accuracy (classifier)
No info	0.9792	77.92%
EDU distance	0.9501	78.36%
RD	0.9453	78.79%
all features	0.7107	**86.83%**

If we have no information at all about the EDUs, we should guess the average degree of coreference, which is 0.39 mentions in common between any two EDUs in the training data. This gives a root-mean-square error (RMSE) of 0.9652, meaning the regressor may be off by about 0.96 mentions on any given pair in the test data. Using EDU distance or RD alone only gives an improvement of about 3% (almost 3.5%) over this baseline, again confirming Tetreault and Allen's (2003) results. The best RMSE for the regressor using the multilayer features in Figure 6.10 is 0.71. Although this improvement may not seem large, it is actually a fairly good result, especially given that the regressor has no information about the lexical items, or even the number of nouns found in the EDUs: It is only looking at global features of the EDU pairs situated in the discourse graph and is attempting to predict exactly how many coreferent pairs will be shared by two EDUs.

For classification of binary coreferentiality, we use the decision 'always predict no coreference' as a baseline, which would be right 77.9% of the time. Using all features gives a gain of ~9% over this baseline accuracy, close to 87% accuracy, or ~8% gain compared to RD (about 79%) and EDU distance (about 78%). This is perhaps the more interpretable result in terms of the original formulation of Veins Theory: Using pure graph topography gives a very minimal improvement over the baseline, but using all features can get a rather good performance, again given that we know almost nothing about the contents of the segments. The feature importances as estimated by the classifier (based on Gini indices, see Section 4.3) are shown in Figure 6.10, which reveals that both distances, and the position of the EDUs within the text, are actually helpful.

As we can see in Figure 6.10, the ensemble of decision trees overall prefers features that relate to a priori high likelihood of coreference, such as unit length (more tokens mean more chances for coreferent entity mentions) and document position (later positions in the document have access to a larger subset of previously mentioned entities). In fifth place, we begin to see graph-topological properties: EDU distance, RD and immediately afterwards genre and the direct/indirect parentage distinction. This means that although these features are not as powerful as some of the more obvious length- and position-based ones, they are helpful in combination with other features: We can use RD and EDU distance, but they are only valuable after factoring in the expected effects of length and position. It is also interesting to observe that the genre effect is on par with these predictors in terms of the Gini index, suggesting the rather different a priori coreference likelihood in different genres that we have already seen in Section 5.4, but also perhaps an ability to combine genre with the other predictors in decision trees giving other features different thresholds in different genres.

The next two relatively strong predictors are features of the antecedent EDU, including whether it is a subordinate clause (which relates to discourse accessibility in the DRA model, because subordinate clauses are usually satellites)[7] and the sentence type (based on the scheme presented in Section 3.2). Sentence type can be relevant in many ways, but considering, for example, the fact that imperatives and fragments lack a subject argument already makes it useful to know that an EDU is one of these types, because subjects add an argument to refer to and are also the most

---

7. See also Trnavac and Taboada (2012) on the importance of subordination for the potential to have cataphora.

likely argument to be coreferential. The tail of the feature importance plot consists of specific labels, including the specific RST labels (rel1 for the antecedent's EDU and rel2 for the anaphor) and dependency labels for the head of each clause, indicating the function of the clause (e.g. 'advcl' for adverbial clauses). Although these help somewhat, they are clearly weaker indicators. Although this may seem surprising for the RST labels, the reason is likely related to the fact that we are looking at any, even indirect, coreference (not immediate antecedents). This means that often the function labels designating the two units have little to do with the relationship between them. Instead, the algorithm merely learns the effects of each function on referential potential.

In terms of applying this model in practice, it is clear that a real use of this information for the description of entity models, and for coreference resolution in particular, will have to be combined with an examination of the properties of actual entity mentions within the discourse units in question. However, we can use the classifier or the regressor constructed here to reformulate the idea of DRAs in quantitative, multifactorial terms and conceptualize the relative path of accessibility as a type of 'heat map', indicating where we expect references to occur for entities in each target EDU. Figure 6.11 shows such a heat map, which offers a more 'distant reading' view of the interrelations between the discourse graph and expected referentiality using our model. Starting from a targeted 'anaphoric' EDU framed in bold (number [47] in the graph), earlier EDUs predicted to contain antecedents for its mentions are shaded by their predicted coreference density with respect to entity mentions in the targeted EDU.

As we can see in Figure 6.11, the regressor has learned to assign higher coreference likelihood in areas that are similar to the paths anticipated by Veins Theory, but the distinctions are probabilistic rather than absolute. Units that are more likely than not to contain no coreferent mentions have been left completely white. Greater expected densities are shaded darker, with units [43], [44] and [46] ranging expected coreferent pairs between 1.7–2.13 common mentions. Note that based on the dependency conversion following Li et al. (2014), as described in Section 6.1, unit [44] is directly linked to [47], placing it in its direct parentage path. Unit [45], by contrast, is a satellite of [44], making it have an indirect path, as well as greater RD, and ends up below the threshold for highlighting. Earlier units, such as [39] and [40] have lower density estimates, around 0.64 and 0.5, leading to lighter shades, but are still more likely to contain coreferent mentions than [41] and [42], which are closer in surface distance to the target EDU [45], but farther in RD (especially [41]). Function labels too, and all other features considered earlier, play a role in shaping the heat map. To illustrate coreferent positions falling along the lines of these predictions, we can look at the pronoun 'we', which has been highlighted wherever it appears in the heat map. We can clearly see that the repeated

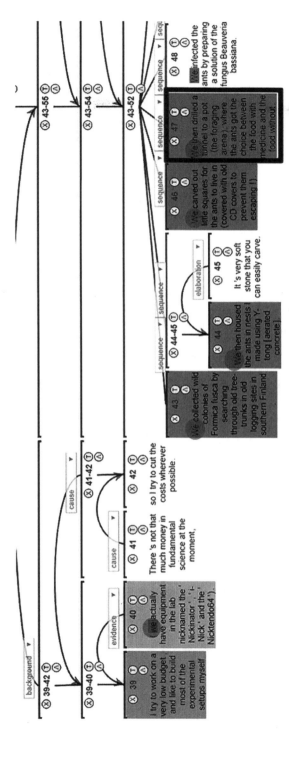

Figure 6.11 Heat map for expected coreference density, based on the framed unit [47] containing the anaphor. The pronoun 'we', which seems to follow the expected distribution, has been highlighted

mention of 'we' within the temporal sequences overlaps neatly with the predictions but is absent from the white nodes (although the related 'I' appears in [42]). Needless to say, the regressor is unaware of the presence of such pronouns in the EDUs, and is also not particularly attuned to finding this particular word: The heat map corresponds more generally to expected coreference density in these EDUs across all mention types. The result is an aggregated view of what we can learn about the shape of annotations in one layer by simultaneously looking at the contents of other, largely independent layers.

6.4   Neural Models for Relation Signaling

So far the discussion has been focused on what we can learn about discourse structure from discrete annotation layers above the level of the primary textual data. In this section we will look more closely at what marks or signals specific discourse relations in our corpus, complementing our use of categorical annotations with continuous information by introducing a neural network approach to the study of discourse connectives and other signals. The topic of signaling has been a substantial strand of research in RST and related frameworks for a long time and centers on finding language-specific cues which indicate the presence of discourse relations to the reader or hearer. Although there has been some interest in syntactic cues for discourse relations, most work has focused on lexical indicators, and particularly on function words in various languages and genres (Sweetser 1990; Sanders et al. 1992; Knott and Dale 1994; Knott 1996; Taboada and Lavid 2003; Stede and Grishina 2016; Toldova et al. 2017), including projects specifically aimed at annotating such signals on multiple layers (notably Taboada and Das 2013).

A straightforward approach to evaluating signals in corpora with functional discourse annotations is to extract frequency counts for all lexical types or lemmas and cross-tabulate them with discourse relations, such as *cause*, *elaboration*, etc. This approach quickly reveals the core inventory of cue words in the language, and in particular the class of discourse markers (DMs), such as 'but' or 'also' (see Fraser 1999 on delimiting the class of explicit DMs), potentially including multiword expressions, if this is applied to multitoken spans (e.g. 'as a result'). Because this approach is language independent, it also allows for a straightforward comparison of connectives and other DMs across languages. Results may also converge across frameworks, as the frequency analysis may reveal the same items in different corpora annotated using different frameworks. For example, the inventory of connectives found in work on the Penn Discourse Treebank (PDTB, see Prasad et al. 2008) largely converges with findings on connectives using RST (see Stede 2012: 97–109; Taboada and Das 2013): For example, conjunctions such as 'however' can mark different kinds of contrastive relations, and adverbs such as 'meanwhile' can convey contemporaneousness, among other things.

Two main caveats of the frequency-based approach are over/under-fitting and ambiguity. The issue of overfitting is more problematic in small datasets, in which certain content words appear coincidentally in discourse segments with a certain function. Table 6.2 shows the most distinctive lexical types for several discourse relations in GUM based on pure ratio of occurrence. On the left, types are chosen which have a maximal frequency in the relevant relationship compared with their overall frequency in the corpus. This quickly overfits the contents of the corpus, selecting irrelevant words such as 'touched' for *solutionhood*, or 'ammonium' for *sequence*. This problem can be alleviated by requiring that the types occur more than a certain threshold of times across the corpus, thereby suppressing rare items. The items on the right of the table are limited to types occurring more than 10 times.

Looking at the items on the right, several signals make intuitive sense, especially for relations such as *solutionhood*, which is mainly used for marking questions: the items are wh-words, the question mark and 'did', most likely due to inversion with 'do' support in polar questions. However, other relations show more lexical items, some easier to justify than others: For *circumstance*, we find month and day names, due to the guideline tagging datelines in GUM as a *circumstance* (the time at which something occurs may be considered circumstantial information).

Table 6.2 Most distinctive lexemes for some relations in GUM, with different frequency thresholds

Relation	Most distinctive collexemes by ratio	
	f > 0	*f > 10*
solutionhood	*viable, contributed, 60th, touched, Palestinians*	*What, ?, Why, did, How*
circumstance	*holiest, Eventually, fell, Slate, transition*	*October, When, Saturday, After, Thursday*
result	*minuscule, rebuilding, distortions, struggle, causing*	*result, Phoenix, wikiHow, funny, death*
concession	*Until, favored, hypnotizing, currency, curiosity*	*Although, While, though, However, call*
justify	*payoff, skills, net, Presidential, supporters*	*NATO, makes, simply, Texas, funny*
sequence	*Feel, charter, ammonium, evolving, rests*	*bottles, Place, Then, baking, soil*
cause	*malfunctioned, jams, benefiting, mandate, recognizing*	*because, wanted, religious, projects, stuff*

For other relations, lexical items still appear to be coincidental – 'Phoenix' and 'wikiHow' for *result* seem arbitrary, as do 'NATO' and 'Texas' for *justify*. At the same time, some expected strong signals, such as the word 'since' are absent from the table: The words 'religious', 'projects' and even 'stuff' are ranked higher for the expression of the *cause* relation, despite 31 occurrences of 'since' in GUM, 8 of which are inside *cause* units (the most frequent relation for this word). This is because the distribution of 'since' is not specific enough to *cause*.

The second and more problematic issue of ambiguity flows out of the specificity problem. It is difficult to predict or explain accurately when a discourse marker, such as the adverb 'meanwhile', will mark one of two or more possible relations: For example, in some cases 'meanwhile' is a purely temporal signal, whereas in others it might be contrastive. And to make matters even more difficult, a connective does not always achieve its function in isolation and can mean rather different things depending on the presence of items which are not themselves seen as connectives. As an example, we can search for cases of the word 'if', which is usually a very dependable signal for the *condition* relation, which appear in GUM within EDUs annotated with other relations, as in (89)–(90).

(89)   *there are a number of "safe" harbours for shelter **if** the need arises.*

(90)   *So **if** we go to the pregnant woman, she doesn't get enough iodine, she won't make enough thyroid hormone, and the foetus won't get the amount of thyroid hormone it needs for adequate and proper development of the brain, so you 'll then see consequences being loss of IQ, learning difficulties [. . .]*

Although annotation decisions in RST are often open to debate, and their ambiguity may in fact be inherent to the subjective interpretation process to some extent (see Das et al. 2017), these casses do seem to deviate from 'normal' conditional uses of 'if'. In (89), need arising is not literally a condition for the existence of safe harbors; but a different choice of predicate in the nucleus could have changed that (e.g. in a hypothetical "harbors are constructed if the need arises"). In (90), an ostensible conditional is in fact used to introduce or shift the topic, more specifically by focusing attention on one example of the consequences of iodine deficiency. Beyond the need to circumvent the clearly unintended literal force of the utterance (the sense is not 'if we go to the pregnant woman, then she will not receive sufficient iodine'), the reader is meant to recognize that this is a hypothetical situation, or an unspecific or generic pregnant woman, in effect expressing 'as for pregnant women, the consequences of any one of them not receiving'. This, too, is not signaled by the word 'if' in itself, but by a more complex inference process involving the interpretation of the pronoun 'we', the surrounding context, etc.

Although it is difficult to imagine a general annotation framework to describe such interactions between connectives and context, it is possible to apply modeling techniques that learn to recognize contexts in which connectives are and aren't signaling a specific relation, as well as more generally to quantify what signals might be responsible for a postulated relation and to what extent, while taking that specific sentence into consideration. To do so, we will use recently developed computational techniques from the area of Deep Learning using Recurrent Neural Networks (RNNs). Deep Learning in general and RNNs in particular have had a profound effect on recent computational linguistics approaches to classifying high-level discourse phenomena and have been likened to a 'tsunami' in the force with which they have recently reshaped research in the area (see Manning 2015). Nevertheless, they have found little application so far in theoretical studies of language in usage, in part because of the difficulty in interpreting their results (see Karpathy et al. 2016; Krakovna and Doshi-Velez 2016). Although neural networks can learn patterns in large amounts of texts and annotations, and subsequently yield excellent predictive power for unseen cases, they are even more difficult to interpret than ensemble methods such as Random Forests (see Section 4.3 on interpreting non-linear models). In this section we will attempt to learn about connectives and other signaling devices using an RNN by using it not to classify relations in unseen corpus data, but rather to inspect the degree with which each word in a running text 'convinces' the network of the correct relation, or in other words, to quantify the importance of each word in a given sequence.

To model the probability of each word belonging to each relation, we will use a bi-LSTM (bidirectional Long-Short Term Memory, see Greff et al. 2016 for an overview) feeding into a CRF decoder (Conditional Random Fields, i.e. a bi-LSTM/CRF architecture, see Ma and Hovy 2016). The network receives input sequentially, token after token, in two dedicated sub-networks, reading the data from left to right and from right to left. At each time-step a token is fed to both directional networks, which predict a label for the current EDUs discourse function; if the prediction is wrong, a loss function propagates a penalty back to those connections which caused the false classification within connections representing the network's current time-step. The loss is then also propagated back through 'time' to network connection weights representing earlier inputs. Finally, the CRF decoder computes the optimal path through the decisions of all time-steps to maximize correct predictions for whole discourse units. The schematic structure of the network, adapted from Ma and Hovy (2016), is shown in Figure 6.12.

Inputs to the network come from the running tokens of the text, encoded in three ways. The first encoding converts each lexical type in the data into a 300-dimensional vector space representation, which places words that appear in similar contexts in very large corpus data at similar coordinates.

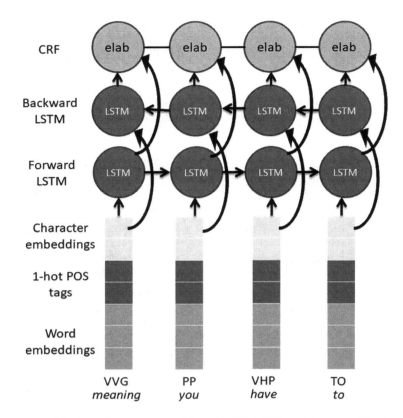

Figure 6.12 Schematic structure of the bi-LSTM/CRF architecture. Word and character embeddings are concatenated into a vector for each input word along with POS tag representations, feeding both LSTMs, and LSTMs into a CRF layer constraining predictions by estimating an optimal sequence of labels

For this purpose we use the precomputed GloVe embeddings, extracted from 6 billion tokens of data from Wikipedia and the Gigaword corpus (Pennington et al. 2014). The vector is then supplemented with a second one-hot representation of the token's part of speech tag, giving some access to grammatical structure as well. The third representation is a character n-gram embedding, which represents sub-strings of each word in a vector space computed from the network's own training data. The proximity of sub-strings and words in both this and the word embedding space can be altered by the network as it learns (in other words, words which behave similarly in terms of predicting relations effectively edge closer together in the vector space representations that are fed to the network during training). The CRF component ensures that labels form a plausible sequence, and because all adjacent tokens in an EDU have the same label (e.g. *elaboration* for the entire EDU), it quickly learns to avoid 'chimerical' outputs switching from one label to the other every few words. This offers an advantage for evaluating signaling behavior, because decisions are not made based on individual words, but rather a globally optimal path through the EDU is computed, resulting in much more uniform predictions.

To train the network, we reserve 10% of the GUM data for validation and 10% for testing, while dividing as close as possible to document borders. An important reason for not shuffling the data, even into large coherent units, is that the network should not learn about document-specific lexical items which predict relations. For example, if a how-to guide routinely mentions a 'hammer' during *sequence* relations for content reasons, then this idiosyncratic fact should not be learned (unless it is helpful also for the validation partition, in which case it is not idiosyncratic anymore). We use mini-batch training in batches of 20 EDUs, a recurrent drop-out rate of 50%, batch normalization, a learning rate of 0.001 and the Adam optimizer.[8] Training is stopped after no improvement in performance is achieved on the validation set for five consecutive epochs.

Whereas in an NLP context we might be interested in encoding the entire network's output for all words in an EDU into one classifier, for the purpose of this study on signaling we will be interested in the emissions of the bidirectional network at each time-step. To test which words 'excite' the network most in the direction of the true discourse relation, we apply the softmax function (ensuring the probabilities of all relations for each token sum up to 1) to each time-step's bidirectional LSTM representation and visualize the probability that the relation is in fact the one in question using color depth, normalized to the probabilities of all words predicting all relations. In other words, the most certain predictor of a correct relation is colored black, and the weakest of all predictors is colored a very light gray. The two most powerful cues in favor of the correct relation in each EDU are additionally marked in bold. Examples (91)–(92) below render such visualizations for some excerpts from the test data, which the network has not seen during training.

(91)   [**This** occurs for two reasons :]~preparation~ [**As** it moves over land ,]~circumstance~ [it is cut off from the source of energy driving the storm . .]~cause~

(92)   [**Combine** 50 milliliters of hydrogen peroxide and a liter of distilled water in a **mixing** bowl .]~sequence~ [A ceramic bowl **will** work best ,]~elaboration~ [**but** plastic works too .]~concession~

---

8. Dropout refers to randomized disabling of a different subset of cells at each step, reducing overfitting; batch normalization, the learning rate and the optimizer are important components in finding the optimal network weights during gradient descent, see Pascanu et al. (2013), Kingma and Ba (2015), Ioffe and Szegedy (2015) for details.

Example (91) exhibits typical explicit signals: In the first unit, a sentence initial 'This' without a following noun is a possible signal for the *preparation* relation; however, although it is difficult to see, the strongest signal for the relation according to the network is actually the unit-final colon (also bold and slightly more black). This makes sense, as colons are good cues for a *preparation*. The second unit is a *circumstance*, predictably marked by 'as'; however, we note that not every 'as' is a discourse marker (in fact, most cases of 'as' are not highlighted by the network in the test data). In this case, the information that 'as' is initial, capitalized and followed by a pronoun and verb is readily available to the network. The final unit is in a *cause* relation to a further EDU (not displayed), but the network has detected no strong cue of this fact (all light gray).

In (92), the network is most confident of the classification of the first unit as *sequence* based on the initial verb 'Combine'. Several factors likely contribute to this: The utterance is verb initial, with a verbal base form (tagged 'VV' as an imperative, not present 'VVP'); the position of this word as initial is recognizable to the sequentially operating LSTM in general, but the character-based representation may also flag the initial capital to indicate that this is the first clause in the sentence; and the vector space semantic representation gives some indication of the type of activity denoted by the verb. It is likely that the network has learned that sentence initial imperatives (at least of some kinds of verbs) may begin a *sequence* in how-to guides, based on documents in the training data. In the next clause, the word 'best' ranks highest for identifying the *elaboration*, with 'will' as a close second. Whereas a word such as 'best' might normally be associated with an *evaluation*, its combination with 'will' would be less usual in this function, and the network may be exploiting the presence of both words together. Finally the third clause contains a *concession*, marked by the somewhat ambiguous 'but', which can also indicate *contrast* or *antithesis*, among other relations. However, we note that next to 'but', the network also selects 'too' as a signal, and it seems reasonable to assume that the combination is a particularly good signal for the *concession* relation.

The network can also pick up on rather subtle lexical cues in some cases, provided that it has seen similar cases in the past. For example, in (93) we can see that it is sensitive to dates, and in particular the year in a dateline, as a signal for the *circumstance* relation, which is always used for the dateline in news articles. A subsequent caption for an image of the flag of New Zealand has the country's name flagged, quite possibly because image captions in the corpus often mention place names (especially in the travel guides), and these are often annotated as either *background* or *preparation*. Using the vector space model, network cells can easily recognize the similarity between 'New Zealand' and other place names in the training data, although the name New Zealand does not appear in the training data at all.

(93) [Thursday , May 7 , 2015]$_{circumstance}$ [The current flag of **New Zealand .**]$_{preparation}$

(94) [I cannot comment **directly** on **how** the Indian government was prepared for this cyclone .]$_{concession}$ [**However** , the news reports (BBC etc.) were very encouraging]$_{joint}$

In (94), we see the word 'directly' being marked rather confidently as a signal for *concession*. This may be hard to understand initially; however, the classification is not entirely unreasonable: Without the word 'directly', the sentence may be a flat statement. But after refusing to comment directly, the speaker in fact proceeds to comment 'indirectly', making the statement about lack of direct comment a concession. To see how the network may have learned to recognize this, we can look at other *-ly* adverbs in concessions in the training corpus, as in (95)–(97).

(95) *even if that animal is as special as these **clearly** are*
(96) *We're quite far from our goals **currently**,*
(97) *I don't care if a girl is **absolutely** exquisite looking --*

In all of these examples, annotated as *concession* EDUs, the adverbs support the relation by intensifying a conceded property: Despite being not just special, but 'clearly' special in (95), or in spite of being not just exquisite looking but even 'absolutely exquisite looking' in (97). The LSTM has at least three sources of information to learn such patterns from: the POS tags (all are tagged RB); the vector space representations of these lexemes, which were derived from very large corpus data; and the character-based LSTM input, which can recognize the suffix *-ly*. A similar picture can be seen in (98), where adverbs such as 'ideally' and 'slightly', both not common in the training data, are recognized as markers of elaboration in context, next to more classic syntactic signals, such as 'so that' marking a purpose clause in the next EDU.

(98) [Place the quaffle **and** three bludgers in the **middle** of the field .]$_{sequence}$ [**Ideally** the quaffle and bludgers should be **slightly** deflated]$_{elaboration}$ [**so that** they are easier to throw and catch .]$_{purpose}$

Beyond the qualitative evaluation of such analyses, the neural model can help us to quantify the reliability of signals in context, as well as the degree of ambiguity for different DMs as they are used in the test data. Table 6.3 gives the top ten most reliable cues as estimated by the network in context. The probabilities in the second column correspond to the average likelihood with which the system believes that that word indicates the relationship in question, and the third column gives the most strongly predicted function in any context.

Table 6.3 Most reliable cues on average based on the bi-LSTM/CRF's classification probabilities

Token	Mean probability	Favored relation
If	0.758153	condition
When	0.608065	circumstance
How	0.529172	preparation
Image	0.507956	elaboration
?	0.385541	solutionhood
October	0.381028	circumstance
International	0.364706	elaboration
his	0.363948	circumstance
if	0.363922	conditional
statement	0.355041	joint

We can see that only the very first few cues are truly low in ambiguity, such as a capitalized sentence initial 'If' or 'When' signaling a *condition* or *circumstance*, or the question mark signifying *solutionhood*, that is, a literal (non-rhetorical) question. On average, these items are given around 35% to 75% of the probability mass that must be distributed between 20 possible relations whenever they are encountered. Some items lower in the list are rather corpus specific, such as the fact that image credits, which usually begin with the word 'Image', are annotated consistently as an *elaboration*, or the annotation guidelines for datelines making 'October' a strong cue for *circumstance*. Other words, such as 'International', are more spurious, in this case, probably a result of several travel guides listing various airports containing the word 'International' inside elaborations about possible flights to take to a destination.

We can also look at how the network evaluates some of the distinctive collexemes from Table 6.2 which are also attested in the test data (some items from the table, for example 'NATO' and 'Phoenix', coincidentally do not appear in the held out data). Figure 6.13 shows boxplots for several such tokens, plotting the probability assigned by the LSTM softmax layer to the correct relation in each instance in the unseen data. Here we can see the advantage of the network in giving not one number per item, but a whole range of probabilities based on the individual contexts in which items appear.

For example, the word 'stuff', which makes it into the top five of signals for the *cause* relation based on count data in Table 6.2, is correctly assigned a low probability in the figure as a predictor of relations in the test data, because it does not appear to be part of the context identifying the relation in the unit as a whole, for example in (99). The spurious item 'death', which was in the top five for *result*, is similarly not assigned a high

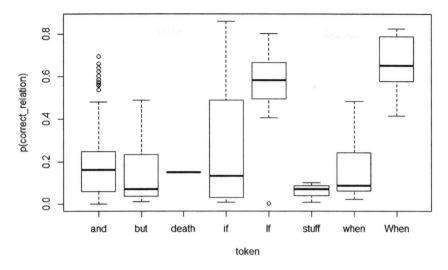

Figure 6.13 Boxplots for range of LSTM correct class probabilities associated with signals as encountered in context in the test data

probability of predicting the correct relation in the boxplot (although this is based on only a single occurrence in the test data). By contrast, capitalized 'If' and 'When' are very strong cues (usually for *condition* and *circumstance* respectively), but both are seen as much more reliable than uncapitalized variants. We can see why in (100)–(101).

(99) [*you probably don't have this **stuff** lying around the house (hopefully not)*]~motivation~

(100) [*and ask people **if** they want to play*]~sequence~

(101) [***If** a player is pegged . .*]~condition~

The annotation guidelines specify that object clauses are not segmented, meaning that a lowercase 'if' is also likely to appear within a non-conditional segment, for example, within direct or indirect speech. The network therefore learns to be more skeptical of such markers. However, at the same time, we note that the spread of the boxplot for lowercase 'if' (and to a substantial extent, lowercase 'when') also reaches rather high probabilities on occasion: These are cases where context promotes a likely *condition* or *circumstance* reading, in which the conjunction can also participate, as in (102)–(103).

(102) [*Therefore, **if** you are staying overnight in York and arriving by car, . .*]~condition~

(103) [*. . **when** you are cramped in such a small, tight space.*]~circumstance~

In both cases, the adjacent subject pronoun 'you' and possibly also the proximity to the beginning of the sentence cause the network to put more stock in the role of lowercase 'if' and 'when'. Finally, looking at some of the typically very ambiguous uses of 'and' and 'but', we can again note a low median probability for both items, but some quite strong cue cases as well, with many outliers especially for 'and'. These occur in contexts in which the role of 'and' or 'but' is more obvious, such as (104)–(105).

(104)   [*and the game ends*]$_{joint}$
(105)   [*but over the last few years there has been a dramatic rise in the number of community teams*]$_{contrast}$

In (104), a simple coordination of rules of a game is recognized as part of a *joint*, perhaps due to the brevity of the segment and lack of other discourse markers. In (105) there is much more material to interpret, but possibly the temporal PP after the initial 'but' strengthens the impression of a contrast. In both of these cases, the segment-initial position of the coordination seems important, but the network can use a variety of other signals to assign high probabilities to the relations *joint* and *contrast*, such as the existential construction with 'there has been' (also recognizable through the POS tag EX for expletive 'there', which is available to the network), or the semantic nature of some of the predicates, such as 'ends' (because the network has access to large-scale vector space embeddings).

Although the results of the network's output are not easy to analyze, and are certainly open to multiple interpretations, they give us access to an operationalizable way of quantifying contextualized cue validity using automatic methods and revealing subtle interactions that we may not have been aware of. System probabilities can show us which cues are generally valid, which ones are likely spurious and which ones vary strongly by context (those with a high variance, only sometimes reaching high contextualized probabilities). In so far as the behaviors of the network seem plausible, they strongly suggest that further research on signaling discourse relations should seek to capture different profiles of discourse markers in context, across all levels of signaling elements (and not only discourse marking conjunctions and adverbials, but also lexical, syntactic, morphological and other semantic devices, see Taboada and Das 2013). Models seeking to contextualize the issue of signaling must also incorporate not only the lexical semantic identity of surrounding content words, but also their semantic neighborhood or similarity profile, which can alter the effect of other markers, including in novel cases featuring unfamiliar context items for which we can establish some analogy to similar entities and predicates. Vector space representations can contribute to this effort by grouping similar familiar and novel items in the same continuous semantic space.

6.5 Interim Conclusion

In this chapter we looked at the structure of discourse relations across sentences in the different genres and documents in the GUM corpus and explored hypotheses about the identification of Domains of Referential Accessibility (DRAs) and discourse cues that signal the presence of specific relations. The availability of multiple layers of information made it possible to approach the complex, interacting nature of discourse structure and to create predictive models of intricate phenomena.

After comparing some discourse annotation frameworks and discussing different representations of discourse parses, an examination of the distribution of relation types in four different genres revealed the close relationship between the communicative goals of texts and the types of discourse relations most frequently realized. For example, how-to guides and travel guides frequently employ *condition* clauses to present different contingencies and use *motivation* clauses to recommend courses of action, whereas interviews use relations such as *justify* and *evaluation* and join news articles in discussing *cause* relations often. Looking at graph-topological relations in discourse parses through a distant reading lens, the shapes of RST graphs showed some differences in the typical elaborating 'staircase' of news narratives as compared to the more spread out and 'list-like' organization of instructional texts.

By cross-referencing the discourse graph structures in the corpus with the entity and coreference annotation layers, it was shown that although a binary notion of DRAs as formulated in Cristea et al. (1998) is too rough to form a predictive model, combining different annotation layers enables us to recast the concept of DRAs as a probabilistic 'heat map', identifying the likely location in the discourse graph for coreferentiality between any two given discourse units in a document. Although our results could likely be improved and need to be integrated with text and entity level cues to be applied in practice, they already indicate the potential of a multifactorial approach to model referential accessibility in discourse.

Finally in the previous section, memory-based Recurrent Neural Networks (RNNs) using vector space models of word and substring semantics were employed together with CRFs to shed more light on the ambiguous nature of discourse markers used to signal the presence of specific relations. We do not normally think of the primary textual data as a form of annotation (see Section 2.2); however, its structure can also be explored by converting words in context into vector representations that persist through state changes in an RNN. The results not only relativize the reliability or cue validity of cue words obtained via pure frequency counts, but also show the role of neighboring words that are not usually identified as discourse markers but are crucial for the interpretation of signals in context.

The results in this chapter leave many open questions, some of which point to directions for further study in a multilayer corpus paradigm. One avenue of research that is possible using data such as GUM, but was not approached in this chapter, is the use of layout information and its relevance as part of a multifactorial description of discourse structure (see e.g. Bateman et al. 2001: 418–430). Preliminary experiments using the GUM data suggest, unsurprisingly, that the document structure annotations on the TEI XML layer are highly predictive of both relation types and RST graph topology (e.g. presence of headings, paragraph divisions, bullet points and fonts). For cue identification, too, the focus of this chapter, and especially the last section, has been more on lexically identifiable material and less on syntactic- and genre-based cues (see Taboada and Das 2013). It is highly likely that constructing more complex architectures blending evidence from multiple layers of annotation, including syntax trees, will shed more light on the contributions of different types of information in marking discourse relations and identifying the reflexes of discourse structures in other levels of linguistic description.

7 Non-Standard Language

7.1 Introduction

In the previous chapters we focused on predicting high-level annotations and alternation phenomena using a range of predictors across layers and explored discourse structure from a 'distant' perspective, looking at documents as multilayer annotation graphs. However throughout the discussion so far, the concept of an underlying 'text' was relatively straightforward: Documents consist of primary textual information which we can tokenize (cf. Section 2.2), and subsequent annotation layers build more complex structures above the tokens (see Section 2.3). This chapter explores two broad types of corpora in which the 'simple text' assumption breaks down: corpora of non-native language, and in particular learner corpora, and historical texts in multilayer diachronic corpora.[1] Although these kinds of data can often be used for the same kinds of studies explored in previous chapters, here the focus will be on specific challenges in such corpora of non-standard language.

A connection between historical corpora, which contain information from epigraphy, manuscripts and early prints, and modern learner corpora or other non-native sources may seem strange to assume; however, there are important similarities in the ways in which such sources can be represented using multilayer architectures and some of the methodologies that can be employed to study them. The most important concept in representing both types of data is that of *normalization*, that is, to what extent a representation of the original, often heterogeneous data, as it was produced is complemented by a more homogenized version that has been edited by the corpus creators (see Archer et al. 2015 on normalizing historical English, and Reznicek et al. 2013 for the concept

---

1. A third and very important class of data with related challenges is found in multimodal corpora of both spoken and sign languages; these remain outside the scope of the current discussion, but see Allwood (2008) and Adolphs and Carter (2013) on multimodal corpora in general, and Schembri et al. (2013) and Orfanidou et al. (2015) on corpora of sign languages.

of target hypotheses for learner data, discussed further in Section 7.2).[2] The examples in (106)–(107) are a case in point.

(106) *at this the King* **laught** (for 'laughed', Archer et al. 2015: 14)
(107) *Therefore, we can* **interpretate** *and understand the data* (for 'interpret', CityU Corpus, Lee et al. 2015)

In (106), including a normalized layer in which 'laughed' can be searched for is the only way to ensure that researchers searching for that item will find it no matter how it is spelled. Even if we allow for fuzzy searches or regular expression searches, with which users may find other plausible spellings of specific words, some research questions, such as targeting precisely the alternation seen here (realization of the devoiced past-tense marker), will be difficult or impossible across all verbs. Similarly in (107), the issue is not merely the ability to find a form likely standing in for the intended verb 'interpret', but also the ability to examine more general questions of L2 word formation, for example, the productivity of affixes such the verbal suffix '-ate'. Knowing that this word exhibits a discrepancy between normalized 'interpret' and actual 'intepretate' gives us more information than not marking up this token, but also more than a general error annotation without a corresponding annotation encoding the target hypothesis 'interpret' explicitly. More generally speaking, we can never fully anticipate the range of variations and deviations from a given norm that we will find in a corpus.

The challenges in using multilayer architectures for non-standard language are many and go well beyond supplying normalization, for example, by creating problems for annotation graph anchoring: If we wish to provide further layers of annotation, such as syntax trees, semantic or discourse annotations, we must decide how the borders of spans or edges in a graph relate to the various, potentially conflicting, representations of the underlying texts (cf. Sections 2.3–2.4). Nevertheless, the trend for such corpora has been growing, and the ensuing complexity of data models is likely to be inevitable in the face of the complex research questions and rich data at hand. The following sections of this chapter are therefore devoted to studies using complex corpora of non-standard language. Section 7.2 presents studies of two types of multilayer learner corpora: Falko, the error annotated learner corpus of German (Reznicek et al. 2012), whose target hypothesis layers will be used to examine alternative verbalizations of compounds in L2 German; and the parallel aligned Hong Kong City University Corpus of English Learner Academic Drafts (Lee et al. 2015), which is used to study L2 textual

---

2. The concept of an 'original' text is itself often problematic, especially for historical data: Do we mean a physical manuscript? Or a faithful transcription? If there are many copies, which one is the original?

revision practices. Section 7.3 focuses on historical data and examines case studies using corpora from the Coptic Scriptorium project (Schroeder and Zeldes 2016), which document the complex structure of Coptic manuscripts from the first millennium alongside linguistic analyses, and the multilayer RIDGES corpus (Odebrecht et al. 2017) of Early Modern German scientific texts.

7.2   Non-Native Language

A unique property of non-native data from a linguistic perspective is the fact that there is no 'ideal speaker hearer' in the sense often postulated in generative linguistics (Chomsky 1965: 3; see Fillmore 1979 for criticism): learners vary significantly in the ways in which they speak and deviate from target language norms, and it is therefore essential, but also challenging, to distinguish consistent tendencies in L2 language from residual variation between L2 speakers.

One important way in which multilayer corpora help us to approach this challenge is in making the differences between L2 usage and postulated target norms explicit. Foundational research in learner corpora has led to the development of error annotation schemes which identify and classify deviations from L1 norms in the original data (e.g. the International Corpus of Learner English, ICLE, Granger 2003; see also Nagata et al. 2011; Lüdeling and Hirschmann 2015 for discussions of various schemes). Error annotations were initially done using inline formats (see Section 3.3), and in some cases supplemented by inline corrections, as shown in the L2 French example in (108), from Granger (2003: 470).

(108)   *L'héritage du passé est très* <G><GEN><ADJ>#*fort$ forte* </ADJ></GEN></G>
         'the heritage of the past is very strong'

The nested tags in this example indicate a grammatical error (G) related to gender (GEN), specifically due to erroneous adjectival (ADJ) agreement: the word *héritage* is feminine, mandating the feminine form *forte* for the adjective 'strong'.

Although explicit error tags and possible corrections of this kind can be powerful tools in evaluating the prevalence of errors and the environments promoting them, subsequent research has shown the limitations of inline approaches to error annotation from both technical and theoretical standpoints. From a technical point of view, it is clear that errors and their corrections can require access to discontinuous, overlapping and hierarchy-breaking spans of text, for example, an erroneous English discontinuous phrasal verb, such as "pick the bag along" for "pick the bag up". From a theoretical standpoint, a substantial problem is that multiple corrections are often conceivable – we could correct the same example to the target hypothesis "take the bag along", placing the error on the choice of verb rather than the particle. Lüdeling (2008) shows in an inter-annotator agreement experiment that even trained foreign language teachers can differ rather substantially in their target hypotheses (TH), suggesting that error annotation without explicit TH annotation is highly ambiguous. Like all forms of annotation, TH annotation therefore involves subjective interpretation, which is ideally constrained by clear guidelines and used cautiously in the context of a specific research question. Following this approach, the following section presents a corpus annotated with target hypotheses which will be used to investigate differences between native and non-native formation of compounds in German, and the next section looks at a special case of original and corrected versions of learner texts by examining a corpus of annotated learner revisions of their own texts.

Target Hypotheses and L2 German Compounds

Second-language writing, and in particular by advanced learners, often differs from native speaker writing not only in the presence of errors, but also in quantitative ways with regard to their over and underuse of constructions found in both populations. In this section, we will look at a challenging but rather frequent construction in L1 and L2 German: the formation of complex compound nouns, for which German is well known (see Gaeta and Schlücker 2012). In particular, we would like to answer some questions about L2 compounding: Do learners use compounds as often as natives? How often do they make errors, and what kinds of errors are most frequent? Do learners use compounds where they shouldn't or vice versa, and if they replace compounds with other constructions, which? These questions involve comparing actual L2 usage with hypothetical target-like behavior which they could assume. To examine how learner usage of German compounds differs from native norms, we will therefore use a corpus annotated with the kind of target hypotheses outlined earlier.

The Falko corpus (Fehlerannotiertes Lernerkorpus, 'error annotated learner corpus', Reznicek et al. 2012) is a richly annotated multilayer corpus of advanced L2 German writing containing a complex TH architecture. It consists of several L2 and comparable L1 subcorpora, which encompass data from essays (about 275,000 L2 and 70,000 L1 tokens) and summaries (approximately 40,000 and 21,000 tokens for L2 and L1, respectively), as well as a longitudinal L2 corpus (about 78,000 tokens). The corpus can be searched using ANNIS (see Section 3.5) at https://korpling.german. hu-berlin.de/falko-suche. Annotations in the corpus include POS tags (using the German STTS tag set, Schiller et al. 1999), lemmatization and dependency syntax trees (using the parser from Bohnet 2010), but also cover several layers of alternative target hypotheses, which are themselves tagged and lemmatized. There is a total of three TH layers: in TH1, learner data are corrected in the most minimal way possible that would make the learner text grammatical, using very strict guidelines, which promote high inter-annotator agreement (e.g. consistently preferring to correct the subject rather than the verb in cases of morphological disagreement). The result on TH1 is a minimally correct text with predictable orthography which can be used for lexical search and to find formal discrepancies in the original learner text. TH2, by contrast, corrects text based on meaning, as well as style, and is therefore more free and target language-like, but less predictable or consistent in terms of inter-annotator agreement. Finally, TH0 is a version of TH1 in which word order corrections are not carried out, resulting in a text that follows the original word order but has consistent and predictable orthography, morphology, etc. Target hypotheses are produced for both the L2 data and comparable L1 data, because both contain some similar errors (see Reznicek et al. 2013). The data are parsed automatically based on the contents of TH1, which is likely to produce fewer parsing errors than the more aberrant data in the learner text. Example (109) gives an example of a learner utterance requiring some corrections.

(109) *wenn mann lieber im   Wirtschaftleben arbeiten möchtet*
      if   one   rather in.DEF industry-life   work   would-like
      'if one would rather work in industry life'

In this example, several errors render the utterance ungrammatical: On the orthographic level, the word for generic 'one' has been spelled with two n's, like its homophone *Mann* 'man'. A morphologically almost valid but semantically incorrect compound 'industry-life' is also used to designate work in industry. From a formal perspective, this compound would require a linking element -s to be well-formed, that is, it should read *Wirtschaftsleben* 'industry life'. Finally, the verb *möchte* 'would like', is inflected incorrectly with a final -*t*. The target hypotheses for this example are given in (110)–(111) (TH0 is identical to TH1 in this case, because there are no word order errors).

(110)   TH1: *wenn ma**n** lieber im **Wirtschaft**s**leben** arbeiten **möchte***
(111)   TH2: *wenn ma**n** lieber **in der Wirtschaft** arbeiten **möchte***

On the TH1 level, the orthographic error in *man* 'one' and the inflectional error in *möchte* 'would like' have been corrected, as these result in completely unacceptable target language forms. The aberrant compound has been repaired with the missing linking -s but has not been replaced, despite being an odd choice of words. On the TH2 level, by contrast, the morphological repairs to the subject and verb are retained, but the compound is replaced by a simplex *Wirtschaft* 'industry', which sounds much more target-like, assuming the learner meant to say 'work in industry'. However, the substitution entails adding a required feminine article, which leads to the sequence *in der Wirtschaft* 'in the industry'. With these target hypotheses at hand, the Falko architecture then adds annotations to each layer, including not only POS tags and lemmas for each hypothesis, but also automatically generated 'diffs', or difference layers, which indicate whether a TH contains changes, deletions, insertions or movement of items with respect to the original learner text.

Although target hypotheses do not encompass explicit error annotations that allow us to directly examine learner error types, such as compounding errors, they are in fact extremely versatile in allowing us to search for any type of discrepancy we may be interested in, even if it was not originally envisioned during the construction of the corpus. In the following, I will leverage the target hypotheses and difference annotations to examine some aspects of cases where a compound is replaced across layers, indicating issues with compounding. For a more detailed examination of L2 compounds in Falko and some further applications of its corpus architecture for this purpose, see Zeldes (2018b).

To gain a first idea of whether or not, or to what extent, German learners in Falko make errors in compounds, we use ANNIS to export all tokens tagged as nouns in the original text, along with their TH and TH diff values, then tag them automatically to detect compounds using the morphological analyzer described in Zeldes (2013). Applying this process to both the L2 data and the native controls, we find 4,355 compound tokens within a total of 43,268 nouns, a ratio of almost exactly 10% as compared to about 15% of the 11,431 nouns found in the L1 data. This suggests that learners substantially underuse compounds, a possible sign that compounds are difficult to use (see Zeldes et al. 2008). This could be either because fewer compounds are acquired or because compounding is avoided, possibly in order to avoid potential morphological errors (e.g. omitting or choosing incorrect linking elements, such as the -s noted earlier).

Of the 4,355 L2 compound tokens, 483 cases show differences in TH1, indicating an error rate of just over 11%. Manual inspection of these errors reveals different causes, which are presented in Table 7.1 (the total exceeds 483, because a single compound can contain multiple errors).

Table 7.1 Error type breakdown in L2 German compounds in the Falko corpus

	Frequency	*% compounds*	*% errors*
Derivation	10	0.2	2.0
Linking	172	3.9	33.9
Inflection	139	3.2	27.4
To simplex	11	0.3	2.2
Lexical	38	0.9	7.5
Modifier	68	1.6	13.4
Head	70	1.6	13.8
Total	508	—	100

Some of these errors are not specific to compound formation and are therefore less interesting for the question of L2 compound formation in particular: For example, the last two categories in the table, indicating orthographic errors within the compound head or modifier (e.g. misspelled compound parts), can occur within any word, including the respective compound constituents when they appear in isolation. The same applies to inflection and derivation errors: Although the entire compound can have incorrect number or gender inflection applied to it, this affects the compound in much the same way as it would affect its head alone – for example, the erroneous nominative plural form *Hauptproblemen* 'main problems' has an incorrect plural suffix -en instead of -e, but the same error is found with the simple head *Problemen* 'problems'.

The more interesting cases for the behavior of L2 compounds in particular are linking errors, which occur when the head and modifier are not connected with the correct linking morpheme (see Kürschner 2005; Nübling and Szczepaniak 2013). These form the single largest group of compounding errors, covering almost 34% of cases. Identifying frequent erroneous items among these in terms of both problematic linking elements and specific lexical items or patterns is of interest not only for the description of L2 compounds per se, but also for the development of teaching materials based on L1 and L2 usage information. Two results that emerge very clearly from a qualitative inspection of items on the list are the disproportionately high number of errors using the linker -s (cf. Nübling and Szczepaniak 2011 on inconsistent use of this element in L1 German), which, among the six main productive German linkers, is responsible for almost two-thirds of linking errors (see Zeldes 2018b for more detailed analysis and some pedagogical implications).

The second broad class of interest is infelicitous compounds, which are either substituted with a different compound by changing the head or modifier lexeme, or both (the category 'lexical' in the table). In some cases, no appropriate substitute compound is selected, leading to the 'to simplex' category. Simple examples of lexical substitution result when learners are missing the appropriate lexical item and replace it with an inappropriate one, often a loanword, as in (112)–(113).

(112) *Tenniswoman* 'tennis woman' (TH1: *Tennisspielerin* '(female) tennis player')
(113) *Chancespielen* 'games of chance' (TH1: *Glücksspiele* lit. 'luck games')

In (112) the learner did not use the expected German *Spielerin* '(female) player', either due to difficulties with that lexeme or perhaps due to the need to derive the feminine *Spielerin* rather than the simpler masculine *Spieler* 'player'. Although the source language for the loan is, of course, English, the writer's native language, encoded in the corpus metadata, is, in fact, French in this example, showing a frequent learner strategy to use

English loanwords to cover for missing German vocabulary. Example (113), from a different writer who is coincidentally also French speaking, exhibits a similar situation, also likely inspired by English *game of chance* (the corresponding French expression is *jeu de hasard*, rather than the French word *chance* 'luck'). In both cases the compound therefore contains a 'loan item' either as a head or as a modifier.

Other cases are more complex and involve loan translations from compounding patterns in the respective native languages of the writers or in other foreign languages, primarily English. For example, in (114) a Ukranian writer is likely constructing a loan translation from English 'hometown', despite the fact that the corresponding Ukranian expression has a different structure. The morphemes used for the compound are, however, non-loans, creating the appearance of a native-like formation.

(114) *oft   befindet sich das Studiumort nicht in der <u>Heimstadt</u>*
       often finds REFL the study-place not   in the home-town
       'often the place of study is not in the <u>hometown</u>' (TH1=*Heimatstadt*)

In Ukranian, the most idiomatic translation of 'hometown' is probably рідне місто 'native town', with an adjectival modifier. However, possibly by analogy to English 'hometown', the author has constructed a compound from German *Heim* 'home' and *Stadt* 'city, town'. The expected form in the TH1 layer uses a more specific word, *Heimat*, itself meaning 'native place', which is combined with *Stadt* to form the idiomatic *Heimatstadt* 'hometown'.

Although the Falko corpus is not annotated for compounding errors, it is therefore possible to find different kinds of errors by cross-referencing the TH layer with the original text and its annotations. At the same time, TH1 does not contain all errors we may be interested in, because many infelicitous compounds are not ungrammatical, meaning that they will be retained in TH1. We can therefore also look at compound changes on TH2, which are more rare and mostly occur due to complete reformulations on the part of annotators. Some of the more interesting cases involve compounds which are formally possible but would not be used to express the desired meaning, as in (115)–(116).

(115) *Müllarbeiter* lit. 'garbage worker' (TH2: *Müllman* 'garbage man')
(116) *Raubplan* lit. 'rob plan' (TH2: *Planung* 'planning (of a robbery)')

In (115), a conceivable compound 'garbage worker' is used instead of lexicalized 'garbage man'. Suspicion that the writer may have been familiar with the expected form but wanted to avoid a gendered form with '-man' is unlikely, because the chosen head *Arbeiter* '(male) worker' is also gendered (cf. feminine *Arbeiterin* '(female) worker'). The form is also not a loan translation from English, nor from the author's native Danish, which uses a very similar compound headed by 'man', Danish *skraldemand* (where *mand* corresponds to English *man* and German *Mann*). Here the learner either didn't think of the head *Mann* or perhaps rejected it as inappropriate. In (116) as well, which originates from an English speaker, 'rob plan' is not a direct loan, though 'robbery plan' is possible. In both cases, it seems likely that learners are applying German compounding rules productively to form novel combinations that are not directly coined after existing sources but result from the application of combinatory rules operating on nominal and verbal stems, such as N+N ('garbage' + 'worker'), or V+N ('rob' + 'plan').

Finally, we can also examine cases where compounds appear in target hypotheses but not in the learners' original texts, suggesting cases of underuse (i.e. environments appropriate for compounding but where compounding was not realized). Because annotators are conservative in altering learner texts, there are only 113 cases of this kind in the entire corpus, such as examples (117)–(118). This corresponds to only 0.2% of all nouns produced by the learners.

(117)   *in Zeit von Kriegen* 'in time of wars' (TH2: *Kriegszeiten* 'war times')
(118)   *eine Position von Autorität* 'a position of authority' (TH2: *Führungsposition* 'leadership-position')

In both of these examples, learners use a periphrastic phrase with *von* 'of', instead of forming the compound which annotators felt would have been more appropriate on the TH2 layer. Such examples, coupled with the overall lower compounding rate in L2 data compared to native controls (about 10% compared to 15%, see earlier), lead to a possible hypothesis that learner compounds are less common due to the use of competing constructions.

If this is the case, we would expect a rise in the frequency of such competitors, such as prepositional phrases with *von* 'of' or other perpositions, or perhaps the use of adjectives, genitives or relative clauses, all of which can substitute for modification using a compounding construction. The relative frequencies of these competing constructions can be checked using the POS tags for the original text layer (for prepositions, the tags APPR and APPRART, for attributive adjectives, the tag ADJA, and for relative pronouns, PRELS), or the dependency trees (to look for adnominal genitive modifiers, annotated with an edge labeled GMOD). Table 7.2 gives differences in frequencies for these constructions in L2 and comparable L1 data, as well as statistical significance levels for those differences using a χ^2 test.

As we can see, learners underuse all modification constructions, except for *von* phrases and attributive adjectives, both of which are overused, but not yet significantly so. These results fall in line with other studies which have shown consistently that L2 German is lower in its rate of modification

Table 7.2 Underuse and overuse of constructions competing with compounds in L2 vs. L1 data

	Count (L1)	Norm (L1)	Count (L2)	Norm (L2)	Ratio	Significance
pos=ADJA	2753	0.040	5052	0.041	+2.34%	ns
deprel=GMOD	942	0.013	1569	0.012	–7.11%	ns
pos=PRELS	666	0.009	991	0.008	–17.02%	***
pos=APPR (ART)?	4766	0.069	8092	0.065	–5.31%	***
with *von*	410	0.005	797	0.006	+8.41%	ns
not *von*	4356	0.063	7295	0.059	–6.60%	***

Significance codes: 0 '***' 0.001 '**' 0.01 '*' 0.05 '.' 0.1 'ns' 1

than native German in a variety of constructions (Hirschmann et al. 2013; Vyatkina et al. 2015). In other words, the main answer to the question of what learners use instead of compounds given their 5% lower compound ratio is most likely just unmodified nominal heads, which do not amount to an error that would trigger a TH correction.

Using the TH layers concurrently with other traditional annotations such as POS tags and dependency parses, we can thus explore the relationship between actual learner language and a formalized concept of 'what a native would have said'. In some senses this is a way of pinning down the 'context' and 'meaning' parts of the equation proposed by the Probabilistic Syntax framework presented in Section 4.1, because we are looking at alternative verbalizations under the same given conditions for communicative intent. At the same time it is important to reiterate that target hypotheses, much like any kind of annotation, are not ground-truth data, but an interpretation, which in the case of TH2 may be particularly volatile. In the next section we move on to explore a different kind of non-native corpus, which does provide multiple versions of 'ground-truth' data for comparison, by looking at the behavior of learners' own textual revisions in the process of writing and rewriting their own texts in the face of language tutor feedback.

Multiple Texts and Textual Revision

In the previous section we concentrated on learner data as a complete, final product, without considering the process by which a text, such as an essay, comes into being. In actuality, texts, and especially academic writing, are often produced in an iterative process of revision and correction of errors, both in L2 writing and in general. The special and very interesting characteristic of textual revision in non-native language is that learners can improve their texts not only from a stylistic or goal-based point of view (simply making an essay 'better'), but also from the perspective of approaching target-like language. This can occur both through intrinsic revision processes without intervention and using a variety of structured feedback techniques to improve learner writing (see Graham and Perin 2007 for a meta-study surveying various approaches).

In order to study how learners iteratively craft and improve a text over multiple revisions,[3] examine whether and how texts become more target-language like and what the effect of instructor feedback might be we require a special type of corpus data and architecture: At the textual level, we need multiple, successive versions of texts revised by the same authors. To study the effects of instructor feedback, we also need a systematic annotation scheme codifying such feedback, which should ideally contain the same information supplied to students during the language instruction process. Finally, we will need technical infrastructure to model the data and make them searchable: In particular, we will require some kind of alignment between versions of texts indicating what has been altered and in what ways.

The Hong Kong City University Corpus of English Learner Academic Drafts (Lee et al. 2015) was created to meet these requirements. Data for the corpus were collected from over 4,200 predominantly Cantonese-speaking English learners over the course of seven semesters, spanning the academic years of 2007 to 2010; the complete corpus contains over 7.7 million tokens in just over 11,000 drafts (see Webster et al. 2011 for details). Learners used the Blackboard web interface (www.blackboard.com/) to edit and submit essays, and tutors responded with comments highlighting spans of texts that contained problems or should be revised. The comments came in two formats: simple, predetermined error categories from a list called the Comment Bank, such as 'pronoun missing' or 'gerund needed', and free-text comments detailing more complex issues. After each round of comments, authors were allowed to resubmit a revised version for further comments as often as they liked until they felt satisfied with the text and submitted a final version. As a result, all texts have an initial and final version, but the number of intermediate versions varies: The maximum number of versions was 5, but only for a handful of texts, with the average number of revisions being approximately 2.7. This can complicate comparisons across documents, as we will see later.

To make the corpus searchable for research questions about the revision process, each draft was automatically POS tagged and lemmatized. Consecutive versions of the same essay were then automatically sentence

---

3. A related and very interesting question regarding how learners compose and revise a single draft as they type or write it incrementally is beyond the scope of this study.

and word-aligned, including the possibility of null alignments and split/ merge for 1:2 or 2:1 alignments between sentences across versions (see Lee et al. 2015 for details and evaluation). The data from these automatic processes were merged with the closed and free-text error tags from tutors and serialized in PAULA stand-off XML (see Section 3.3) – alignment edges were realized as different types of pointing relations ('SentenceAlign' and 'WordAlign') and labeled with the alignment types 'identical' or 'replace' for unchanged or edited segments, 'shift' for reordered items and 'split' or 'merge' for 1:2 or 2:1 alignments. For deleted or inserted text, which cannot be aligned by means of a concrete edge (because it would have either no source or no target), a token annotation was introduced marking tokens destined to be delete in the next version as 'del', and conversely, tokens introduced since the last version as 'ins'. An example of data from the corpus is shown in Figure 7.1, visualized using ANNIS (see Section 3.5).

In this example, one version of an essay on wine making contains the phrase 'well known'. This span is commented on in the grid at the bottom of the figure using the span annotation CommentBank="92", a very general error type code which was rendered for learners as 'Word choice', suggesting the wording was somehow not appropriate but without a clear indication of what a better formulation might look like. The word 'known' has been automatically aligned to 'popular' in the next version, shown in the middle of the figure along with token annotations (alignment edges are not visualized in this view). The word 'well' in the earlier version at the top of the figure did not receive an alignment, and as a result it receives the 'del' annotation indicating that it would not appear in the next version. We can see that the error annotation CommentBank="92" belongs to the 'ver1' layer, which groups together

Yeasts	are	well	known	in	wine	making	.	They
		del						
yeast	be	well	know	in	wine	making	.	they
NNS	VBP	RB	VBN	IN	NN	NN	.	PRP
.	Yeasts	are	popular	in	wine	making	.	They
.	yeast	be	popular	in	wine	making	.	they
.	NNS	VBP	JJ		IN	NN	NN	.	PRP

⊟ grid (ver1)

CommentBank			92			
Paragraph	p					
Sentence	s					
tok	Yeasts	are	well	known	in	wine	making	.

Figure 7.1 Aligned data from the CityU corpus

all annotations belonging to the first revised version of the essay (the original version is 'ver0' and the final one is 'verfinal'; see Section 2.3 on grouping annotations in complex layers).

Using the different layers in this corpus architecture in conjunction, we can approach a range of questions regarding the revision process. First, we may consider how often texts are revised at each version and, generally speaking, whether comments precipitate most changes to learner texts or not. This is an important question for drawing pedagogical consequences from the data in this corpus, because the topic of the effectiveness of corrective feedback in improving L2 writing has been hotly debated (see Truscott 1996; Russell and Spada 2006; Ferris 2006; Bitchener and Ferris 2012). Although the coarse and partly automatic nature of the annotation process of our data is subject to the presence of errors, we can expect to be able to get coarse answers if the disparities across versions and commented/uncommented material are sufficiently large (for estimates of annotation error rates in this corpus see Lee et al. 2015). Table 7.3 gives the number of instructor comments per sentence pair in sentence pairs automatically aligned as 'identical' (no changes at all) or not (including edits, but also shifts, splits and merges). Separate counts are given for open and closed comment formats, as well as totals covering both types.

The table clearly shows that the number of comments reduces from revision to revision, suggesting that essay quality is (unsurprisingly) improving with subsequent revisions. Sentence pairs that were revised (right half of the table) consistently contain more open and closed comments. All differences across revised/unrevised sentences for both open and closed comments are significant at $p < 0.0001$ in a Bonferroni adjusted chi-square test, except for open comments in version 3–4, which are not significantly different in both revised and identical sentences. Starting out at a level of between 0.73 and 1.17 comments of any kind for all sentence pairs in the first revision, learners drop to 0.19 to 0.55 comments per sentence in the second revision, and then exhibit a more modest drop to 0.17 to 0.51 comments per sentence in the third revision.

Table 7.3 Open, closed and total comments per sentence pair for identical and revised pairs in the CityU corpus. All cells on the 'identical' side differ significantly from 'revised' counterparts unless marked 'ns'

Revision	Identical			Revised		
	Open	*Closed*	*Total*	*Open*	*Closed*	*Total*
1 to 2	0.10	0.63	0.73	0.23	0.94	1.17
2 to 3	0.04	0.14	0.19	0.11	0.44	0.55
3 to 4	0.08(ns)	0.08	0.17	0.12(ns)	0.39	0.51

The large drop between the first two rows indicates that the impact of the first revision is the greatest. The fact that the tallies for the second and third revisions are rather close could suggest that the third version solves very few further issues, or it could be showing some residual level of comments which tutors are likely to make at any revision, because one could always suggest some changes. It is likely that a combination of both of these possibilities holds, that is, that learners are able to correct few additional issues in a third revision and that some baseline level of comments would be present even after many revisions.

Looking at the difference between revised and identical sentences, we see that although revised sentences predictably contain more comments per sentence, many sentences carrying comments are not revised at all. In the case of open comments, this could be the result of informative comments without an actual suggestion to revise, as shown in (119), or rather abstract comments as in (120).

(119)   *I will say having learnt a logical way of thinking is the greatest benefit I have gained from this course.* (free comment: "good introduction!")

(120)   *Everything can relate to and rely on computers.* (free comment: "if you give an example here, such as 'Everything from business and transport to personal relationships', your argument will be fortified, less generalised")

However with closed comments, which generally indicate the type and more or less exact location of errors, the rather high number of about 0.63 cases per sentence without any revision to the sentence in the initial revision is somewhat surprising. Taken together with the number of closed comments in revised sentences, which is about 50% higher at 0.94, it seems likely that there are simply more comments than the learners can effectively handle in a single revision. The dramatic drop in closed comments without revisions in the second and third revisions suggests that these do eventually get altered, whether or not the result is an error-free sentence (and we note that even at the third revision, there are 0.39 closed comments per sentence in revised sentences).

Turning to the actual errors involved in generating these numbers, we can focus on the more common error types. Because the corpus data model directly allows us access to the closed comment annotation spans and the sentence alignment in segments containing them, we can easily get a breakdown of error types within revised and unrevised sentences to examine which types of error feedback are associated with bringing about revisions. Figure 7.2 shows the association of chi-square residuals (cf. Section 4.1) across all revisions for the eight most common error

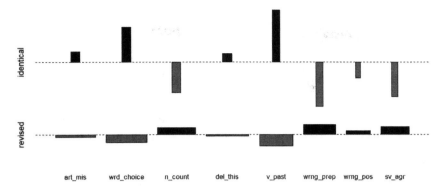

Figure 7.2 Association plot of common error type prevalence in revised and unrevised sentences across all consecutive version pairs

types in revised and unrevised sentences (i.e. ones showing the 'identical' alignment type).[4]

Although sentences often contain multiple errors, meaning that revision behavior cannot be attributed solely to the errors in question, given enough data and assuming a random distribution of other errors, an association between revisions and error types can still emerge. What's more, in cases of 'identical' alignment, we can be certain that learners ignored the corrective feedback, because no changes took place. Unsurprisingly given the large number of categories, the data in the figure strongly deviate from an assumption of independence between presence of revisions and the specific error tags (p < 0.005). Four comment types are associated with higher-than-expected revision rates: 'wrong preposition', 'wrong part of speech', 'subject-verb agreement' and 'noun—countable' (the latter refers to pluralization errors). By contrast, categories such as 'article missing', 'word choice', 'delete this' and 'verb—past' tend to be revised less.

Initially it may seem surprising that learners ignore a comment such as 'delete this', but in fact, this type of comment may not be so helpful if the localized comment does not indicate how the surrounding sentence might need to be changed in view of this correction (cf. Ashwell 2000). The same can be said about 'article missing', and even more so about 'word choice', because the learner may not be certain which article should be inserted

4. Naturally this should not be taken to say that these are the most common error types in general: Results from this corpus are influenced by the categories made available to tutors, the nature of the specific texts (college level essays), writers (students), native language (predominantly Cantonese), etc., and agreement on error categories is also imperfect (see Lee et al. 2015 for evaluation).

(definite or indefinite) and may not be able to establish a better word choice by themselves. In the case of 'noun—countable', by contrast, the correct solution is almost always simply adding a plural 's', and in cases such as 'subject-verb agreement', students can rely on English instruction they have received to realize that a present tense verb must be -s marked (if they intended a singular subject), or the other way around – the location and extent of the correction are therefore virtually unambiguous. Errors such as wrong preposition or part of speech may be similar to 'word choice', but are more constrained and are perhaps easier to respond to by, for example, looking up verbs and associated prepositional arguments in a dictionary, which was available to writers in the writing process.

A more fine-grained analysis of responses to corrective feedback in revision data would require either a manual inspection of the correspondences (see Lee et al. 2015: 674–676 for a detailed analysis of tense changes in a random subset of sentence pairs from this corpus) or an additional annotation layer aligning changes more directly or indicating whether feedback was acted upon for individual cases. We can get partial information of this kind using the word alignment information for certain types of errors: For example, it is not difficult to use word alignment between tokens annotated with the POS tag 'NN' (singular noun) in an earlier version and tokens tagged 'NNS' (plural noun) in a later version. The proportion of such cases within closed comment annotations in the category 'noun—countable' can give us an idea of the specific uptake rate for this comment, and not just about the presence of changes in sentences containing it. The AQL query retrieving such cases is given in (121), and an example is given in (122).

(121)   `CommentBank="42" _i_ pos="NN" ->WordAlign pos="NNS"`

(122)   ver1: *Taking a risk of losing credit in such a public way, little* [***enterprise***]$_{noun-countable}$ *will cheat here to attract loans.*
ver2: *Taking a risk of losing credit in such a public way, little* [***enterprises***] *will cheat here to attract loans.*

The query specifies a search for the appropriate error code (#42), which includes a 'pos' annotation with the value 'NN'. This node points to a second node annotated with the tag 'NNS', using the WordAlign pointing relation type. This query retrieves 1,989 cases in the corpus, but normalizing to get the proportion of comment uptake is not completely trivial: On the one hand, dividing this number by all errors with the code #42 ignores the fact that some 'NN' tags might get changed even without a corresponding error annotation. On the other hand, if we get the number of all NN -> NNS changes in the corpus, we would need to relativize this number based on how many nouns could have conceivably had a change NN -> NNS. This latter number cannot be based on the total count of NN tags in the corpus, because at least nouns in the final version never get the chance to be changed (the final version is no longer subject to correction).

To obtain a correct estimate of the uptake and compare it to chance modification of noun number, we therefore begin by collecting all NN tags which are not in the final version of a document (this can be done thanks to the layers grouping document nodes into 'verfinal' and other layers). Out of 1,537,708 tokens tagged 'NN' in the corpus, 1,341,235 belong to a non-final version, and within these, 5,880 are automatically aligned to plurals (NNS), that is, an overall change rate of just 0.43%. Of 6,955 singular nouns contained within an error with the code #42, the 1,989 cases found earlier to be aligned with NNS tags constitute 28.6%. Although this uptake rate is not very high, we should keep in mind that relative to the overall chance of changing NN to NNS, these cases are addressed by authors rather often. However some other caveats also remain, including the following:

1. There is always the possibility of resolving an error by a reformulation that does not involve pluralizing the relevant word.
2. It is possible that some of the error annotations come from the same position in different versions, where the error was eventually addressed, but persisted for some of the earlier revisions.
3. Revising a word into the plural form does not necessarily produce a correct, or even better, sentence.

To address these and many other questions about the effects of corrective feedback in this dataset, other layers of information could be added given time and resources, including target hypotheses and direct annotations of revision type and level of success for aligned segments.

7.3   Historical Multilayer Corpora

Historical corpora have become substantially richer in recent years, covering the same kinds of information found in multilayer corpora of modern languages along the lines of the OntoNotes corpus used in Chapter 4. Historical corpora with syntax trees (e.g. the Perseus treebanks for Classical Greek and Latin, Bamman and Crane 2011), named entities (Neudecker 2016) and even coreference annotations (see e.g. the PROIEL corpora in a variety of Indo-European languages, Haug et al. 2009) are now no longer exceptional, and have joined earlier work on architectures for historical corpora focusing more on preserving document layout or properties of manuscripts. In the following section we will look at some of the challenges and opportunities in representing a linguistically annotated corpus of diplomatic manuscript transcriptions, which can be used for both linguistic and paleographic purposes in the study of the Coptic language of Hellenistic Egypt. The next section then examines a historical corpus of academic Early Modern High German used to study the development of German as a language of science.

Coptic Scriptorium

The Coptic language of ancient Egypt in the first millennium CE represents the last stage of the indigenous language of Egypt, the oldest documented human language, which goes back to the hieroglyphs starting at the end of the fourth millennium BC (see Loprieno 1995 for a historical overview). The designation of Egyptian texts as Coptic, as opposed to Late or Demotic Egyptian, is based on their orthography using Greek letters rather than hieroglyphs or hieratic script, which attests to the centrality of Greek culture in the region during this period. The influence of Greek on Coptic can be seen not only in the use of Greek letters to write Coptic, but also in the massive influx of Greek loanwords into Coptic, which appear in a variety of texts to varying degrees and participate in a range of grammatical change phenomena in the language (see Torallas-Tovar 2010; Grossman 2014, as well as Richter 2009 on the later influence of Arabic).

Representing historical Coptic texts is challenging for a number of reasons related both to the nature of the surviving manuscripts and grammatical properties of the language. In a series of projects outlined in Schroeder and Zeldes (2016), a digital corpus initiative called Coptic Scriptorium (http://copticscriptorium.org/) has undertaken the task of digitizing Coptic manuscript materials while attempting to meet the challenges of encoding the data in a way that is adequate for representing both linguistic and paleographic information. Beyond the need to deal with the fragmentary nature of the texts and attempt to preserve and normalize heterogeneous source documents, the system of word segmentation in Coptic imposes complex architectural requirements for this project. Coptic is an agglutinative language in which multiple morphemes which we might consider to be words are spelled together in at least two levels of granularity. The units which are separated by spaces in Coptic are conventionally referred to as bound groups, which represent units that probably carried one main stress in the spoken language (see Layton 2011: 12–20). Bound groups represent sequences of morphemes which cannot be interrupted, for example, by enclitic particles imported from Greek, such as *de* 'and, but'. Similarly to Semitic languages such as Arabic or Hebrew, a bound group may contain a noun with accompanying articles, possessive pronouns or proclitic prepositions, all of which form units which we might typically want to tag for part of speech. Similarly, and again like Arabic or Hebrew, verbal bound groups may also contain enclitic subject and object pronouns, but also a long chain of auxiliaries and conjunctions. However unlike Arabic or Hebrew, the constituent units of a bound group may themselves be complex, for example, when a noun or verb is itself a

compound, as compounds are spelled together in conventional Coptic.[5]
The example in (123) illustrates all of these levels of segmentation for two
consecutive bound groups, separated by white space.

(123)   ⲉⲛⲛⲉϥⲍⲃⲏⲩⲉ   ⲙⲙⲛⲧⲣⲉϥⲍⲉⲧⲃⲯⲩⲭⲏ
          hn-nef-hbēue   m-mṇt.ref.hetḫ.psyxē
          in-his-deeds   of-ness.er.kill.soul
          'in his deeds of soul-killing'
          (Besa, Letter to Aphthonia, urn:cts:copticLit:besa.aphthonia.
          monbba)[6]

In the gloss for the first bound group in (123), a prepositional phrase
which translates as 'in his deeds', three constituent word units are separated by dashes: the preposition for 'in', a possessive determiner and a
plural noun. This type of phrasal orthographic unit is typical in many
languages, particularly in the Semitic language family, where articles and
prepositions behave as proclitic elements, and the entire phrase is spelled
together to match the prosodic foot of the stressed lexical noun. The second bound group shows the added complexity in Coptic: Here, a complex
incorporated verb form *hetḫ.psyxē* 'soul-kill' combines the native Coptic
verb *hōtḫ* 'kill' with the Greek loan *psyxē* 'psyche, soul'. The incorporated
status of the verbal object can be recognized both by the lack of a definite
article on the object and the phonological reduction of *hōtḫ* 'kill' to the
shortened *hetḫ* (see Grossman 2014). This complex verb is subsequently
prefixed with the agent nominalization *ref-* (similar to the English agent
nominalization in -*er*) and then further derived into an abstract noun with
mnt- (similar to English abstract -*ness*) to produce 'soul-killing' (literally
'soul-kill-er-ness'). The entire derivation constitutes a single noun, which
is then preceded by the preposition 'of', a separate word unit with the
same status as the preposition 'in' in the first bound group. The segmentation into multiple levels is necessary not just to enable morphological
search in the corpus (e.g. for all nominalizations in *mnt-*), but also for
lexical search for an item such as *psyxē*, because that morpheme is part
of a larger word. Additionally, items such as *psyxē* in particular can carry
other annotations, such as a language of origin annotation indicating that
it (but not the entire complex noun) is a Greek loanword.

There are several further complications in representing the text in
(123) beyond the morphological complexity of Coptic word forms. One

5. It should be noted that these conventions were generally established much later than the
manuscripts presented later in this section, all of which were written in *scriptio continua*,
i.e. without any spaces at all.
6. The stable urn identifier can be used to retrieve the corpus data at http://data.copticscrip
torium.org/.

problem is that the form as listed in the example is not actually the form as spelled in the manuscript: a variety of diacritics have been removed for the purpose of normalization. In order to represent both the diplomatic spelling as found in the manuscript and the normalization, further layers of annotation are needed. A second problem is that although the segmentation in (123) is linguistically adequate, there may be facts about the manuscript that require further and different segmentations. In this particular case, the manuscript line ends before the letter *x* of *psyxē*, meaning we need a more fine-grained 'timeline' of segmentations (cf. Section 2.1) in order to correctly represent its location. Figure 7.3 gives the complete annotation grid representing the position of the second bound group of example (123) in its manuscript using the ANNIS search and visualization platform (Krause and Zeldes 2016, see Section 3.5).

The annotations 'orig' and 'norm' in the figure represent diplomatic and normalized versions of the text, respectively, in units sized to correspond to what we would think of as words bearing parts of speech in English. The 'pos' annotation layer shows that we are looking at a preposition (PREP) and a noun (N) ('of' + 'soul-killing'), and the 'morph' annotation shows that the noun is complex, consisting of four morphemes. The final morph, ⲯⲩⲭⲏ *psyxē* is also annotated on the 'lang' layer as 'Greek'. The series of layers 'pb_xml_id', 'cb_n' and 'lb_n' give page, column and line identifiers, respectively. We can see that line 5 (lb_n="5") ends before the final part of the last morpheme, indicating a line break mid-word.

Having access to page layout information such as page and line breaks can be important not only in order to reproduce faithful representations

norm_group	ⲙ̄ⲛ̄ⲧⲣⲉϥϩⲉⲧⲃ̄ⲯⲩⲭ︦ⲏ				
norm	ⲙ	ⲙⲛ̄ⲧⲣⲉϥϩⲉⲧⲃⲯⲩⲭⲏ			
pos	PREP	N			
lemma	ⲛ	ⲙⲛⲧⲣⲉϥϩⲉⲧⲃⲯⲩⲭⲏ			
morph		ⲙⲛ̄ⲧ	ⲣⲉϥ	ϩⲉⲧⲃ	ⲯⲩⲭⲏ
orig_group	ⲙ̄ⲙⲛ̄ⲧⲣⲉϥϩⲉⲧⲃ̄ⲯⲩⲭⲏ				
orig	ⲙ̄	ⲙⲛ̄ⲧⲣⲉϥϩⲉⲧⲃⲯⲩⲭⲏ			
lang					Greek
translation	And he is the one that the devil will have power over in his deeds of soul killing.				
p_n	III.3				
pb_xml_id	BA49				
cb_n	1				
lb_n	4			5	6
tok	ⲙ̄	ⲙⲛ̄ⲧ	ⲣⲉϥ	ϩⲉⲧⲃ̄	ⲧⲩ	ⲭⲏ

Figure 7.3 Annotation grid for example (123) shown in ANNIS

for visualization purposes, but also for a correct analysis of the text and a variety of paleographic and codicological purposes. To illustrate this, we can look at two examples using these annotation layers. The text in (124) gives an unusual-looking sentence from the same manuscript as in (123), taken from the Letters of Besa, an abbot of the White Monastery in Upper Egypt in the fifth century CE.

(124) ⲬⲈ-ⲡⲁ-‖ⲡⲁⲖⲓⲛ ⲟⲛ ⲛ-ⲧⲈⲧⲛ-ⲕⲈⲧ-ⲧⲏⲩⲧⲛ Ⲉⲡⲁ?ⲟⲩ ?ⲓ-ⲛⲓ-ⲙⲛⲧ.ⲣⲈ?.ϯ.Ϭⲱⲛⲧ
  je-pa-‖palin on ṇ-tetn-ket-tēutṇ epahu hi-ni-mṇt.ref.ti.čōnt
  <small>that-my-again also conj-you-turn-you back   upon-these-ness.er.give.strife</small>

  <small>'that also my(?) again you return to these provocations'</small>

The basic structure of the sentence is not unusual, using a 'that' clause marked by *je-*, a main verb supported by the conjunctive auxiliary *n-* and a reflexively used object pronoun ('you-turn-you' = 'you return'),[7] and a complex prepositional object similar in structure to the second bound group in (123). What is unusual is the apparent inclusion of *pa* 'my' before the Greek loanword *palin* 'again', which is not normally combinable with a possessive. This would roughly translate to 'my again', which seems odd. However, it should be noted that if we examine all layers of information from the manuscript, we can see that there is a page break in this example, whose location is marked by the double vertical line in (124). The location of the page break indicates that the difficult word *pa* 'my' happens to stand at the end of the page, immediately before a new page beginning with the word *palin* 'again', which starts with the same letters *pa*. Knowing this last fact is a strong indication that one of the two instances of *pa* is actually redundant, likely a scribal error resulting from the repetition of letters across page borders.[8] Access to page break locations is therefore crucial in analyzing text from the corpus, including for linguistic tasks such as normalization and POS tagging.

As a second example of the importance of diplomatic layout information, we can consider the application of fragment identification. Many ancient Coptic manuscripts have been preserved in relatively good condition thanks to the dryness of the Egyptian desert. However, a large number of texts are fragmentary, at times containing lacunae that result

7. There is also a stronger, unambiguous reflexive pronoun which could be translated as 'oneself', but in this instance the object form of 'you' is used, which is indistinguishable from non-reflexive cases.
8. In some ancient manuscripts, preparing the reader for the next page by supplying redundant letters was done intentionally to facilitate reading out loud. In the case of this particular manuscript, this example is unusual, and the phenomenon is not repeated elsewhere in this text.

in small portions of text being missing, and at times amounting to no more than a few scraps. An extreme example of the latter case can be found in the Candle Room Fragments, found in a previously sealed part of the White Monastery near Sohag in Upper Egypt during an archeological excavation in December 2011 (see Davis et al. 2014). Many of the fragments found are very small and cannot be pieced together to form larger folia, as shown in Figure 7.4 on the left.[9] Side 'a' of the fragment in the figure bears part of two lines, the first of which contains an omega (ⲱ) and the second a sequence which is likely the Coptic letters alpha-pi-djandja (ⲁⲡϫ).

Although the text on the fragment is extremely little, we can try to search for similar constellations in Coptic Scriptorium corpora, which include data from codices originating in the White Monastery. Specifically, some of the data digitized using the architecture outlined above in the Coptic Scriptorium project come from texts authored

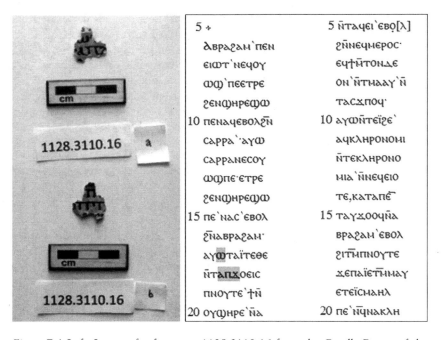

Figure 7.4 Left: Image of a fragment 1128.3110.16 from the Candle Room of the White Monastery Church, courtesy of Stephen J. Davis and the Yale Monastic Archaeology Project (YMAP). Right: digital corpus position matching the configuration of the letters on the fragment shown at the top-left

9. For more images see: http://egyptology.yale.edu/archaeological-expeditions/white-monastery-project/candle-room-project/parchment-coptic-1128-3110-and-1131-3150.

by Shenoute of Atripe, archimandrite of the White Monastery in the fourth to fifth centuries CE. Because the fragments come from the White Monastery, and some of the fragments identified by Davis et al. (2014) also belong to texts by Shenoute, it is possible that the fragments contain some texts for which digitized duplicates exist. To search for text matching the two-line fragment in Figure 7.4 we can use the AQL query in (125).[10]

```
(125)   lb_n  _i_  norm_group=/.*ꙍ.*/ &
        lb_n  _i_  norm_group=/.*ⲁⲡⲝ.*/ &
        #1  .  #3
```

The first line of the query searches for a node annotated with lb_n (some line break annotation), which includes a normalized group matching a regular expression containing the letter omega (ꙍ). The second line similarly searches for a line containing a group with the letters alpha-pi-djandja. Finally in the third line, a constraint specifies that the first node (#1), that is, the first line annotation, immediately precedes the third node (#3), that is, the second line, meaning that the two lines must be consecutive. The visualization on the right side of Figure 7.4 shows the only match for such a text in some 47,000 tokens of data for which we have manual diplomatic transcription annotations. This result comes from a well-known text by Archimandrite Shenoute called "Abraham Our Father", a long sermon, this part of which is preserved in codex YA, page 518. Although it is impossible to say for a fragment of this size whether it truly comes from another manuscript of this same text, this result shows that, at the very least, the words on the fragment could be the result of a similar text, in which the lower line could be part of the bound group ⲁⲡⲝ [ⲟⲉⲓⲥ] 'the Lord did', which begins with the same three letters as the fragment. That the omega could belong to the word [ⲁⲩ]ꙍ 'and' is somewhat less interesting, because a single letter is much more ambiguous and the word in question is very common, but the configuration is at least possible as the corpus evidence shows.

It should also be noted that the visualization on the right of Figure 7.4 can be generated automatically from the corpus data model exposed in Figure 7.3, and that this visualization is in fact essential for judging the plausibility of the spatial configuration of the characters for comparison with the fragment. This is because although the annotations indicate that the lines are adjacent, we do not have annotations indicating the width of different lines or characters (e.g. that iotas 'ⲓ' are thin and pi 'ⲡ' is wider – a type of annotation which is conceivable but harder to exploit). It is therefore essential to visualize the manuscript if we wish to quickly scan results without accessing and analyzing manuscript images

10. For more on AQL see Section 3.5.

in detail, which is a time-consuming and potentially costly operation (because many manuscripts images must be ordered from libraries by interested researchers and paid for). The visualization itself is generated using a fairly simple stylesheet, which translates the annotation layers into HTML elements using the following three-colunm format (column 3 can be empty):

```
pb_xml_id      table
pb_xml_id      tr
cb_n           td
lb_n           div:line       value
tok            span           value
```

The first column in the stylesheet specifies the annotation names which trigger HTML elements specified in the second column. For example, the presence of a 'pb_xml_id' annotation triggers the generation of an HTML table and table row (<tr>). Because each manuscript page contains exactly one 'pb_xml_id' annotation, the visualization creates a table with one row per manuscript page. A separate CSS stylesheet coupled with the configuration ensures that the table will be surrounded by a solid border, giving it the appearance of a page. Inside each row, the column break annotation 'cb_n' generates a table cell (<td>); because the manuscript has two columns, each page 'row' has two cells, which are rendered as the columns in Figure 7.4. The 'lb_n' annotation generates HTML divisions (<div>) which appear as stacked blocks of text, forming the lines. This instruction also specifies the presence of an HTML attribute 'line', which is filled with the value of the 'lb_n' annotation based on the presence of the reserved word 'value' in the third column. This allows the line numbers to be visualized every five lines, as shown in Figure 7.4. Finally the token value itself is spelled out for each token, generating the actual text, which is given a Coptic font in the CSS stylesheet.[11]

The same type of visualization facilities can be extended to cover a variety of other research goals by using a mapping between annotation layers and HTML elements. For example, we can use the same richly annotated multilayer architecture outlined earlier to examine the role of Greek loanwords in different kinds of texts represented using the same

---

11. For more information on generating visualizations of this kind using the ANNIS platform, and how to couple them with CSS stylesheets, see http://corpus-tools.org/annis/documentation.html/. An important aspect of this type of stylesheet-generated visualizations is their ability to capitalize on generic data models of the type introduced in Chapter 2 – the same logic mapping the presence of certain annotations to specific HTML elements can be reused for a variety of applications, including visualizing the same multilayer data from different perspectives.

data model. We can define a visualization which highlights the position of loanwords using the following configuration:

```
norm_group    span
norm          span          value
lang          a:lang        value
```

This configuration focuses on normalized forms, rather than the diplomatic structure of the document, but is generated in ANNIS from the same underlying representation (realized in the Salt object model, see Section 2.3). Here the 'norm_group' annotations are realized as HTML <span> elements, which contain further spans corresponding to the 'norm' annotations (i.e. the word units inside bound groups, see Figure 7.3). Whenever a 'lang' annotation is present, it is mapped to an HTML anchor (<a>) carrying an attribute 'lang', which is filled with the content of the 'lang' annotation layer (e.g. Greek). A CSS stylesheet coupled with this configuration can then highlight <a> elements which have a 'lang' attribute 'Greek'. Figure 7.5 shows the distribution of such loanwords in excerpts from two Coptic texts: the Gospel of Mark on the left and the Apophthegmata Patrum (Sayings of the Desert Fathers) on the right.[12]

Looking at the two texts from a distance, the contrast in the prevalence of Greek loanwords is clear, because the Biblical text on the left contains far more highlighted words. What is not immediately discernable without reading the text more closely is the nature of loanwords appearing in each case. The text on the right uses primarily function words such as the common Greek particle *de* 'but, and' (twice), or the adverb *mōnon* 'only, just'. Only two Greek content words appear: the verb *tʰlibe* 'torment, distress' and the noun *eidos* 'form, shape'. These are relatively general terms, compared to the Greek words in the Gospel text, which are exclusively religious in nature. The words on the left include the common *de*, as well as a similar enclitic particle *gar* 'for, indeed', but the large majority are content words, such as *euangelion* 'gospel', *pisteue* 'believe', *diakoni* 'minister' or *angelos* 'angel'. Although the presence of Greek loanwords in the Bible is not surprising given that the text was translated into Coptic from the Greek, it is generally agreed that the Coptic version of the Apophthegmata Patrum was also translated from Greek (Chaîne 1960: VIII), so the Greek origin in itself does not account for this disparity. However, if we consider the subject matter of the texts, the difference makes more sense, because the Apophthegmata Patrum text recounts sayings and stories of Coptic hermits from the Egyptian desert and contains many conversations in

---

12. I would like to thank Carolin Odebrecht, who has suggested to me the term 'annotation-assisted close reading' for the use of visualizations of this kind. This term aptly describes situations where we are interested in reading the running text while being made aware of the presence of certain annotations.

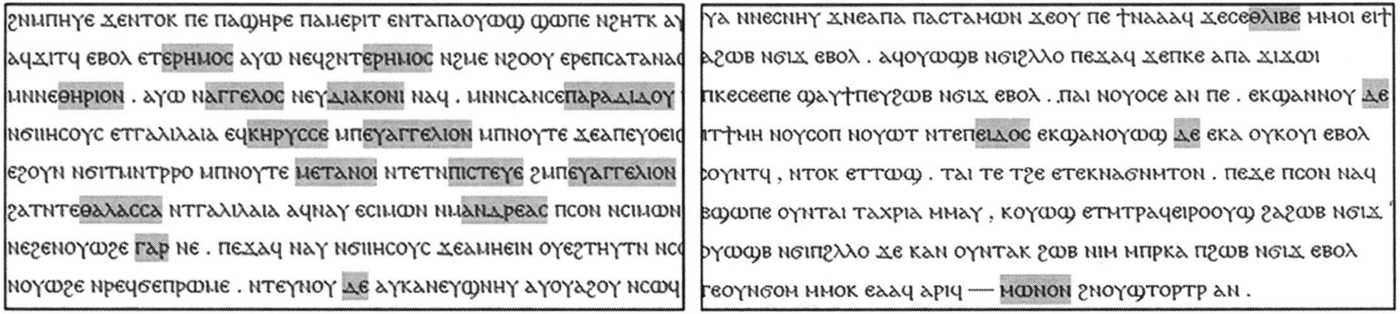

Figure 7.5 Greek words highlighted in Coptic Scriptorium corpus data. Left: Gospel of Mark 1; right: Apophthegmata Patrum 27

direct speech between Coptic figures. As a result it is a less 'foreign' text, and may be using more day-to-day Coptic words than the non-indigenous narrative in the Gospel of Mark.

The impression gained from comparing the text excerpts in Figure 7.3 can be confirmed quantitatively by checking for the frequencies and part of speech tags of foreign words in the Gospel of Mark and the Apophthegmata Patrum. These are presented in Table 7.4, and complemented by numbers for a sermon by Shenoute of Atripe, titled *I See Your Eagerness*, an untranslated native Coptic text. For each text, four columns give the number of loans in that row's part of speech tag, the percentage of all words in the text that this amounts to (first % column), then the total number of words carrying that tag in that text and the percentage of those instances which are loans (second % column).

The data in the table do suggest loanwords are more frequent in the Gospel of Mark, at a total of 7.94% versus 6.06% in the Apophthegmata Patrum (AP) and almost identical 6.07 in the native sermon. The difference is fairly small but highly significant due to the deviation in Mark (χ^2 = 59.185, p < 0.0001). However, the more interesting differences can be seen by looking at the individual POS tags, which reveal stark contrasts in the first % column (% loans out of all words): 3.33% of all words in Shenoute's sermon are loan nouns, compared to 2.82% in Mark and 2.61% in the AP, suggesting that at least for nouns, Mark is situated between the two texts. Conversely, Mark has the highest rate of foreign particles (PTC, 1.94%) compared to the AP (1.66%) and Shenoute (0.67%). The reason for these fluctuations is in large part due to the different text types being examined: Whereas Mark and the AP are narrative texts, Shenoute's sermon is in large part a first-person monologue with much less narration. Greek particles such as the frequent *de* 'but, and' are more typical to narrative texts, leading to the discrepancy. It is therefore more appropriate to examine the proportion of loanwords within each category, regardless of that category's frequency.

The last % column (percentage of loans within the POS tag category) for each text shows that the ratio of loans within nouns is similar, though AP is slightly behind the other two texts (19% versus around 23% of nouns). A bigger difference can be found for foreign verbs, which are typologically 'harder' to integrate (see Grossman 2014 on integration of Greek loan verbs in Coptic). Here we see that about 8% of verbs are loans in both translated texts, but only 4% in the native sermon by Shenoute. Other striking differences involve proper names (NPROP) and conjunctions (CONJ). Whereas Biblical texts and the sermon are rife with foreign names, the AP contain more native Coptic names, because although the characters discussed often had Greek names, some names were of non-foreign origin. The Bible and sermon alike mention primarily Biblical figures bearing foreign names. The cause for the inflation in 'foreign' conjunctions in the sermon, by contrast, is less linguistically meaningful and

Table 7.4 Prevalence of loanwords for major tags in three Coptic corpora

Tag	Shenoute (N = 16,634)				Mark (N = 19,941)				AP (N = 7,161)			
	Loans	%	Tag	%	Loans	%	Tag	%	Loans	%	Tag	%
N	554	3.33	2415	22.94	563	2.82	2446	23.02	187	2.61	976	19.16
PTC	112	0.67	152	73.68	387	1.94	511	75.73	119	1.66	212	56.13
NPROP	74	0.44	80	92.50	302	1.51	307	98.37	28	0.39	55	50.91
V	59	0.35	1415	4.17	191	0.96	2289	8.34	59	0.82	730	8.08
ADV	16	0.10	436	3.67	26	0.13	535	4.86	7	0.10	172	4.07
PREP	19	0.11	2526	0.75	12	0.06	2885	0.42	7	0.10	1007	0.70
CONJ	176	1.06	750	23.47	103	0.52	1089	9.46	27	0.38	321	8.41
total	1010	6.07	7774	12.99	1584	7.94	10062	15.74	434	6.06	3473	12.49

has primarily to do with Shenoute's use of *ē* 'or' in presenting alternatives to his audience. Coincidentally, the Coptic word for 'and', which is frequent in narratives, is not a loan, whereas 'or', which is almost completely absent from narratives, is of Greek origin. However, this word was so integrated that it does not really stand in contrast to a native alternative. As a result, and bearing in mind that much more could be said about the distribution of loanwords across Coptic text types, the finding for CONJ tentatively reflects a difference in communicative purposes which leads to a contrast between disjunctions and coordinations in the genres examined here.

The results in this section highlight the versatile applications of multilayer historical corpora for paleographic and linguistic research, enabling flexible visualizations for the examination of manuscript materials and distant reading of linguistic categories. The same underlying data model can be used to produce different views of the data, which can be mapped for example to HTML, allowing us to reuse the same corpora for different purposes. The last example also showed the relevance of considering metadata categories, such as text types of genres and translated vs. original texts, in the analysis of the results, as well as the crucial importance of examining the individual texts, sentences and words in the interpretation of quantitative results. In the next section, we will examine a multilayer built to examine language and genre change across time.

The Language of German Science in RIDGES

The multilayer RIDGES Herbology corpus was created in the RIDGES project (Register in Diachronic German Science, see https://korpling.org/ridges) as a class-sourced corpus of historical German documents tracing the development of German as an autonomous language of science (Odebrecht et al. 2017; see also Section 3.1 on class-sourcing). Although German was written throughout the second millennium CE, early scientific writing in Germany was carried out primarily in Latin, which only gradually gave way to native scientific texts being written in German, starting in the late Middle Ages (see Klein 1999; Pörksen 2003). In order to follow the development of German scientific language, the RIDGES corpus focuses on a specific field of science which was chosen for its relative stability over time, specifically botanical texts. Many scientific fields experienced very strong changes in focus and nature over time, such as astronomy, which begins with astrological works, and gradually changes into what we would consider to be studies in astronomy. Botanical texts, by contrast, are focused on the description of plants and their (often medicinal) properties relatively early on. Although there is still considerable variation in the purposes of texts (focus on alchemical versus medical use, practical cooking instructions and later more narrowly scientific and theoretical texts), the subject matter is more comparable across time than in many other disciplines, and the corpus is therefore more readily suitable for language-change studies.

The multilayer architecture of RIDGES covers a wide range of linguistic and structural phenomena relating to the types of texts included in the corpus (as of Version 7.0, which is described here). The corpus was designed to include documents coming from 30 year 'bins' starting from the 1480s and reaching into the twentieth century, with the earliest and latest texts currently coming from 1482 and 1914, respectively. The entire corpus contains 58 text excerpts, covering over 257,000 tokens, all of which come from early German prints made available via Google books and transcribed or corrected manually from OCRed images by students at Humboldt University in Berlin. Annotation layers include both properties of print layouts using TEI XML (similar to GUM annotations discussed in Section 3.2) and linguistic annotations such as POS tagging (again using the German STTS tag set), morphological annotations (e.g. case, number, gender, person and tense; not available for all texts), two layers of normalization (see below), automatic constituent and dependency parses (currently only for a subset of texts), language of origin annotations (especially for Latin vs. German), a manual analysis of compound types and verb placement for much of the corpus and some content annotations regarding the style and referentiality of terms in the texts. The latter set of annotations includes explicit markup of references to the author (i.e. self-references) and to the reader (addressee annotations), as well as an annotation scheme for terminology covering plants, health conditions (diseases, etc.) and other technical terms. Figure 7.6 shows part of the annotation layers in RIDGES.

As we can see at the top of Figure 7.6, the layers 'norm', 'clean' and 'dipl' are distinct versions of the same text, with 'dipl' representing the original print most faithfully, much like the Coptic Scriptorium 'orig' layer in the previous section. This layer includes older German characters which were also in use for English at one point, such as the long 's' written as <ſ> in *weiſe* 'wise', as well as a faithful division of segments based on the page layout, with the word *vnₐwiſſenheit* 'lack of knowledge' split into two due to its position across a line break. The word was hyphenated in the original using a double diagonal hyphen, which is represented using the appropriate Unicode character. The layer 'clean' replaces archaic or variant characters such as the tall 's' with modern equivalents, and groups segments based on modern orthographic word division, including the removal of the word internal line break division. This allows for a more predictable search behavior, again similarly to the normalization in the Coptic corpora in the previous section.

However, RIDGES contains a further layer of normalization beyond the two-tiered approach found in the previous section, which normalizes characters that would be admissible in Modern German, but are not in fact used to spell the relevant words. For example, in Figure 7.6, the word

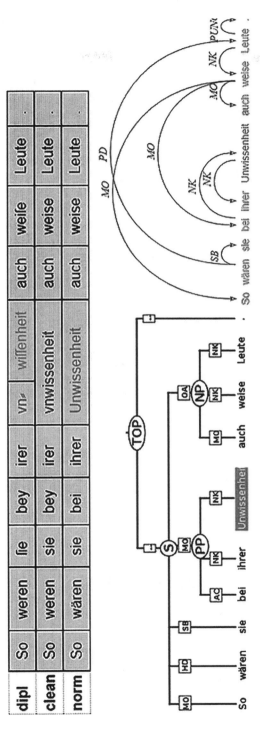

Figure 7.6 Excerpt of annotation layers in the RIDGES corpus for the sentence: *So wären sie bei ihrer Unwissenheit auch weise Leute* "Thus they would also be wise people in their lack of knowledge"

normalized as *Unwissenheit* 'lack of knowledge', is spelled in the original in lowercase and with the character for 'v', not 'u'. Whereas the 'clean' layer retains the 'v' (because it is a valid Modern German character), users searching for the equivalent Modern German word (or morphological categories, such as negation with *un-*) would not be able to guess the spelling used here. As we will see later, examining the text through the 'norm' versus 'clean' layers leads to some different results.

Finally we note that the syntax trees used in the corpus, shown at the bottom of Figure 7.6, both use the 'norm' layer to represent their terminal nodes, even though there are in fact more granular tokens in the data model (e.g. the position corresponding only to the prefix *vnʒ* 'un-' in the layer 'dipl'). The reason for this is twofold: From a user-oriented perspective, it is likely that syntax tree searches will be performed on the normalized text (e.g. searches for predicates of the normalized verb *wären* 'would be', not just its variant spelling here, *weren*). From a technical point of view, the norm layer is also used as the basis for obtaining automatic parses of the data, because parsers will perform better on data closely matching the Modern German orthography used in their training data. As a result, normalization is performed on the RIDGES data first, before applying automatic parsers to the normalized text and merging the results using the tools described in Section 3.4.

To see how normalized and cleaned text differ across the corpus, we can examine the development of standardization as a function of time. Because, unlike the learner corpora in Section 7.2, RIDGES contains no target hypotheses in terms of grammatical or other word order deviations, we are primarily looking at orthography. However, the layers 'clean' and 'norm' differ in this respect: Whereas 'clean' removes variation in terms of the characters chosen to represent the language, 'norm' also removes morphological forms that are non-standard in Modern German. This also means that regional or dialectal forms preserved in 'clean' will be effaced in 'norm'. Example (126) illustrates a case with such as difference.

(126)   dipl: *daſz ſolche Deutſche werck*
        clean: *dasz solche Deutsche werck*
        norm: *dass solche deutschen Werke*
        'that such German works' (Alchymistische Practic, Libavius, 1603)

In this example, the 'clean' layer only replaces cases of long 's' with the standard modern 's'. In particular, the regional lack of final 'n' in the definite plural adjectival declension of *Deutsche* 'German (pl.)' is not normalized, whereas in 'norm' we have the form with final 'n'. Similarly, the non-standard zero-plural for *Werk* 'work' is left intact in 'clean' but standardized in 'norm'. To examine how normalization progresses with time in the corpus, Figure 7.7 plots the proportion of cases in which

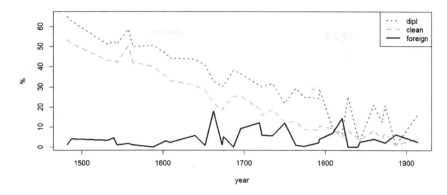

Figure 7.7 Normalization proportion and foreign words over time in the RIDGES corpus, showing two kinds of normalization

'norm' differs from 'dipl' and from 'clean' in two separate lines.[13] In a first attempt to plot these data, it was noticed that some of the texts that appear to have lower-than-expected rates of normalization also contain large amounts of Latin words, which generally do not require normalization. Data for the figure therefore remove these tokens and refer only to native German words, using the language of origin annotation layer. At the same time, it can still be noticed that texts using large amounts of Latin still require less normalization than neighboring texts, as shown by comparing the top two normalization curves with the 'foreign' curve at the bottom of the plot.

As is turns out, texts rich in Latin vocabulary (and occasionally other foreign languages) contain more standardized spelling overall, leading to noticeable spikes in the 'foreign' line towards the second half of the seventeenth century and early in the eighteenth century. Remarkably, the same positions are associated with comparably low rates of normalization, seen in the dells in the corresponding regions of the top lines. Although this suggests that those Latin-leaning texts are at least somewhat more standard than their contemporaries, the tendency is not significant overall; the correlation is somewhat apparent (Pearson's r = −0.2236), but not significant, due to many other texts violating the apparent relationship.

Looking at the differences between 'clean' and 'dipl' we notice, unsurprisingly, that the rate of normalization from 'clean' drops off earlier than 'dipl' as German orthography is standardized. This is because the inventory of characters used to print German texts is reduced over time,

---

13. This is, of course, a very coarse analysis: Ideally, we would like to analyze differences qualitatively, categorize them and examine the results quantitatively as well. This goal is outside the scope of the present chapter, but see Odebrecht et al. (2017).

stabilizing towards the latter half of the nineteenth century. Virtually all texts up to the 1820s require some 10% more token adjustments than the amount required for the transition from 'clean' to 'norm' (i.e. the gap between the 'orig' and 'dipl' curves is constant). In the latter part of the nineteenth century, the gap oscillates, with some texts using completely standard modern characters and some still showing older glyphs. The 'clean' curve itself reduces from over 50% at the beginning of the corpus, indicating strong spelling variation (e.g. contextual spelling of 'u' and 'v' in common words such as *und* 'and'), down to less than 20% in the eighteenth century and below 10% in the nineteenth century. This development folds in several parallel strands of standardization, including narrowly linguistic phenomena, such morphological and other superregional developments, and more purely orthographic ones, such as the standardization of capitalization rules for nouns in German (see Nerius 2003).

Although the amount of normalization seen in the normalization layers in the corpus gives an idea as to the extent and velocity of standardization processes, it does not reveal any specific characteristics of the relevant periods found in the data. To extract distinctive features of each period, we can segment the data into subcorpora – for example, by century – and use text classification methods to find features that distinguish one period from another. However, it should be noted from the outset that any discrete model binning texts into units such as centuries uses an arbitrary cutoff point for membership in one class or the other: The border between 1699 and 1700 is not more meaningful or interesting than the one between 1698 and 1699. The reason for using such bins is therefore a convenience that is only justified in so far as it allows the use of otherwise unavailable statistical methods which are limited by the small dataset at hand: We have only a sparse attestation of texts, which are thematically close but still quite distinct, and examining them each individually will lead to recognizing primarily idiosyncratic, content-related features. As a result, it is easy to overfit a classifier by allowing an algorithm to memorize which predictors or interacting sets of predictors uniquely identify the documents in our dataset. Using training and unseen test dataset splits similar to the ones in Section 4.3 is less feasible here, because we have little data to work with. If a classifier is given access to all lexical types in small bins (or even per-text bins), it will quickly pick out those words which appear specifically in training documents from each bin, without those terms necessarily appearing in other documents or in the test set at all.

A good baseline for text classification given a discrete multinomial response variable, such as 'century', is the Naïve Bayes classifier used for a variety of linear prediction tasks based on lexical frequencies in natural language processing. Given a sparse matrix of term frequencies for each text and all terms in a corpus (including potentially many zeros for each particular text), the classifier can learn the individual conditional probabilities linking each term with a possible classification, without risking overfitting the data by memorizing specific combinations of terms. At the same time, given the relatively small training corpus available to us, it is essential to rule out items uniquely identifying specific texts. To ensure this, we extract only features which are attested non-sparsely; for this purpose we set a minimum amount of documents that a term must appear in in order to be considered, and a minimum total frequency, so as to avoid rare items, which are usually content specific. The document count threshold is set somewhat arbitrarily to 3 and up (no less than a third of the documents in any century), and the term count threshold is set to 15, effectively restricting the list of lexical items considered to a little under the 500 most frequent types. Because we have only small amounts of data at the 'tail-end' centuries, we will restrict the eligible data to texts from the sixteenth through the nineteenth centuries, for which we have more dense attestation.

As predictive features it could potentially be useful to consider all words, part-of-speech sequences and annotations in the data. However, in order to combat data sparseness, we will attempt to use representations of the data which are ideally more dense than the surface forms in 'dipl' or 'clean'; in fact, using these will lead to overfitting because archaic spellings are easy to spot and the model will exploit them at the expense of linguistically more interesting categories. Instead, we can use the 'norm' and 'lemma' annotations, which are naturally less sparse and more evenly distributed. Next to the lemmas, we select POS tag bigrams as a more grammatical feature level, because longer n-grams would be too sparse for this corpus.[14] Finally, we also consider the author and reader reference annotations, which have only a few feature values encoding lexical NPs or different types of pronouns referring to the reader or author of the text. These are fairly densely attested and can therefore be used directly. The total number of features, including normalized and lemma forms, POS bigrams and referentiality annotations, amounts to 1,462.

The Naïve Bayes classifier is trained using the Python implementation in the sklearn library (Pedregosa et al. 2011) and achieves a fit of 96% (predicting the same data it was trained on) and unseen classification accuracy of 71.8%, obtained by leaving out each text in the training data

---

14. In a larger corpus, trigrams would probably deliver more interesting results, because they can capture more intricate constructions. The same reasoning can be applied to syntax trees, in which features such as dependency subgraph types can be used in lieu of, or next to, POS tag n-grams for large enough corpora. A caveat in all of these cases is that, at least for an automatically tagged dataset such as RIDGES, errors generated by NLP tools are more likely than usual due to the non-standard language and its deviations from the standard data used to train those tools.

Table 7.5 Most distinctive lemma, norm, POS-bigram and referential features by
century in RIDGES

	1500s	z	1600s	z	1700s	z	1800s	z
	Feature	*z*	*Feature*	*z*	*Feature*	*z*	*Feature*	*z*
lem	heißen 'called'	1.72	Nutzen 'use'	1.72	ohne 'without'	1.66	kurz 'short'	1.73
norm	darin 'therein'	1.73	werden 'become'	1.72	unten 'below'	1.71	länglich 'elongated'	1.73
POS	NE_ VAFIN	1.72	ADJA_ VVPP	1.72	PIS_ APPRART	1.67	PRELS_ PPER	1.72
ref	read_ pron3sg	1.65	read_ pron2pl	1.62	auth_ pron1sg	1.48	auth_ pron1pl	1.05

and predicting its class using the other texts for training.[15] Table 7.5 gives
the top lexical features (from 'norm' and 'lemma'), top POS-based feature, and most striking referentiality-based feature for each century based
on the classifier's estimates. Because the estimates are scaled to the frequencies of each feature across the centuries, we rank them not by absolute values but by z-scores, effectively selecting for each century those
features for which it is the strongest outlier. Note that because we are
not measuring z-scores from document frequencies but from the classifier's estimates (four data points per feature, one for each century), values
should not be interpreted as implying p-values (an 'outlier' in a sample of
four points is unlikely to be highly significant).

Although the results in the table are not immediately interpretable
without reference to the underlying data, they can reveal trends in each
sub-corpus when coupled with some qualitative inspection. The first thing
to notice is that none of the items in the table are precluded or ungrammatical in any century: The lexical items are all in use throughout Early
Modern High German, and the POS tag bigrams correspond to sequences
found in German texts to this day. This is because categorical changes
in German over the past few centuries are few: Much like most Early
Modern English constructions are considered grammatical today, if sometimes sounding dated, so are changes in the German corpus data mainly
a matter of quantitative variation between competing constructions (cf.
Rissanen 2008). Furthermore, it is certainly possible that the use of a
single modern tag set, in this case STTS, obscures certain differences that
would otherwise be noticeable: By assuming a Modern High German

15. Note that although the gap between these two accuracy scores suggest substantial
overfitting, it is comparatively robust compared to a model with variable interactions: A
Random Forest classifier similar to the one in Section 4.3 easily achieves 100% accuracy
on the entire dataset, but only 65.6% cross-validation accuracy with the same features,
because it effectively encourages memorizing the data.

part of speech tag set, we are ignoring categorical differences that may be justified in a synchronic analysis of older language stages.[16]

Bearing this in mind, if we look at examples of the features of the earlier texts, we can note a connection for those differences that are nevertheless found by the model with primarily instructional communicative intent. The prevalence of third-person singular references to the reader in the 1500s comes from descriptions of a hypothetical patient, to whom instructions are addressed, as in (127), using a 'whom-so-ever' type construction, which can then be resumed with imperatives without explicit addressees, or with repeated references of the type 'he shall'. The form *darin* 'therein' most often refers to effects on pains or 'foulness' in certain organs ('the foulness therein', etc.), whereas the lemma 'called' is primarily used to introduce alternate popular names of medicinal herbs. The POS tag sequence NE + VAFIN, a proper noun followed by a finite auxiliary, is related to this and usually refers to the name of a herb and the copula verb, as in the bold tokens in (128), which again gives advice.

(127) *Wem die Lenden weh tun. Astreus. Nimm Meyenwurzel*
       'Whom the loins pain: Astreus. Take meyen-root.'
       (Artzney Buchlein Der Kreutter, Tallat, 1532)
(128) *Bolus **armenus**/NE **ist**/VAFIN gut den bösen Blattern und
       Geschwüren*
       'Bolus armenus is good for bad scabs and ulcers'
       (Artzney Buchlein Der Kreutter, Tallat, 1532)

The 1600s resemble the previous century, with vocabulary put to similar use: *werden* 'become' is the passive auxiliary, and stands in most often as the substitute of the more popular *heißen* 'be called' to name herbs in the combination *genannt werden* 'be called', as well as often next to the passive participle for 'distilled', shown in (129). This likely reflects the simple historical fact that distillation had become popular and widespread in the 1600s, after initially being introduced in Germany through the popular work *Liber de arte destillandi* (*The Book of the Art of Distillation*) by Hieronymus Braunschweig in the early 1500s. The same example also shows the construction in which an inflected, attributive adjective (ADJA), precedes the passive participle (VVPP), which is more usually preceded by a predicative adjective (ADJD). The construction most often uses a nominalized superlative, which must carry a case ending and therefore be tagged (ADJA), again for the purpose of recommending something, in (129), an optimal distillation technique. The word *Nutzen* 'use' describes medicinal uses of herbs. In contrast to the 1500s, the second-person plural

---

16. I thank Carolin Odebrecht for raising this point. A likely candidate for such differences may be found in participles, which in older texts serve a variety of functions more similar to modern finite verbs, but are all tagged in the same way as their morphologically identical modern counterparts.

address is more popular in our data, as in (130), rather than the more archaic 'whom-so-ever' style construction seen in (127).

(129)   *dadurch die Wasser . . . aufs **allersubtilste**/ADJA **destilliert**/VVPP* *werden*
'thereby the waters **become distilled** . . . to **the subtlest of all**'
(Alchymistische Practic, Libavius, 1603)

(130)   *Greift zu welchem ihr wollt*
'Take whichever you want'
(Schweizerischer Botanicus, von Roll, 1687)

In the latter two centuries, texts begin to resemble modern scientific writing more closely. The item *unten* 'below' in particular is well attested in all centuries in reference to bottom parts of plants, but now begins to appear frequently in a second meaning, referring to text further below, as in (131). This new construction, or at the very least usage profile or sense, therefore increases the frequency of this lexical item. The lemma 'without', which again appears frequently in all centuries, is perhaps more frequent in the 1700s due to more occurences of a concessive or antithetical discourse function (cf. Chapter 6 for RST analyses of this relation) – this is shown in (132), one of several examples using clausal 'without' to debate with other scholarly texts. Much like the 1800s, this century sees references to the author outweighing references to the reader, preferably in the first-person singular in the 1700s (133) and in the scientific authorial plural in the 1800s (131). The item 'short' in the 1800s also gains frequency in part due to abstract, text-organizing usages unattested earlier, such as in (134). The form *länglich* 'elongated', by contrast, seems to be a spurious result, which coincidentally appears with above-average frequency in three nineteenth-century texts, but without any apparent special or qualitatively different usage compared to previous centuries.

(131)   *wie **wir unten** (in Nr. 149, 451, 597) näher darlegen werden*
'as **we** will present **below** in more detail (in Nr. 149, 451, 597)'
(Deutsche Pflanzennamen, Grassmann, 1870)

(132)   *Wer es indes nur nehmen und sich aneignen will, **ohne** die ursprüngliche Quelle anzugeben, der greift mir ans Herz.*
'Meanwhile whoever wishes to only take and appropriate it to himself, **without** giving the original source, attacks my heart'.
(Flora 6, Wilbrand, 1821)

(133)   *so fand **ich** 6 bis 7 Unzen Wasser in der Vorlage*
'so **I** found 6 to 7 ounces of water in the model'
(FloraSaturnizans, Henckel, 1722)

(134)   *Wir stellen daher hier in **kurzem** Überblick die Grundsätze auf*
'We therefore present the foundations here in a **brief** overview'
(Deutsche Pflanzennamen, Grassmann, 1870)

These few but suggestive examples show the interplay between the contents and communicative purposes of different texts, as well as other diachronic changes in data from just one domain: botanical scientific texts. The discussion in this section is therefore limited in scope and cannot do justice to the complexity of the developments in the German language of science in the early modern period as a whole. However, by looking at differences in annotation value frequency distributions, it is possible to notice some interesting changes in the types of texts available in each period and the interactions between the lexical, grammatical and discourse levels of one kind of scientific texts across time, which is one part of a whole system of scientific writing that evolves for German in a range of domains during the latter half of the second millennium. Because many of the categories involved are attested to some extent in multiple, or even all periods of the corpus, the quantitative results exposed by multilayer annotations give the added value of being able to point out distinctive outliers in each period, which can be examined qualitatively and grouped with other conspicuous results to form a better understanding of the characteristics of each successive period. The same could potentially be done in comparison to the development of other domains and text types from the language in each successive period. However, in all cases, the nature of such a data-driven analysis by itself is always somewhat superficial, and ideally its results should serve as starting points for in-depth qualitative and quantitative study of specific phenomena.

7.4 Interim Conclusion

In this chapter, the multilayer approach was applied to resources with multiple layers of textual representation in an attempt to expose patterns in non-standard data from different points of view. For both historical and non-native texts, this inevitably involves a tension between maximally literal renditions of the source data and more standardized ones which allow for easier search and grouping of results, but at the cost of eliminating potentially important idiosyncrasies.

The examination of learner data showed the potential of multiple annotation paradigms in learner corpus research: Error annotations and target hypotheses offer complementary sources of evidence which can be used to study L2 grammar (see Lüdeling and Hirschmann 2015), the effects of corrective feedback and dynamic processes such as textual revision (Lee et al. 2015). Using target hypotheses, it is also possible to harness automatic NLP tools to enrich data which would otherwise not be amenable to automatic processing: By feeding a tagger or parser a corrected version of the text which more closely resembles its training data, corpora such as Falko are able to include target hypothesis POS tags and syntax trees. Using edit tags describing the differences between two layers, such as insertion, deletion and other edit tags between original texts and target hypotheses, such annotations can then also be projected back to the original text

(Reznicek et al. 2013). The same can be said to some extent of alignment across multiple revisions of a text, which enable the creation of automatic insertion and deletion tags for the study of correction behavior.

For historical data, we also saw the importance of using features from different lexical levels, as well as harnessing document structure annotations for research questions, such as supporting fragment identification or charting out standardization processes through time. Having simultaneous access to document structure and linguistic annotations allows us to visualize historical data with superimposed linguistic analyses for distant reading, looking at the distribution of Greek words in Coptic texts (see also Zeldes and Schroeder 2015) or Latin words in early scientific writing in German (Odebrecht et al. 2017). Part of the challenge is reconciling the original structure of documents while exposing standardized linguistic units for evaluation, using appropriately granular levels of word segmentation and normalization. In many cases, this means abandoning the equation of token units in the underlying corpus architecture and lexical word units on the linguistic level. Using a graph-based multilayer architecture, it is then possible to build subgraphs such as syntax trees on top of non-terminal word form units, which are themselves spans above multiple complex units (morphemes, or even arbitrary sets of characters annotated for their graphical appearance in a manuscript, see Krause et al. 2012). The same technical devices presented in Chapters 2–3 are therefore not only applicable to the representation of non-standard data, but also indispensable in order to create multipurpose and maximally reusable corpus resources that enable these types of applications.

8 Conclusion

This chapter takes stock of the main findings from the preceding chapters and discusses some consequences and remaining desiderata. Section 8.1 condenses the main results from each chapter and serves as an executive summary of the main ideas in this book. Section 8.2 presents some of the implications and application of multilayer corpora for usage-based paradigms in linguistic theory and makes the case for the use of such data in probabilistic models of high-level language phenomena. Section 8.3 discusses some of the lessons learned from the datasets used in this book and reiterates the importance of making reusable corpus data, both in the creation of new corpora and in the expansion of existing ones. Section 8.4 concludes with a discussion of the place of richly annotated data looking forward, in particular with Deep Learning approaches in mind, which are increasingly focusing on more shallowly annotated corpora of Big Data.

8.1 Summary

The two parts of the present volume present a methodological paradigm within corpus linguistics which promotes the encoding of many independent, and potentially conflicting, analyses of the same running texts. In the first part of the book, some of the main notions were laid out which separate multilayer corpora from other types of corpus work in general, and multifactorial approaches to language in particular. On the one hand, the notion of conceptual independence of multiple analyses was presented as a distinctive characteristic of multilayer resources, which can be expanded by different researchers at different times and merged together to obtain results that each single analysis would not be able to produce. On the other hand, the focus on complete annotated corpora was contrasted with the rich annotation of a very narrow subset of results in a targeted multifactorial study, such as annotating a table of instances of a specific construction taken from a larger corpus and subjecting only these to analysis.

Although targeted datasets of this type can be extremely valuable, the advantages of running corpora annotated completely for categories we assume to be omnipresent (e.g. information structure, discourse function, etc.) become clear, especially in domains such as those studied in the second half of this book, such as the introduction and identification of discourse referents, or the study of discourse markers used to signal relations between utterances. The multilayer paradigm allows studies targeting complex alternations involving broad categories, for example, the ordering of referential NPs, or pronoun choice, or even ubiquitous types of errors in learner language, or changes in frequencies of constructions across time in historical corpora.

The survey of corpora in Section 1.4 makes it clear that multilayer resources vary widely in the types of texts covered, the annotations chosen and the development history of each one, as some projects create richly annotated data from the outset, whereas others emerge organically through iterative addition of analyses, often by different teams at different times. Chapter 2 gave an overview of data models capable of representing the different types of information available in such corpora and made the case for the use of graph-based models which clearly separate primary textual data (whose original, white space–preserving form should ideally be retained), tokens or even multiple tokenizations and a web of annotated and interconnected non-terminal nodes as required, all the way to document nodes forming a graph of subcorpora and metadata annotations. Several ontological types of nodes and relations between nodes were distinguished based on some existing data models, such as hierarchical or flat span nodes, as well as dominance relations and non-dominant pointing relations. These were subsequently used to encode different data structures used in the corpora that were analyzed in the chapters of Part II of this book.

Chapter 3 took the abstract concepts from Chapter 2 and discussed specific formats, data types and tools used to create and annotate multilayer corpora. Much of the chapter focused on a case study using a class-sourced corpus called GUM, collected and annotated by students on very many levels as part of the curriculum at Georgetown University (see Section 3.2). The discussion then moved on to technical issues in the preparation of such datasets, including the merging and validation of information from different source formats and tools (Section 3.4) and search and visualization for multilayer corpora, primarily using the ANNIS search engine (Section 3.5). ANNIS and the SaltNPepper converter framework described in this chapter were instrumental in assembling and using the corpora queried in the chapters of Part II.

The second part of the book explored multilayer corpora in four chapters, moving between different research questions, levels of linguistic representation and types of data. Chapters 4–6 looked mainly at standard contemporary English data and were concerned with a variety of discourse phenomena, including contextual effects on word order and morphological agreement, entity models and referentiality and formal analyses of discourse structure. Chapter 4 began with a discussion of the research program of Probabilistic Syntax (Manning 2003), which casts predictive modeling as a main goal of linguistics. Given a context and a meaning to express in language production, we wish to be able to predict the specific lexical realization (or at the very least select or rank the most likely ones) that speakers of a language will prefer. In language understanding, we wish to model the cues in specific linguistic utterances in specific contexts which give rise to the meanings which hearers perceive. Modeling these types of probabilities is at the heart of all multifactorial work, and for several areas of corpus-based studies of discourse processes, a multilayer corpus allows us to identify categories that are predictive of such processes in a way that goes beyond linear correlations with individual predictors. In Section 4.2, multilayer data were used to compare the relative impact of information structure, phrase length, grammatical function and voice on word order in all sentences in a corpus, using linear mixed-effects models. Section 4.3 then applied non-linear decision tree ensemble techniques to the prediction of a highly complex and seemingly unpredictable alternation between singular and plural pronoun anaphors for so-called 'committee nouns' (e.g. "the committee says/say that it/ they"). The results made it clear that many interacting factors influence variation, both in word order and pronoun choice, and that an overall model of the behavior of the categories in question can only be developed using richly annotated data.

Chapter 5 shifted the discussion to the area of entities and their semantic properties. By studying the distribution of entity terms, and especially singletons (items mentioned only once) and repeated mentions, it became possible to identify typical occurrence and recurrence patterns for entity mentions, but also genre-specific effects which distinguish news narratives from more conversational, informative and instructional texts. These patterns can be observed through quantitative analysis and regression modeling by plotting aggregate corpus annotation data and by visualizing whole documents and using distance reading techniques, which give an intuitive idea of differences in the distributions of coreferent entity mentions. The chapter's ultimate goal was to characterize the properties of repeatedly mentioned entity terms, as opposed to singletons, by constructing a multifactorial model predicting anaphoricity. Such a model has not only practical applications to steer candidate selection for coreference resolution systems, but also theoretical value in clarifying how language-specific, and to some extent genre-specific, cues signal to hearers/readers that speakers/writers presuppose entities in the common ground which can anchor newly introduced referring expressions. These signals turn out to involve a wide range of annotation layers, which can be used to construct a profile of 'antecedent marking' expressions (NPs likely to be second or later mentions) versus new or even unique mentions in a given document.

In Chapter 6, the same multilayer corpus was re-examined from the point of view of discourse annotation graphs in the framework of Rhetorical Structure Theory. Using aggregate metrics and distant reading techniques, it was again possible to identify far-reaching differences which can be attributed to genre variation. A qualitative analysis of these results strongly suggested that a large part of the differences observed could be attributed to the typical communicative intent associated with different text types, which is reflected directly in the functional analysis of relations between discourse units. Two detailed multifactorial studies then showed the importance and some of the limitations of multilayer data: Again using ensemble methods, it was possible to create quantitative 'heat maps' of areas of discourse accessibility which predicted the level of entity-based coherence between discourse units. This study refined previous work in the area of Domains of Referential Accessibility (DRAs), and notably some categorical predictions on possible domains for anaphora in Veins Theory (Cristea et al. 1998). Then in Section 6.4, it was shown that using discourse parses alone to identify terms that serve as discourse markers or relation signals is insufficient due to the high level of ambiguity and context sensitivity with which some words occasionally do or do not serve as meaningful cues. Here we opted for the use of Recurrent Neural Networks which use distributional meaning representations of words, as well as character n-grams and part-of-speech annotations to feed a memory-based model which can learn to identify discourse markers in context. In this case, the relationship between corpus annotations and the target phenomenon of relation signals required access to distributional properties of individual words above and beyond explicit annotations.

Chapter 7 concluded the case studies in Part II by looking at two areas with similar challenges but rather different types of text: non-native data and historical data, both of which require us to confront an original text separately from a normalized notion of what a standard version of the same content might look like. Section 7.2 first approached a quantitative study of advanced L2 German compound formation, showing that learners underuse compounds and sometimes use different kinds of erroneous compounds or simple nouns where native speakers might have used compounding. This was made possible by the existence of multiple target hypothesis layers aligned to the original learner data. In a second study, textual revisions from learners of English were examined, which offer a series of texts from each individual which are progressively nearer to the standard. Using automatic alignment between earlier and later revised versions of the same texts, as well as English tutors' feedback and error tags at each step, the multilayer corpus allowed us to examine the effects of corrective feedback on revision behavior. In Section 7.3, two studies of historical corpora showed the use of multilayer architectures to represent manuscript-near text next to linguistically more accessibly normalized versions. In a study of Coptic corpora, it was possible to use manuscript layout information to recognize scribal errors and attempt to identify manuscript fragments by finding similar positions in annotated corpus data. Using normalized and tagged text with language of origin labels, we also looked at the distributions of loanwords in different part of speech categories in several autochthonous and translated Coptic literary text types. The final section of the chapter used a diachronic corpus of the development of German as a language of science, focusing on language change and standardization in botanical texts from the fifteenth to the early twentieth centuries. By comparing normalized texts to two layers of more or less standardized grammar and orthography, the trajectory of standardization could be traced. Then using a Naïve Bayes classifier, pertinent lexical items, lemmas, POS tag bigrams and referential annotations were extracted for separate centuries, opening a quantitative window to differences most characteristic of each period with categories that are well attested throughout the entire corpus, rather than being swayed by rare items with particular associations to particular texts. Although the studies in this chapter addressed rather different questions than the preceding studies, they used much of the same underlying architecture and methods introduced in Part I, showing the breadth of applications that multilayer corpora can contribute to.

8.2 Probabilistic Usage-Based Models

Much of the theoretical framework and many of the underlying assumptions in this book are couched in the tradition of usage-based models of grammatical description. An in-depth discussion of the properties of such models is beyond the scope of this book, and it is hoped that most of the studies in the previous chapters should be valuable to researchers, regardless of their theoretical framework. However, several important features of the usage-based and especially probabilistic point of view mentioned earlier should be addressed in the context of the growing trend toward multilayer corpus work. Most usage-based models, and in particular work within different frameworks falling under the broad umbrella of construction grammar or constructivist approaches (e.g. Fillmore 1979; Croft 2001; Goldberg 2006), assume that speakers store information about usage and frequencies in their mental lexicon alongside phonological, morphological and grammatical information (part of speech and more fine-grained categories, associated argument structures). The quantitative aspects of this usage information have often been discussed in terms of 'entrenchment' brought on by repeated exposure to language usage (cf. Langacker 1987; Bybee 2006), and more recently have led to controversial discussions regarding the role of entrenchment in steering language acquisition and preventing overgeneralization errors (e.g. 'negative entrenchment', Stefanowitsch 2008, preemption, Boyd and Goldberg 2011; see Ambridge et al. 2012; Yang 2015 and Goldberg and Boyd 2015 for discussion). Much of the evidence discussed in the articles cited above is experimental, and many of the categories involved are fairly 'close to the text', involving phonological and morphological distinctions, but with less reference to discourse-level cues. Here I would like to suggest that much work remains to be done in connecting research on constructional alternatives, entrenchment and preemption which integrates higher-level information across utterances and the persistence of entities in memory, for which corpus and experimental evidence can converge and complement each other (see e.g. Spalek and Zeldes 2017 on converging evidence for reflexes of Alternative Semantics across sentences).

A second important property of many usage-based models in the context of multilayer corpora is the postulation of constructions as arbitrary form–meaning pairings, including fully lexicalized, partially lexically specified (with open 'slots') or fully abstract constructions, such as unfilled argument structure constructions (e.g. 'caused motion'). To some extent, we can view consistently recurring combinations of annotations on multiple layers as evidence of a possibly entrenched construction. For example, some typical types of 'obvious' singleton mentions in coreference chains (Chapter 5) or typical discourse graphs serving a specific function (advice and concession, 'staircase' elaborations, etc., Chapter 6) are perhaps discourse-level constructions with partially unpredictable semantic and distributional properties. But much rather than approaching the search for constructions purely exploratively, one gap that could be filled using multilayer corpus architecture is the lack of a corpus annotated introspectively for the presence of constructions. Even if only a small, ideally manageable subset of constructions could be handled in an annotation scheme at first, coupling such a form of annotation with existing treebank-style layers and other morphological, syntactic, semantic and discourse annotations could make a contribution to usage-based grammar theory building in a very tangible way.

Finally, much work remains to be done in using multilayer corpora to answer questions regarding the architecture of the language faculty (see e.g. Jackendoff 1997) in terms of interfaces, modularity and compositionality. Most usage-based approaches are monostratal, non-derivational and non-modular (see Fischer and Stefanowitsch 2006: 3) and admit an infinite depth of interactions in principle. Multilayer corpora embody many of the analytical tools that fit within such a framework. For example, postulating separate layers of representation for information structure, illocutionary force and other categories can alleviate much of the complexity integrated into syntax trees in cartographic approaches (Rizzi 1997) which assume empty categories and functional projections representing, for example, topic, focus, etc. Similar notions of concurrent layers have been gaining prominence in multidimensional approaches to semantics in discourse (see Marx and Venema 1997; Petukhova and Bunt 2009) and discourse representation approaches such as Layered Discourse Representation Theory (LDRT, Geurts and Maier 2013). In the context of predictive models, the independence of layers encoding such information (cf. Section 1.3) can significantly improve our ability to use modeling tools and achieve higher accuracy using more orthogonal cues. All of these converging properties of multilayer corpora and usage-based approaches make the case for the application of the architectures and methods explored in this book for the development of predictive approaches to high-level phenomena which are not yet well understood.

8.3 Reusability and Multilayer Corpora

As was pointed out in Section 1.4 and at several points over the course of this book, it is increasingly the case that existing corpus resources are reannotated in order to capitalize on the high level of investment in existing resources (and especially syntactically annotated treebanks) and benefit from the synergies of old and new annotations. This development, made possible by the growing landscape of sophisticated and open corpora, brings both opportunities and challenges. On the one hand, better resources are becoming available that can do 'more than the sum of their parts'. On the other hand, the pool of annotated texts and text types grows more slowly than it might otherwise, and improving existing resources becomes difficult due to errors carried over from existing projects. For example, if we find a tokenization error in a benchmark corpus we are extending with a new layer, we may hesitate to correct it for fear of falling out of sync with other projects using the same underlying data.

These considerations make openly available, well documented and version-controlled corpora more important than ever in the age of multilayer resources. Without open licenses, the ability to reannotate data is limited to a small set of researchers with institutional licenses or appropriate funding, and many of the most useful datasets are only available to commercial companies. Although it is clear that not every type of resource can be made available under an open license, it is crucial looking forward for researchers working on multilayer corpora to do whatever they can in order to make data accessible online. Version-control platforms such as GitHub (https://github.com/) have made it easier than ever to share data online, see how it has been altered and corrected and allow others to contribute to corpora. The GUM corpus introduced in Section 3.2, for example, is developed openly on GitHub, allowing users and contributors to open issues in an issue tracker when they encounter problems and to suggest error corrections, which are released periodically. Corpus practitioners often run into annotation errors in their daily work, but correcting them in a static, rarely updated corpus, such as the Penn Treebank, is much more difficult than for a corpus that is updated and re-versioned transparently online. It is my hope that this type of collaborative, open corpus development work will become more widespread in the near future.

A second issue revolves around explicit licensing: Many more corpora could be shared freely than are specifically made available under such licenses. I would like to stress that not licensing data explicitly is a lose-lose situation for all involved. Corpus creators who have a potentially open resource lose the benefit of external contributions to their project, whether through error corrections as mentioned earlier or the addition of completely new layers contributed by others. Corpus users can use data that they can obtain for their own research, but get into murky waters whenever they need to publish results or tools based on such data. This also works against the interests of corpus creators, whose resources end up being more obscure and less widely used or cited in the community as a result of the unclear status of the materials. It is therefore highly desirable to choose materials which can be made available under explicit licenses whenever research questions or applications allow this and to make the license itself explicit and clear.

The third and final point I wish to consider with future corpora in mind is the use of open, well-documented exchange formats, including official international standards and de facto community standards. Researchers working in a specific area usually know the formats that are accepted in their community, and in computational linguistics these are often the formats of shared tasks, such as datasets from the various CoNLL conferences (Conference on Computational Natural Language Learning). Different XML and tabular formats often express the same things in different ways, and it is important to understand which ones can represent what kinds of data structures (see Section 3.3). However, often it is possible to offer the same corpus data in multiple formats, thereby increasing its usefulness to a broader community and opening new opportunities for collaboration, which can result in more and better multilayer corpora. The GUM corpus, for example, is made available in a variety of formats, some of which only contain some of the annotation layers in the corpus. Many of the formats in which GUM is available via its GitHub repository are not actually in active use in the research group that generates GUM: They are made available as a service to the community, among other reasons because it is not difficult to do so. Using converter frameworks such as SaltNPepper (see Section 3.4) it is increasingly possible to automatically generate multiple output formats from a single underlying data representation, with little or no added effort for corpus creators. Doing so, and avoiding the invention of new formats if possible, is a goal that can be tricky to adhere to in practice but is worth keeping in mind as a best practice.

8.4   Rich Annotations in the Age of Deep Learning

A few final remarks are due with respect to the place of multilayer corpora within the growing subfield of Deep Learning in computational, and more recently also corpus linguistics, using neural networks such as the one introduced in Section 6.4. Much of the current work within the Deep Learning 'tsunami' (see Manning 2015) in NLP has capitalized on Big Data, often by using unannotated plain text as input to predict categories that are 'naturally occurring' or 'found' on the Internet, such as review ratings (e.g. Tang et al. 2015) or images with captions (Karpathy and Fei-Fei 2017). Creative uses of such existing datasets have pushed computational linguistics progress enormously in the past few years and have gone hand in hand with the creation of annotation tasks, interfaces and Games With A Purpose (e.g. 'referit', http://tamaraberg. com/referitgame/ for object labeling, see also Section 3.1). Lines of work in this vein work very well for many of the more semantic tasks in NLP, and there is no way that manually created multilayer corpora can serve the same purposes.

That said, I believe that expert and machine annotated multilayer datasets have many important roles to play in the age of Deep Learning, both in corpus linguistics and NLP. To begin with, many Big Data resources are parsed and tagged automatically for various categories using tools that are trained on smaller gold-standard corpora. Although tasks such as coreference resolution and discourse parsing are increasingly approached from 'plain text' (see Lee et al. 2017 and Braud et al. 2017, respectively), the target categories for these tasks are annotated fully manually and categorically and are not inferred from plain text corpora.[1] In many approaches, multilayer annotations are used to pre-train neural networks, including using data from multiple corpora. For example, in the 'multi-view/multi-task' approach to discourse parsing in Braud et al. (2016), coreference annotation and parse trees from OntoNotes (see Section 1.4) and discourse relations from PDTB (see Section 6.1) are used to train a network ultimately modeling RST relations from RST-DT (Section 6.1). Recent extensions of the work on relation identification presented in Section 6.4 (Zeldes 2018c) have also shown that supplementing word and character embeddings with further categorical annotations from a multilayer corpus improves the performance of neural networks on the task substantially.

But a more important issue from the perspective of corpus linguistics is that, even if we can use plain text to predict phenomena like pronoun realization (cf. Section 4.3), without categorically labeled multilayer data, we can't gain insight into the relationships between categorically different linguistic phenomena. For example, if we want to know how discourse structure constrains which areas of a text are accessible for pronominalization (see Section 6.3), then it's no use to look at plain text alone. Examining multiple layers of categorical information tells us more about

---

1. It can also be noted that virtually all NLP work using 'plain text' corpora relies on word embeddings, i.e. multidimensional vector space representations of word meaning based on neighboring word distributions in large corpora. The embeddings assigned to each word can themselves be seen as a form of automatic semantic annotation, different in scope but not in principle from existing semantic annotation schemes such as the UCREL Semantic Analysis System (USAS, Rayson et al. 2004). Some forms of embeddings even integrate annotation categories to assign distinct embedding outputs, e.g. Levy and Goldberg (2014).

how a discourse 'plan' is implemented, in the sense of a structured graph, and how constraints on the referential potential of entities are signaled in terms of sentence, entity and relation types. In other words, even if we could predict the response variable from text using sufficient amounts of data (and for this particular task NLP performance is not currently good enough to do so), this will not answer our research question any more than asking a human to successfully complete the task without understanding how she or he did it. The goal as stated inevitably requires a richly annotated corpus.

For purely task-driven NLP as well, it seems that many interesting categories, such as syntactic, semantic and discourse parsing, coreference, bridging and more, cannot be trained against purely 'found' datasets, and in some cases, cannot be crowd-sourced reliably, requiring the types of gold-standard, often richly annotated, treebanks used in this book. The same applies to evaluation: Knowing how well a system can predict any of these categories, even if more sparsely annotated training materials are used, ultimately relies on having gold-standard data. This means that existing Big Data resources often go hand in hand with smaller, richly annotated corpora for many practical purposes.

From the opposite point of view, I also believe that studies using small, richly annotated datasets have a lot to gain from incorporating both Deep Learning and Big Data resources into their methodology. For many interesting questions, especially in semantics and discourse studies, we assume that speakers' mental models incorporate vast amounts of world knowledge, presuppositions and common ground that are not mentioned as part of running corpus text. Giving our modeling tools access to parallel sources of data, including textual Big Data but potentially also images or video data from the Web, paired with image labels or closed captions, is a way of introducing some of that world knowledge into our explanatory process. The challenge as I see it is to retain the interpretability and separability of theoretically disjoint predictors and building models which give us new and generally applicable insights into how language works, rather than just raising accuracy metrics on a handful of available test sets. It is my hope that corpus linguistics research will take up these challenges in the near future and advance theories formalized in annotation schemes by illuminating their relationships with one another, and with the masses of data that are now available to us on the Web.

Bibliography

Adolphs, Svenja and Ronald Carter (2013), *Spoken Corpus Linguistics: From Monomodal to Multimodal* (Routledge Advances in Corpus Linguistics). London: Routledge.

Adolphs, Svenja and Dawn Knight (2010), Building a Spoken Corpus: What Are the Basics? In: Anne O'Keeffe and Michael McCarthy (eds.), *The Routledge Handbook of Corpus Linguistics*. London: Routledge, 38–52.

Afantenos, Stergos, Pascal Denis, Philippe Muller and Laurence Danlos (2010), Learning Recursive Segments for Discourse Parsing. In: *Proceedings of LREC 2010*. Valletta, Malta, 3578–3584.

Afantenos, Stergos, Eric Kow, Nicholas Asher and Jérémy Perret (2015), Discourse Parsing for Multi-Party Chat Dialogues. In: *Proceedings of EMNLP 2015*. Lisbon, Portugal, 928–937.

Aguilar-Guevara, Ana, Bert Le Bruyn and Joost Zwarts (eds.) (2014), *Weak Referentiality* (Linguistics Today 219). Amsterdam and Philadelphia, PA: John Benjamins.

Allwood, Jens (2008), Multimodal Corpora. In: Anke Lüdeling and Merja Kytö (eds.), *Corpus Linguistics: An International Handbook*. Vol. 1. Berlin: Mouton de Gruyter, 207–225.

Ambridge, Ben, Julian M. Pine, Caroline F. Rowland and Franklin Chang (2012), The Roles of Verb Semantics, Entrenchment, and Morphophonology in the Retreat From Dative Argument-Structure Overgeneralization Errors. *Language* 88(1), 45–81.

Anderson, Anne H., Miles Bader, Ellen Gurman Bard, Elizabeth Boyle, Gwyneth Doherty, Simon Garrod, Stephen Isard, Jacqueline Kowtko, Jan McAllister, Jim Miller, Catherine Sotillo, Henry Thompson and Regina Weinert (1991), The HCRC Map Task Corpus. *Language and Speech* 34, 351–366.

Annala, Henri (2008), *Changes in Subject-Verb Agreement With Collective Nouns in British English From the 18th Century to the Present Day*. PhD Thesis, University of Tampere.

Archer, Dawn, Merja Kytö, Alistair Baron and Paul Rayson (2015), Guidelines for Normalising Early Modern English Corpora: Decisions and Justifications. *ICAME Journal* 39, 5–24.

Ariel, Mira (1990), *Accessing Noun-Phrase Antecedents*. London: Routledge.

Artstein, Ron and Massimo Poesio (2006), Identifying Reference to Abstract Objects in Dialogue. In: *Proceedings of BRANDIAL 2006: The 10th Workshop on the Semantics and Pragmatics of Dialogue*. Potsdam, Germany, 56–63.

Asher, Nicholas (1993), *Reference to Abstract Objects in Discourse*. Dordrecht: Kluwer.

Asher, Nicholas and Alex Lascarides (1998), Bridging. *Journal of Semantics* 15(1), 83–113.

Asher, Nicholas and Alex Lascarides (2003), *Logics of Conversation* (Studies in Natural Language Processing). Cambridge: Cambridge University Press.

Ashwell, Tim (2000), Patterns of Teacher Response to Student Writing in a Multiple-draft Composition Classroom: Is Content Feedback Followed by Form Feedback the Best Method? *Journal of Second Language Writing* 9(3), 227–257.

Baayen, R. Harald (2001), *Word Frequency Distributions* (Text, Speech and Language Technologies 18). Dordrecht: Kluwer.

Baayen, R. Harald (2008), *Analyzing Linguistic Data: A Practical Introduction to Statistics Using R*. Cambridge: Cambridge University Press.

Bamman, David and Gregory Crane (2011), The Ancient Greek and Latin Dependency Treebanks. In: Caroline Sporleder, Antal van den Bosch and Kalliopi Zervanou (eds.), *Language Technology for Cultural Heritage*. Heidelberg: Springer, 79–98.

Bański, Piotr (2010), Why TEI Stand-off Annotation Doesn't Quite Work and Why You Might Want to Use It Nevertheless. In: *Proceedings of Balisage: The Markup Conference 2010* (Balisage Series on Markup Technologies 5). Montréal.

Bański, Piotr, Bertrand Gaiffe, Patrice Lopez, Simon Meoni, Laurent Romary, Thomas Schmidt, Peter Stadler and Andreas Witt (2016), Wake Up, Standoff! In: *Proceedings of the TEI Conference 2016*. Vienna, Austria.

Bański, Piotr and Andreas Witt (2011), Do Linguists Need a Corpus Query Lingua Franca? In: *ISO TC37 Meeting in Seoul, South Korea, 13 June 2011*. Seoul, South Korea.

Barðdal, Jóhanna (2008), *Productivity: Evidence From Case and Argument Structure in Icelandic* (Constructional Approaches to Language 8). Amsterdam and Philadelphia, PA: John Benjamins.

Barri, Nimrod (1977), *Clause-Models in Antiphontean Greek*. Munich: Wilhelm Fink.

Barsalou, Lawrence W. (1999), Perceptual Symbol Systems. *Behavioral and Brain Sciences* 22(4), 577–660.

Bateman, John, Jörg Kleinz, Thomas Kamps and Klaus Reichenberger (2001), Towards Constructive Text, Diagram, and Layout Generation for Information Presentation. *Computational Linguistics* 27(3), 409–449.

Baumann, Stefan and Arndt Riester (2012), Referential and Lexical Givenness: Semantic, Prosodic and Cognitive Aspects. In: Gorka Elordieta and Pilar Prieto (eds.), *Prosody and Meaning*. Berlin: Mouton de Gruyter, 119–161.

Beckman, Mary E., Julia Hirschberg and Stefanie Shattuck-Hufnagel (2005), The Original ToBI System and the Evolution of the ToBI Framework. In: Sun-Ah Jun (ed.), *Prosodic Typology: The Phonology of Intonation and Phrasing*. Oxford: Oxford University Press, 9–54.

Bejček, Eduard, Eva Hajičová, Jan Hajič, Pavlína Jínová, Václava Kettnerová, Veronika Kolářová, Marie Mikulová, Jiří Mírovský, Anna Nedoluzhko, Jarmila Panevová, Lucie Poláková, Magda Ševčíková, Jan Štěpánek and Šárka Zikánová (2013), *Prague Dependency Treebank 3.0*. Univerzita Karlova v Praze, MFF, ÚFAL, Technical Report, Prague, Czech Republic.

Biber, Douglas (1988), *Variation Across Speech and Writing*. Cambridge: Cambridge University Press.

Biber, Douglas (1993), Representativeness in Corpus Design. *Literary and Linguistic Computing* 8(4), 243–257.

Biber, Douglas (2009), Multi-Dimensional Approaches. In: Anke Lüdeling and Merja Kytö (eds.), *Corpus Linguistics: An International Handbook*. Vol. 2. Berlin: Mouton de Gruyter, 822–855.

Biber, Douglas and Susan Conrad (2009), *Register, Genre, and Style* (Cambridge Textbooks in Linguistics). Cambridge: Cambridge University Press.

Biber, Douglas, Stig Johansson, Geoffrey Leech, Susan Conrad, Edward Finegan and Graeme Hirst (1999), *The Longman Grammar of Spoken and Written English*. London: Longman.

Bitchener, John and Dana R. Ferris (2012), *Written Corrective Feedback in Second Language Acquisition and Writing*. New York, NY: Routledge.

Björkelund, Anders, Kerstin Eckart, Arndt Riester, Nadja Schauffler and Katrin Schweitzer (2014), The Extended DIRNDL Corpus as a Resource for Coreference and Bridging Resolution. In: *Proceedings of the Ninth International Conference on Language Resources and Evaluation (LREC 2014)*. Reykjavik, Iceland, 3222–3228.

Blackwell, Christopher and Thomas R. Martin (2009), Technology, Collaboration, and Undergraduate Research. *Digital Humanities Quarterly* 3(1). Available at: http://digitalhumanities.org/dhq/vol/003/1/000024/000024.html.

Bloomfield, Leonard (1933), *Language*. London: George Allen & Unwin.

Boas, Hans C. (2009), Semantic Frames as Interlingual Representations for Multilingual Lexical Databases. In: Hans C. Boas (ed.), *Multilingual FrameNets in Computational Lexicography: Methods and Applications*. Berlin: Mouton de Gruyter, 59–99.

Boas, Hans C. (2011), Coercion and Leaking Argument Structures in Construction Grammar. *Linguistics* 49(6), 1271–1303.

Bock, Kathryn and Kathleen M. Eberhard (1993), Meaning, Sound and Syntax in English Number Agreement. *Language and Cognitive Processes* 8(1), 57–99.

Bock, Kathryn, Kathleen M. Eberhard, J. Cooper Cutting, Antje S. Meyer and Herbert Schriefers (2001), Some Attractions of Verb Agreement. *Cognitive Psychology* 43, 83–128.

Boersma, Paul and Vincent van Heuven (2001), Speak and unSpeak With PRAAT. *Glot International* 5(9/10), 341–347.

Boguraev, Branimir and Christopher Kennedy (1999), Salience-Based Content Characteristics of Text Documents. In: Inderjeet Mani and Mark T. Maybury (eds.), *Advances in Automatic Text Summarizatrion*. Cambridge, MA: MIT Press, 99–110.

Bohnet, Bernd (2010), Very High Accuracy and Fast Dependency Parsing Is Not a Contradiction. In: *Proceedings of COLING 2010*. Beijing, China, 89–97.

Bosch, Peter, Graham Katz and Carla Umbach (2007), The Non-Subject Bias of German Demonstrative Pronouns. In: Monika Schwarz-Friesel, Manfred Consten and Mareile Knees (eds.), *Anaphors in Text: Cognitive, Formal, and Applied Approaches to Anaphoric Reference* (Studies in Language Companion Series 86). Amsterdam: John Benjamins, 145–164.

Bosch, Peter and Carla Umbach (2007), Reference Determination for Demonstrative Pronouns. *ZAS Papers in Linguistics* 48, 39–51.

Boyd, Adriane, Jirka Hana, Lionel Nicolas, Detmar Meurers, Katrin Wisniewski, Andrea Abel, Karin Schöne, Barbora Štindlová & Chiara Vettori (2014), The MERLIN Corpus: Learner Language and the CEFR. In: *Proceedings of LREC 2014*. Reykjavik, Iceland, 1281–1288.

Boyd, Jeremy K. and Adele E. Goldberg (2011), Learning What NOT to Say: The Role of Statistical Preemption and Categorization in a-Adjective Production. *Language* 87(1), 55–83.

Brants, Sabine, Stefanie Dipper, Silvia Hansen, Wolfgang Lezius and George Smith (2002), The TIGER Treebank. In: *Proceedings of the Workshop on Treebanks and Linguistic Theories, September 20–21 (TLT02)*. Sozopol, Bulgaria, 24–42.

Braud, Chloe, Maximin Coavoux and Anders Søgaard (2017), Cross-lingual RST Discourse Parsing. In: *Proceedings of EACL 2017*. Valencia, Spain, 292–304.

Braud, Chloe, Barbara Plank and Anders Søgaard (2016), Multi-View and Multi-Task Training of RST Discourse Parsers. In: *Proceedings of COLING 2016*. Osaka, 1903–1913.

Bresnan, Joan (1971), A Note on the Notion 'Identity of Sense Anaphora'. *Linguistic Inquiry* 2(4), 589–597.

Bresnan, Joan, Anna Cueni, Tatiana Nikitina and R. Harald Baayen (2007), Predicting the Dative Alternation. In: Gerlof Bouma, Irene Kraemer and Joost Zwarts (eds.), *Cognitive Foundations of Interpretation*. Amsterdam: Royal Netherlands Academy of Science, 69–94.

Bresnan, Joan and Marilyn Ford (2010), Predicting Syntax: Processing Dative Constructions in American and Australian Varieties of English. *Language* 86(1), 168–213.

Broda, Bartosz, Michał Marcinczuk, Marek Maziarz, Adam Radziszewski and Adam Wardyński (2012), KPWr: Towards a Free Corpus of Polish. In: *Proceedings of LREC 2012*. Istanbul, Turkey, 3218–3222.

Brugman, Hennie and Albert Russel (2004), Annotating Multimedia/Multi-modal Resources With ELAN. In: *Proceedings of LREC 2004, Fourth International Conference on Language Resources and Evaluation*. Paris: ELRA, 2065–2068.

Burchardt, Aljoscha, Katrin Erk, Anette Frank, Andrea Kowalski, Sebastian Padó and Manfred Pinkal (2006), The SALSA Corpus: A German Corpus Resource for Lexical Semantics. In: *Proceedings of LREC 2006*. Genoa, Italy, 969–974.

Burchardt, Aljoscha, Sebastian Padó, Dennis Spohr, Anette Frank and Ulrich Heid (2008), Formalising Multi-layer Corpora in OWL DL – Lexicon Modelling, Querying and Consistency Control. In: *Proceedings of the Third International Joint Conference on Natural Language Processing (IJCNLP 2008)*. Hyderabad, India, 389–396.

Büring, Daniel (2010), Towards a Typology of Focus Realization. In: Malte Zimmermann and Carolin Féry (eds.), *Information Structure: Theoretical, Typological, and Experimental Perspectives*. Oxford: Oxford University Press, 177–205.

Bybee, Joan L. (2006), From Usage to Grammar: The Mind's Response to Repetition. *Language* 82(4), 711–733.

Calhoun, Sasha, Jean Carletta, Jason Brenier, Neil Mayo, Dan Jurafsky, Mark Steedman and David Beaver (2010), The NXT-format Switchboard Corpus: A

Rich Resource for Investigating the Syntax, Semantics, Pragmatics and Prosody of Dialogue. *Language Resources and Evaluation* 44(4), 387–419.

Cappelle, Bert (2006), Particle Placement and the Case for 'Allostructions'. *Constructions* SV1(7). Available at: www.constructions-online.de/articles/specvol1/683.

Carletta, Jean, Stefan Evert, Ulrich Heid, Jonathan Kilgour, Judy Robertson and Holger Voormann (2003), The NITE XML Toolkit: Flexible Annotation for Multi-modal Language Data. *Behavior Research Methods, Instruments, and Computers* 35(3), 353–363.

Carlson, Lynn, Daniel Marcu and Mary Ellen Okurowski (2001), Building a Discourse-Tagged Corpus in the Framework of Rhetorical Structure Theory. In: *Proceedings of 2nd SIGDIAL Workshop on Discourse and Dialogue, Eurospeech 2001.* Aalborg, Denmark, 1–10.

Carlson, Lynn, Daniel Marcu and Mary Ellen Okurowski (2003), Building a Discourse-Tagged Corpus in the Framework of Rhetorical Structure Theory. In: *Current and New Directions in Discourse and Dialogue* (Text, Speech and Language Technology 22). Dordrecht: Kluwer, 85–112.

Castilho, Richard Eckart de, Nancy Ide, Emanuele Lapponi, Stephan Oepen, Keith Suderman, Erik Velldal and Marc Verhagen (2017), Representation and Interchange of Linguistic Annotation: An In-Depth, Side-by-Side Comparison of Three Designs. In: *Proceedings of the 11th Linguistic Annotation Workshop (LAW XI).* Valencia, Spain, 67–75.

Chafe, Wallace L. (1976), Givenness, Contrastiveness, Definiteness, Subjects, Topics and Point of View. In: Charles N. Li (ed.), *Subject and Topic.* New York, NY: Academic Press, 27–55.

Chaîne, Marius (1960), *Le manuscrit de la version Copte en dialecte Sahidique des Apophthegmata Patrum.* Cairo: Imprimetie de l'Institut Français d'Archéologie Orientale.

Chamberlain, Jon, Massimo Poesio and Udo Kruschwitz (2008), Addressing the Resource Bottleneck to Create Large-Scale Annotated Texts. In: Johan Bos and Rodolfo Delmonte (eds.), *Semantics in Text Processing: STEP 2008 Conference Proceedings.* London: College Publications, 375–380.

Chambers, Nathanael and Dan Jurafsky (2009), Unsupervised Learning of Narrative Schemas and Their Participants. In: *Proceedings of the 47th Annual Meeting of the ACL and the 4th IJCNLP of the AFNLP.* Suntec, Singapore, 602–610.

Chen, Chen and Vincent Ng (2013), Chinese Zero Pronoun Resolution: Some Recent Advances. In: *Proceedings of EMNLP 2013.* Seattle, WA, 1360–1365.

Chen, Danqi and Christopher D. Manning (2014), A Fast and Accurate Dependency Parser Using Neural Networks. In: *Proceedings of EMNLP 2014.* Doha, Qatar, 740–750.

Chiarcos, Christian (2009), *Mental Salience and Grammatical Form: Toward a Framework for Salience Metrics in Natural Language Generation.* PhD Thesis, Potsdam University.

Chiarcos, Christian, Stefanie Dipper, Michael Götze, Ulf Leser, Anke Lüdeling, Julia Ritz and Manfred Stede (2008), A Flexible Framework for Integrating Annotations From Different Tools and Tag Sets. *Traitement automatique des langues* 49(2), 271–293.

Chiarcos, Christian and Olga Krasavina (2008), Rhetorical Distance Revisited: A Parametrized Approach. In: Anton Benz and Peter Kühnlein (eds.), *Constraints in Discourse*. Amsterdam and Philadelphia, PA: John Benjamins, 97–115.

Chiarcos, Christian, Julia Ritz and Manfred Stede (2009), By All These Lovely Tokens . . . Merging Conflicting Tokenizations. In: *Proceedings of the Third Linguistic Annotation Workshop (LAW III)*. Singapore, 35–43.

Chomsky, Noam (1957), *Syntactic Structures*. The Hague: Mouton.

Chomsky, Noam (1965), *Aspects of the Theory of Syntax*. Cambridge, MA: MIT Press.

Chomsky, Noam (1993 [1981]), *Lectures on Government and Binding*. Berlin and New York, NY: Mouton de Gruyter.

Christ, Oliver (1994), A Modular and Flexible Architecture for an Integrated Corpus Query System. In: *Proceedings of Complex 94: 3rd Conference on Computational Lexicography and Text Research*. Budapest, 23–32.

Clark, Herbert H. and Susan E. Haviland (1977), Comprehension and the Given-New Contract. In: Roy O. Freedle (ed.), *Discourse Production and Comprehension* (Discourse Processes: Advances in Research and Theory 1). Norwood, NJ: Ablex.

Clark, Kevin and Christopher D. Manning (2015), Entity-Centric Coreference Resolution With Model Stacking. In: *Proceedings of the 53rd Annual Meeting of the Association for Computational Linguistics and the 7th International Joint Conference on Natural Language Processing (ACL-IJCNLP 2015)*. Beijing: ACL, 1405–1415.

Cook, Philippa and Felix Bildhauer (2011), Annotating Information Structure. The Case of 'Topic'. In: Stefanie Dipper and Heike Zinsmeister (eds.), *Beyond Semantics: Corpus-based Investigations of Pragmatic and Discourse Phenomena* (Bochumer Linguistische Arbeitsberichte 3). Bochum: Ruhr-Universität Bochum, 45–56.

Crasborn, Onno and Han Sloetjes (2008), Enhanced ELAN Functionality for Sign Language Corpora. In: *Proceedings of the 3rd Workshop on the Representation and Processing of Sign Languages at LREC 2008*. Marrakesh, Morocco, 39–42.

Cristea, Dan, Nancy Ide, Daniel Marcu and Valentin Tablan (1999), Discourse Structure and Co-Reference: An Empirical Study. In: *Proceedings of the Workshop on the Relationship Between Discourse/Dialogue Structure and Reference*. College Park, MD, 46–53.

Cristea, Dan, Nancy Ide and Laurent Romary (1998), Veins Theory: A Model of Global Discourse Cohesion and Coherence. In: *Proceedings of ACL/COLING*. Montreal, Canada, 281–285.

Croft, William (2001), *Radical Construction Grammar: Syntactic Theory in Typological Perspective*. Oxford: Oxford University Press.

Crowdy, Steve (1993), Spoken Corpus Design. *Literary and Linguistic Computing* 8, 259–265.

Cunningham, Hamish, Kevin Humphreys, Robert Gaizauskas and Yorick Wilks (1997), Software Infrastructure for Natural Language Processing. In: *Proceedings of the Fifth Conference on Applied Natural Language Processing*. Washington, DC, 237–244.

Curzan, Anne (2003), *Gender Shifts in the History of English* (Studies in English Language). Cambridge: Cambridge University Press.

da Cunha, Iria, Juan-Manuel Torres-Moreno and Gerardo Sierra (2011), On the Development of the RST Spanish Treebank. In: *Proceedings of the Fifth Linguistic Annotation Workshop (LAW V)*. Portland, OR, 1–10.

Dagan, Ido, Dan Roth, Mark Sammons and Fabio Zanzotto (2013), *Recognizing Textual Entailment* (Synthesis Lectures on Human Language Technologies). San Rafael, CA: Morgan & Claypool.

Das, Debopam, Manfred Stede and Maite Taboada (2017), The Good, the Bad, and the Disagreement: Complex Ground Truth in Rhetorical Structure Analysis. In: *Proceedings of the 6th Workshop on Recent Advances in RST and Related Formalisms*. Santiago de Compostela, Spain, 11–19.

Davies, Mark (2008–), *The Corpus of Contemporary American English: 450 Million Words, 1990-Present*. Available at: http://corpus.byu.edu/coca/.

Davis, Stephen J., Gillian Pyke, Elizabeth Davidson, Mary Farag and Daniel Schriever (2014), Left Behind: A Recent Discovery of Manuscript Fragments in the White Monastery Church. *Journal of Coptic Studies* 16, 69–87.

de Castilho, Richard Eckart and Iryna Gurevych (2014), A Broad-Coverage Collection of Portable NLP Components for Building Shareable Analysis Pipelines. In: *Proceedings of the Workshop on Open Infrastructures and Analysis Frameworks for HLT*. Dublin, 1–11.

de Marneffe, Marie-Catherine and Christopher D. Manning (2013), *Stanford Typed Dependencies Manual*. Technical Report, Stanford University.

Demske, Ulrike (2007), Das Mercurius-Projekt: eine Baumbank für das Frühneuhochdeutsche. In: Gisela Zifonun and Werner Kallmeyer (eds.), *Sprachkorpora – Datenmengen und Erkenntnisfortschritt*. (Jahrbuch des Instituts für deutsche Sprache 2006.) Berlin: De Gruyter, 91–104.

den Dikken, Marcel (2001), 'Pluringulars', Pronouns and Quirky Agreement. *The Linguistic Review* 18, 19–41.

Depraetere, Ilse (2003), On Verbal Concord With Collective Nouns in British English. *English Language and Linguistics* 7(1), 85–127.

de Saussure, Ferdinand (1966[1915]), *Course in General Linguistics*. New York, NY, Toronto and London: McGraw-Hill.

Deshors, Sandra C. and Stefan Th. Gries (2016), Profiling Verb Complementation Constructions Across New Englishes: A Two-Step Random Forests Analysis of *ing* vs. *to* Complements. *International Journal of Corpus Linguistics* 21(2), 192–218.

Dickinson, Markus (2015), Detection of Annotation Errors in Corpora. *Language and Linguistics Compass* 9(6), 119–138.

Dickinson, Markus and W. Detmar Meurers (2003), Detecting Errors in Part-of-Speech Annotation. In: *Proceedings of EACL 2003*. Budapest, Hungary, 107–114.

Diewald, Nils, Michael Hanl, Eliza Margaretha, Joachim Bingel, Marc Kupietz, Piotr Bański and Andreas Witt (2016), KorAP Architecture – Diving in the Deep Sea of Corpus Data. In: *Proceedings LREC 2016*. Portorož: ELRA, 3586–3591.

Dipper, Stefanie (2005), XML-based Stand-off Representation and Exploitation of Multi-Level Linguistic Annotation. In: *Proceedings of Berliner XML Tage 2005 (BXML 2005)*. Berlin, Germany, 39–50.

Dipper, Stefanie and Michael Götze (2005), Accessing Heterogeneous Linguistic Data – Generic XML-based Representation and Flexible Visualization. In: *Proceedings of the 2nd Language & Technology Conference: Human Language*

Technologies as a Challenge for Computer Science and Linguistics. Poznan, Poland, 206–210.

Dipper, Stefanie, Michael Götze and Stavros Skopeteas (eds.) (2007), Information Structure in Cross-Linguistic Corpora: Annotation Guidelines for Phonology, Morphology, Syntax, Semantics, and Information Structure. *Interdisciplinary Studies on Information Structure 7*.

Dixon, Robert M. W. (1977), Semantic Neutralization for Phonological Reasons. *Linguistic Inquiry* 8(3), 599–602.

Druskat, Stephan, Lennart Bierkandt, Volker Gast, Christoph Rzymski and Florian Zipser (2014), Atomic: An Open-source Software Platform for Multi-layer Corpus Annotation. In: Josef Ruppenhofer and Gertrud Faaß (eds.), *Proceedings of KONVENS 2014*. Hildesheim, Germany, 228–234.

Dryer, Matthew S. (2013), Expression of Pronominal Subjects. In: Matthew S. Dryer and Martin Haspelmath (eds.), *The World Atlas of Language Structures Online*. Munich: Max Planck Digital Library. Available at: http://wals.info/chapter/101.

Dukes, Kais and Tim Buckwalter (2010), A Dependency Treebank of the Quran Using Traditional Arabic Grammar. In: *Proceedings of the 7th International Conference on Informatics and Systems (INFOS)*. Cairo, Egypt, 1–7.

Dumitrache, Anca, Lora Aroyo, Chris Welty, Robert-Jan Sips and Anthony Levas (2013), 'Dr. Detective': Combining Gamification Techniques and Crowdsourcing to Create a Gold Standard in Medical Text. In: *Proceedings of the 1st International Conference on Crowdsourcing the Semantic Web (CrowdSem)*. Sydney, 16–31.

Durrett, Greg and Dan Klein (2013), Easy Victories and Uphill Battles in Coreference Resolution. In: *Proceedings of EMNLP 2013*. Seattle, WA, 1971–1982.

Eberhard, Kathleen, J. Cooper Cutting and Kathryn Bock (2005), Making Sense of Syntax: Number Agreement in Sentence Production. *Psychological Review* 112, 531–559.

Eggins, Suzanne and James R. Martin (1997), Genres and Registers of Discourse. In: Teun A. van Dijk (ed.), *Discourse as Structure and Process* (Discourse Studies: A Multidisciplinary Introduction 1). London: Sage, 230–256.

Erjavec, Tomaž (2012), MULTEXT-East: Morphosyntactic Resources for Central and Eastern European Languages. *Language Resources and Evaluation* 46(1), 131–142.

Evert, Stefan and Andrew Hardie (2011), Twenty-first Century Corpus Workbench: Updating a Query Architecture for the New Millennium. In: *Proceedings of Corpus Linguistics 2011*. Birmingham.

Ferris, Dana R. (2006), Does Error Feedback Help Student Writers? New Evidence on the Short-and Long-term Effects of Written Error Correction. In: Ken Hyland and Fiona Hyland (eds.), *Feedback in Second Language Writing: Contexts and Issues*. Cambridge: Cambridge University Press, 81–104.

Féry, Caroline (2006), The Fallacy of Invariant Phonological Correlates of Information Structural Notions. *Interdisciplinary Studies on Information Structure* 6, 161–184.

Féry, Caroline and Shin Ishihara (eds.) (2016), *The Oxford Handbook of Information Structure*. Oxford: Oxford University Press.

Fillmore, Charles J. (1979), Innocence: A Second Idealization for Linguistics. *Proceedings of the Berkeley Linguistics Society* 5, 63–76.

Fischer, Kerstin and Anatol Stefanowitsch (2006), Konstruktionsgrammatik: Ein Überblick. In: Kerstin Fischer and Anatol Stefanowitsch (eds.), *Konstruktionsgrammatik: Von der Anwendung zur Theorie*. Tübingen: Stauffenburg, 3–17.

Fligelstone, Steve, Mike Pacey and Paul Rayson (1997), How to Generalize the Task of Annotation. In: Roger Garside, Geoffrey Leech and Anthony McEnery (eds.), *Corpus Annotation: Linguistic Information From Computer Text Corpora*. London: Routledge, 122–136.

Foland Jr., William R. and James H. Martin (2015), Dependency-based Semantic Role Labeling Using Convolutional Neural Networks. In: *Proceedings of *SEM 2015*. Denver, CO, 279–289.

Fort, Karën (2016), *Collaborative Annotation for Reliable Natural Language Processing: Technical and Sociological Aspects*. London: Wiley.

Fox, Barbara A. (1993), *Discourse Structure and Anaphora: Written and Conversational English*. Cambridge: Cambridge University Press.

Fraser, Bruce (1999), What are Discourse Markers? *Journal of Pragmatics* 31, 931–952.

Frick, Elena, Carsten Schnober and Piotr Bański (2012), Evaluating Query Languages for a Corpus Processing System. In: *Proceedings of LREC 2012*. Istanbul, Turkey, 2286–2294.

Gaeta, Livio and Barbara Schlücker (eds.) (2012), *Das Deutsche als kompositionsfreudige Sprache. Strukturelle Eigenschaften und systembezogene Aspekte* (Linguistik – Impulse and Tendenzen 46). Berlin and New York, NY: De Gruyter.

Garside, Roger, Steve Fligelstone and Simon Botley (1997), Discourse Annotation: Anaphoric Relations in Corpora. In: Roger Garside, Geoffrey Leech and Anthony McEnery (eds.), *Corpus Annotation: Linguistic Information From Computer Text Corpora*. London: Routledge, 66–84.

Garside, Roger and Nicholas Smith (1997), A Hybrid Grammatical Tagger: CLAWS4. In: Roger Garside, Geoffrey Leech and Anthony McEnery (eds.), *Corpus Annotation: Linguistic Information From Computer Text Corpora*. London: Longman, 102–121.

Gatt, Albert and Emiel Krahmer (2018), Survey of the State of the Art in Natural Language Generation: Core Tasks, Applications and Evaluation. *Journal of Artificial Intelligence Research* 61, 65–170.

Gawron, Jean-Mark (2011), Frame Semantics. In: Claudia Maienborn, Klaus Heusinger and Paul Portner (eds.), *Semantics: An International Handbook of Natural Language Meaning* (Handbooks of Linguistics and Communication Science 33). Vol. 1. Berlin and Boston, MA: De Gruyter Mouton, 664–687.

Gerdes, Kim (2013), Collaborative Dependency Annotation. In: *Proceedings of the Second International Conference on Dependency Linguistics (DepLing 2013)*. Prague, 88–97.

Gerdes, Kim, Sylvain Kahane, Anne Lacheret, Arthur Truong and Paola Pietrandrea (2012), Intonosyntactic Data Structures: The Rhapsodie Treebank of Spoken French. In: *Proceedings of the 6th Linguistic Annotation Workshop (The LAW VI)*. Jeju Island, South Korea, 85–94.

Gernsbacher, Morton Ann and Jörg D. Jescheniak (1995), Cataphoric Devices in Spoken Discourse. *Cognitive Psychology* 29(1), 24–58.

Geurts, Bart and Emar Maier (2013), Layered Discourse Representation Theory. In: Alessandro Capone, Franco Lo Piparo and Marco Carapezza (eds.),

Perspectives on Linguistic Pragmatics (Perspectives in Pragmatics, Philosophy and Psychology 2). Cham: Springer.

Geurts, Pierre, Damien Ernst and Louis Wehenkel (2006), Extremely Randomized Trees. *Machine Learning* 63(1), 3–42.

Ghodke, Sumukh and Steven Bird (2010), Fast Query for Large Treebanks. In: *Proceedings of NAACL 2010*. Los Angeles, CA, 267–275.

Ghodke, Sumukh and Steven Bird (2012), Fangorn: A System for Querying Very Large Treebanks. In: *Proceedings of COLING 2012*. Mumbai, India, 175–182.

Gibbon, Dafydd, Inge Mertins and Roger K. Moore (eds.) (2000), *Handbook of Multimodal and Spoken Dialogue Systems: Resources, Terminology and Product Evaluation*. New York, NY: Springer.

Gibbon, Dafydd, Roger Moore and Richard Winski (eds.) (1997), *Handbook of Standards and Resources for Spoken Language Systems*. Berlin: Mouton de Gruyter.

Gildea, Daniel and Daniel Jurafsky (2002), Automatic Labeling of Semantic Roles. *Computational Linguistics* 28(3), 245–288.

Gimpel, Kevin, Nathan Schneider, Brendan O'Connor, Dipanjan Das, Daniel Mills, Jacob Eisenstein, Michael Heilman, Dani Yogatama, Jeffrey Flanigan and Noah A. Smith. (2011), Part-of-Speech Tagging for Twitter: Annotation, Features, and Experiments. In: *Proceedings of ACL 2011*. Portland, OR, 42–47.

Givón, Talmy (ed.) (1983), *Topic Continuity in Discourse: A Quantitative Cross-Language Study* (Typlological Studies in Language 3). Amsterdam: John Benjamins.

Godfrey, John J., Edward C. Holliman and Jane McDaniel (1992), SWITCH-BOARD: Telephone Speech Corpus for Research and Development. In: *Proceedings of ICASSP-92*. San Francisco, CA, 517–520.

Goldberg, Adele E. (1995), *Constructions: A Construction Grammar Approach to Argument Structure*. Chicago, IL: University of Chicago Press.

Goldberg, Adele E. (2006), *Constructions at Work: The Nature of Generalization in Language*. Oxford: Oxford University Press.

Goldberg, Adele E. and Jeremy K. Boyd (2015), A-adjectives, Statistical Preemption, and the Evidence: Reply to Yang (2015). *Language* 91(4), e184–e197.

Götz, Thomas and Oliver Suhre (2004), Design and Implementation of the UIMA Common Analysis System. *IBM Systems Journal* 43(3), 476–489.

Graham, Steve and Dolores Perin (2007), A Meta-Analysis of Writing Instruction for Adolescent Students. *Journal of Educational Psychology* 99(3), 445–476.

Granger, Sylviane (2003), Error-tagged Learner Corpora and CALL: A Promising Synergy. *CALICO Journal* 20(3), 465–480.

Greff, Klaus, Rupesh K. Srivastava, Jan Koutník, Bas R. Steunebrink and Jürgen Schmidhuber (2016), LSTM: A Search Space Odyssey. *IEEE Transactions on Neural Networks and Learning Systems* 99, 1–11.

Gries, Stefan Th. (2002), The Influence of Processing on Grammatical Variation: Particle Placement in English. In: Nicole Dehé, Ray Jackendoff, Andrew McIntyre and Silke Urban (eds.), *Verb-Particle Explorations*. Berlin: Mouton de Gruyter, 269–288.

Gries, Stefan Th. (2003), *Multifactorial Analysis in Corpus Linguistics: A Study of Particle Placement*. London: Continuum.

Gries, Stefan Th. (2005), Syntactic Priming: A Corpus-based Approach. *Journal of Psycholinguistic Research* 34(4), 365–399.

Gries, Stefan Th. (2006), Exploring Variability Within and Between Corpora: Some Methodological Considerations. *Corpora* 1(2), 109–151.

Gries, Stefan Th. (2009), *Quantitative Corpus Linguistics With R: A Practical Introduction*. London: Routledge.

Gries, Stefan Th. (2013), *Statistics for Linguistics With R: A Practical Introduction*. 2nd edition. Berlin: Mouton de Gruyter.

Gries, Stefan Th. (2015), The Most Underused Statistical Method in Corpus Linguistics: Multi-level (and Mixed-effects) Models. *Corpora* 10(1), 95–125.

Gries, Stefan Th. and Stefanie Wulff (2013), The Genitive Alternation in Chinese and German ESL Learners: Towards a Multifactorial Notion of Context in Learner Corpus Research. *International Journal of Corpus Linguistics* 18(3), 327–356.

Grimshaw, Jane (1990), *Argument Structure* (Linguistic Inquiry Monographs 18). Cambridge, MA: MIT Press.

Gross, Derek, James F. Allen and David R. Traum (1993), *The TRAINS 91 Dialogues*. TRAINS Technical Note 92–1, Computer Science Department, University of Rochester.

Grossman, Eitan (2014), Transitivity and Valency in Contact: The Case of Coptic. In: *47th Annual Meeting of the Societas Linguistica Europaea*. Poznań, Poland.

Grosz, Barbara J., Aravind K. Joshi and Scott Weinstein (1995), Centering: A Framework for Modeling the Local Coherence of Discourse. *Computational Linguistics* 21(2), 203–225.

Gruber, Helmut and Birgit Huemer (2008), Two Views on Text Structure: Using Rhetorical Structure Theory and Register & Genre Theory in Improving Students' Academic Writing. In: Nina Nørgaard (ed.), *Systemic Functional Linguistics in Use* (Odense Working Papers in Language and Communication 29). Odense: University of Southern Denmark, 332–364.

Guo, Jin (1997), Critical Tokenization and Its Properties. *Computational Linguistics* 23(4), 569–596.

Habernal, Ivan and Iryna Gurevych (2017), Argumentation Mining in User-Generated Web Discourse. *Computational Linguistics* 43(1), 125–179.

Habernal, Ivan, Omnia Zayed and Iryna Gurevych (2016), C4Corpus: Multilingual Web-size Corpus With Free License. In: *Proceedings of LREC 2016*. Portorož, Slovenia, 914–922.

Halliday, Michael A. K. (1967), Notes on Transitivity and Theme in English: Part 1. *Journal of Linguistics* 3(1), 37–81.

Hardie, Andrew (2012), CQPweb – Combining Power, Flexibility and Usability in a Corpus Analysis Tool. *International Journal of Corpus Linguistics* 17(3), 380–409.

Haug, Dag T. T., Hanne M. Eckhoff, Marek Majer and Eirik Welo (2009), Breaking Down and Putting Back Together: Analysis and Synthesis of New Testament Greek. *Journal of Greek Linguistics* 9(1), 56–92.

Hayashi, Katsuhiko, Tsutomu Hirao and Masaaki Nagata (2016), Empirical Comparison of Dependency Conversions for RST Discourse Trees. In: *Proceedings of SIGDIAL 2016*. Los Angeles, CA, 128–136.

Heiden, Serge (2010), The TXM Platform: Building Open-Source Textual Analysis Software Compatible With the TEI Encoding Scheme. In: *24th Pacific Asia Conference on Language, Information and Computation*. Sendai, Japan, 389–398.

Heim, Irene (1983), File Change Semantics and the Familiarity Theory of Definiteness. In: Rainer Bäuerle, Christoph Schwarze and Armin von Stechow (eds.), *Meaning, Use, and Interpretation of Language*. Berlin: De Gruyter, 164–189.

Heim, Irene (1997), Predicates or Formulas? Evidence From Ellipsis. *Semantics and Linguistic Theory* 7, 197–221.

Heller, Daphna, Kristen Skovbroten and Michael K. Tanenhaus (2009), Experimental Evidence for Speakers' Sensitivity to Common vs. Privileged Ground in the Production of Names. In: *CogSci Workshop on the Production of Referring Expressions*. Amsterdam.

Hess, Wolfgang J., Klaus J. Kohler and Hans-Günther Tillmann (1995), The PHONDAT-VERBMOBIL Speech Corpus. In: *Proceedings of the 5th European Conference of Speech Communication and Technology*. Vol. 1. Madrid, 863–866.

Himmelmann, Nikolaus P. (1998), Regularity in Irregularity: Article Use in Adpositional Phrases. *Linguistic Typology* 2(3), 315–354.

Hinrichs, Erhard W., Marie Hinrichs and Thomas Zastrow (2010), WebLicht: Web-Based LRT Services for German. In: *Proceedings of the ACL 2010 System Demonstrations*. Uppsala, 25–29.

Hinterwimmer, Stefan and Peter Bosch (2016), Demonstrative Pronouns and Perspective. In: Patrick Grosz and Pritty Patel-Grosz (eds.), *The Impact of Pronominal Form on Interpretation*. Boston, MA and Berlin: De Gruyter Mouton, 189–220.

Hirao, Tsutomu, Yasuhisa Yoshida, Masaaki Nishino, Norihito Yasuda and Masaaki Nagata (2013), Single-Document Summarization as a Tree Knapsack Problem. In: *Proceedings of EMNLP 2013*. Seattle, WA, 1515–1520.

Hirschmann, Hagen, Anke Lüdeling, Ines Rehbein, Marc Reznicek and Amir Zeldes (2013), Underuse of Syntactic Categories in Falko – A Case Study on Modification. In: Sylviane Granger and Fanny Meunier (eds.), *20 Years of Learner Corpus Research: Looking Back, Moving Ahead*. Louvain: Presses Universitaires de Louvain, 223–234.

Hobbs, Jerry R. (1979), Coherence and Coreference. *Cognitive Science* 3, 67–90.

Hobbs, Jerry R. (1990), *Literature and Cognition* (CSLI Lecture Notes 21). Stanford, CA: CSLI.

Höder, Steffen (2012), Annotating Ambiguity: Insights From a Corpus-Based Study on Syntactic Change in Old Swedish. In: Thomas Schmidt and Kai Wörner (eds.), *Multilingual Corpora and Multilingual Corpus Analysis* (Hamburg Studies on Multilingualism 14). Amsterdam and Philadelphia, PA: Benjamins, 245–271.

Hovy, Eduard (2005), Text Summarization. In: Ruslan Mitkov (ed.), *The Oxford Handbook of Computational Linguistics*. Oxford: Oxford University Press, 583–598.

Hovy, Eduard, Mitchell Marcus, Martha Palmer, Lance Ramshaw and Ralph Weischedel (2006), OntoNotes: The 90% Solution. In: *Proceedings of the Human Language Technology Conference of the NAACL, Companion Volume: Short Papers*. New York, NY, 57–60.

Hsueh, Pei-Yun, Prem Melville and Vikas Sindhwani (2009), Data Quality From Crowdsourcing: A Study of Annotation Selection Criteria. In: *Proceedings of the NAACL HLT Workshop on Active Learning for Natural Language Processing*. Boulder, CO, 27–35.

Huddleston, Rodney and Geoffrey K. Pullum (2002), *The Cambridge Grammar of the English Language*. Cambridge: Cambridge University Press.

Hunston, Susan (2008), Collection Strategies and Design Decisions. In: Anke Lüdeling and Merja Kytö (eds.), *Corpus Linguistics: An International Handbook*. Berlin: Mouton de Gruyter, 154–168.

Ide, Nancy, Collin Baker, Christiane Fellbaum and Rebecca Passonneau (2010), The Manually Annotated Sub-Corpus: A Community Resource for and by the People. In: *Proceedings of ACL 2010*. Uppsala, Sweden, 68–73.

Ide, Nancy and Keith Suderman (2007), GrAF: A Graph-based Format for Linguistic Annotations. In: *Proceedings of the Linguistic Annotation Workshop 2007*. Prague, 1–8.

Iida, Ryu and Massimo Poesio (2011), A Cross-Lingual ILP Solution to Zero Anaphora Resolution. In: *Proceedings of ACL 2011*. Portland, OR, 804–813.

Ioffe, Sergey and Christian Szegedy (2015), Batch Normalization: Accelerating Deep Network Training by Reducing Internal Covariate Shift. In: *Proceedings of the 32nd International Conference on Machine Learning*. Lille, France.

Isard, Amy, David McKelvie and Andreas Mengel (2000), The MATE Workbench – A Tool for Annotating XML Corpora. In: *Proceedings of Recherche d'Informations Assisté par Ordinateur (RIAO 2000)*. Paris, 411–425.

ISO 24612 (2012), *Language Resource Management – Linguistic Annotation Framework (LAF)*. Available at: https://www.iso.org/standard/37326.html

ISO 24615 (2010), *Language Resource Management – Syntactic Annotation Framework (SynAF)*. Available at: https://www.iso.org/standard/37329.html

Jackendoff, Ray (1997), *The Architecture of the Language Faculty* (Linguistic Inquiry Monographs 28). Cambridge, MA: MIT Press.

Jacobs, Joachim (2001), The Dimensions of Topic-Comment. *Linguistics* 39(4), 641–681.

Jha, Mukund, Jacob Andreas, Kapil Thadani, Sara Rosenthal and Kathleen McKeown (2010), Corpus Creation for New Genres: A Crowdsourced Approach to PP Attachment. In: *Proceedings of the NAACL HLT 2010 Workshop on Creating Speech and Language Data With Amazon's Mechanical Turk*. Los Angeles, CA, 13–20.

Kamp, Hans and Uwe Reyle (1993), *From Discourse to Logic: Introduction to Modeltheoretic Semantics of Natural Language, Formal Logic and Discourse Representation Theory*. Dordrecht: Kluwer.

Karpathy, Andrej and Li Fei-Fei (2017), Deep Visual-Semantic Alignments for Generating Image Descriptions. *IEEE Transactions on Pattern Analysis and Machine Intelligence* 39(4), 664–676.

Karpathy, Andrej, Justin Johnson and Li Fei-Fei (2016), Visualizing and Understanding Recurrent Networks. In: *International Conference on Learning Representations (ICLR 2016)*. San Juan, Puerto Rico.

Kay, Paul and Charles J. Fillmore (1999), Grammatical Constructions and Linguistic Generalizations: The What's X Doing Y? Construction. *Language* 75(1), 1–33.

Kehler, Andrew, Laura Kertz, Hannah Rohde and Jeffrey L. Elman (2007), Coherence and Coreference Revisited. *Journal of Semantics* 25, 1–44.

Kehler, Andy and Hannah Rohde (2013), A Probabilistic Reconciliation of Coherence-driven and Centering-driven Theories of Pronoun Interpretation. *Theoretical Linguistics* 39(1–2), 1–37.

Kingma, Diederik P. and Jimmy Ba (2015), Adam: A Method for Stochastic Optimization. In: *Proceedings of the 3rd International Conference on Learning Representations (ICLR)*. San Diego, CA.

Kipper, Karin, Anna Korhonen, Neville Ryant and Martha Palmer (2006), Extending VerbNet With Novel Verb Classes. In: *Proceedings of LREC 2006*. Genoa, Italy, 1028–1032.

Klein, Wolf Peter (1999), *Die Geschichte der meteorologischen Kommunikation in Deutschland. Eine historische Fallstudie zur Entwicklung von Wissenschaftssprachen*. PhD Thesis, Freie Universität Berlin.

Knott, Alistair (1996), *A Data-Driven Methodology for Motivating a Set of Coherence Relations*. PhD Thesis, University of Edinburgh.

Knott, Alistair and Robert Dale (1994), Using Linguistic Phenomena to Motivate a Set of Coherence Relations. *Discourse Processes* 18(1), 35–52.

Knott, Alistair and Ted Sanders (1998), The Classification of Coherence Relations and Their Linguistic Markers: An Exploration of Two Languages. *Journal of Pragmatics* 30(2), 135–175.

Krakovna, Viktoriya and Finale Doshi-Velez (2016), Increasing the Interpretability of Recurrent Neural Networks Using Hidden Markov Models. In: *NIPS 2016 Workshop on Interpretable Machine Learning in Complex Systems*. Barcelona.

Krause, Thomas, Anke Lüdeling, Carolin Odebrecht and Amir Zeldes (2012), Multiple Tokenizations in a Diachronic Corpus. In: *Exploring Ancient Languages Through Corpora*. Oslo.

Krause, Thomas, Carolin Odebrecht, Amir Zeldes and Florian Zipser (2013), Unary TEI Elements and the Token Based Corpus. In: *Proceedings of the TEI Conference Workshop on Perspectives on Querying TEI-annotated Data*. Rome.

Krause, Thomas and Amir Zeldes (2016), ANNIS3: A New Architecture for Generic Corpus Query and Visualization. *Digital Scholarship in the Humanities* 31(1), 118–139.

Krifka, Manfred (2008), Basic Notions of Information Structure. *Acta Linguistica Hungarica* 55, 243–276.

Kübler, Sandra and Heike Zinsmeister (2015), *Corpus Linguistics and Linguistically Annotated Corpora*. London: Bloomsbury.

Kučera, Henry and W. Nelson Francis (1967), *Computational Analysis of Present-day English*. Providence, RI: Brown University Press.

Kürschner, Sebastian (2005), Verfugung-s-nutzung kontrastiv: Zur Funktion der Fugenelemente im Deutschen und Dänischen. *TijdSchrift voor Skandinavistiek* 26(2), 101–125.

Labov, William (2004), Quantitative Analysis of Linguistic Variation. In: Ulrich Ammon, Norbert Dittmar, Klaus J. Mattheier and Peter Trudgill (eds.), *Sociolinguistics: An International Handbook of the Science of Language and Society*. Vol. 1. Berlin: Walter de Gruyter, 6–21.

Lai, Catherine and Steven Bird (2004), Querying and Updating Treebanks: A Critical Survey and Requirements Analysis. In: *Proceedings of the Australasian Language Technology Workshop*. Sydney, 139–146.

Lambert, Patrik and Rafael Banchs (2005), Data-inferred Multi-word Expressions for Statistical Machine Translation. In: *Proceedings of Machine Translation Summit X*. Phuket, Thailand, 396–403.

Langacker, Ronald W. (1987), *Foundations of Cognitive Grammar: Volume 1. Theoretical Prerequisites*. Stanford, CA: Stanford University Press.

Layton, Bentley (2011), *A Coptic Grammar*. 3rd edition, revised and expanded (Porta Linguarum Orientalium 20). Wiesbaden: Harrassowitz.

Lee, Heeyoung, Angel Chang, Yves Peirsman, Nathanael Chambers, Mihai Surdeanu and Dan Jurafsky (2013), Deterministic Coreference Resolution Based on Entity-Centric, Precision-Ranked Rules. *Computational Linguistics* 39(4), 885–916.

Lee, John, Chak Yan Yeung, Amir Zeldes, Marc Reznicek, Anke Lüdeling and Jonathan Webster (2015), CityU Corpus of Essay Drafts of English Language Learners: A Corpus of Textual Revision in Second Language Writing. *Language Resources and Evaluation* 49(3), 659–683.

Lee, Kenton, Luheng He, Mike Lewis and Luke Zettlemoyer (2017), End-to-end Neural Coreference Resolution. In: *Proceedings of EMNLP 2017*. Copenhagen, 188–197.

Leech, Geoffrey N. (1997), Introducing Corpus Annotation. In: Roger Garside, Geoffrey N. Leech and Tony McEnery (eds.), *Corpus Annotation: Linguistic Information From Computer Text Corpora*. London and New York, NY: Routledge, 1–18.

Leech, Geoffrey N. (2005), Adding Linguistic Annotation. In: Martin Wynne (ed.), *Developing Linguistic Corpora: A Guide to Good Practice*. Oxford: Oxbow Books, 17–29.

Leech, Geoffrey N., Tony McEnery and Martin Weisser (2003), *SPAAC Speech-Act Annotation Scheme*. Technical Report, Lancaster University.

Lehmberg, Timm (2008), Annotation Standards. In: Anke Lüdeling and Merja Kytö (eds.), *Corpus Linguistics: An International Handbook*. Vol. 1. Berlin: Mouton de Gruyter, 484–501.

Le Pesant, Denis (1996), Anaphores associatives et classes d'objets. *Lingvisticae Investigationes* 20(1), 87–116.

Levin, Beth and Malka Rappaport-Hovav (2005), *Argument Realization* (Research Surveys in Linguistics). Cambridge: Cambridge University Press.

Levin, Magnus (2001), *Agreement With Collective Nouns in English* (Lund Studies in English 103). Lund: Lund University.

Levshina, Natalia (2015), *How to Do Linguistics With R: Data Exploration and Statistical Analysis*. Amsterdam and Philadelphia, PA: John Benjamins.

Levshina, Natalia (2016), When Variables Align: A Bayesian Multinomial Mixed-Effects Model of English Permissive Constructions. *Cognitive Linguistics* 27(2), 235–268.

Levy, Omer and Yoav Goldberg (2014), Dependency-Based Word Embeddings. In: *Proceedings of ACL 2014*. Baltimore, MD, 302–308.

Lezius, Wolfgang (2002), *Ein Suchwerkzeug für syntaktisch annotierte Textkorpora*. PhD Thesis, Institut für maschinelle Sprachverarbeitung Stuttgart.

Li, Sujian, Liang Wang, Ziqiang Cao and Wenjie Li (2014), Text-Level Discourse Dependency Parsing. In: *Proceedings of ACL 2014*. Baltimore, MD, 25–35.

Lin, Ziheng, Hwee Tou Ng and Min-Yen Kan (2014), A PDTB-Styled End-to-End Discourse Parser. *Natural Language Engineering* 20(2), 151–184.

Lohmann, Arne (2011), Help vs Help To: A Multifactorial, Mixed-Effects Account of Infinitive Marker Omission. *English Language and Linguistics* 15(3), 499–521.

Loprieno, Antonio (1995), *Ancient Egyptian: A Linguistic Introduction*. Cambridge: Cambridge University Press.

Lüdeling, Anke (2008), Mehrdeutigkeiten und Kategorisierung: Probleme bei der Annotation von Lernerkorpora. In: Maik Walter and Patrick Grommes (eds.), *Fortgeschrittene Lernervarietäten*. Tübingen: Niemeyer, 119–140.

Lüdeling, Anke (2012), A Corpus Linguistics Perspective on Language Documentation, Data, and the Challenge of Small Corpora. In: Frank Seifart, Geoffrey Haig, Nikolaus P. Himmelmann, Dagmar Jung, Anna Margetts and Paul Trilsbeek (eds.), *Potentials of Language Documentation: Methods, Analyses, and Utilization* (Language Documentation & Conservation Special Publications 3). Honolulu: University of Hawai'i Press, 32–38.

Lüdeling, Anke and Hagen Hirschmann (2015), Error Annotation Systems. In: Sylviane Granger, Gaetanelle Gilquin and Fanny Meunier (eds.), *The Cambridge Handbook on Learner Corpus Research*. Cambridge: Cambridge University Press, 135–158.

Lüdeling, Anke and Merja Kytö (eds.) (2008–2009), *Corpus Linguistics: An International Handbook* (Handbooks of Linguistics and Communication Science 29). Berlin and New York, NY: Mouton de Gruyter.

Lüdeling, Anke, Thorwald Poschenrieder and Lukas C. Faulstich (2005), DeutschDiachronDigital – Ein diachrones Korpus des Deutschen. *Jahrbuch für Computerphilologie 2004*, 119–136.

Lüdeling, Anke, Julia Ritz, Manfred Stede and Amir Zeldes (2016), Corpus Linguistics and Information Structure Research. In: Caroline Féry and Shinichiro Ichihara (eds.), *The Oxford Handbook of Information Structure*. Oxford: Oxford University Press, 599–617.

Lüdeling, Anke, Maik Walter, Emil Kroymann and Peter Adolphs (2005), Multilevel Error Annotation in Learner Corpora. In: *Proceedings of Corpus Linguistics 2005*. Birmingham.

Lundborg, Joakim, Torsten Marek, Maël Mettler and Martin Volk (2007), Using the Stockholm TreeAligner. In: *Proceedings of the Sixth Workshop on Treebanks and Linguistic Theories*. Bergen.

Ma, Xuezhe and Eduard Hovy (2016), End-to-end Sequence Labeling via Bidirectional LSTM-CNNs-CRF. In: *Proceedings of ACL 2016*. Berlin, 1064–1074.

Mann, William C. and Sandra A. Thompson (1988), Rhetorical Structure Theory: Toward a Functional Theory of Text Organization. *Text* 8(3), 243–281.

Manning, Christopher D. (2003), Probabilistic Syntax. In: Rens Bod, Jennifer Hay and Stefanie Jannedy (eds.), *Probabilistic Linguistics*. Cambridge, MA: MIT Press, 289–341.

Manning, Christopher D. (2015), Computational Linguistics and Deep Learning. *Computational Linguistics* 41(4), 701–707.

Manning, Christopher D., Mihai Surdeanu, John Bauer, Jenny Finkel, Steven J. Bethard and Davide McClosky (2014), The Stanford CoreNLP Natural Language Processing Toolkit. In: *Proceedings of ACL 2014: System Demonstrations*. Baltimore, MD, 55–60.

Marcu, Daniel (1996), Building Up Rhetorical Structure Trees. In: *Proceedings of AAAI-96*. Portland, OR, 1069–1074.

Marcus, Mitchell P., Beatrice Santorini and Mary Ann Marcinkiewicz (1993), Building a Large Annotated Corpus of English: The Penn Treebank. *Special Issue on Using Large Corpora, Computational Linguistics* 19(2), 313–330.

Marcus, Mitchell P., Beatrice Santorini and Mary Ann Marcinkiewicz (1995), *Treebank-2 LDC95T7*. Philadelphia, PA: Linguistic Data Consortium.

Martens, Scott (2013), Tundra: A Web Application for Treebank Search and Visualization. In: *Proceedings of the Twelfth Workshop on Treebanks and Linguistic Theories (TLT12)*. Sofia, Bulgaria, 133–144.

Martinez-Insua, Ana E. and Ignacio M. Palacios-Martinez (2003), A Corpus-Based Approach to Non-Concord in Present Day English Existential There-Constructions. *English Studies* 84(3), 262–283.

Marx, Maarten and Yde Venema (1997), *Multi-Dimensional Modal Logic* (Applied Logic Series 4). Dordrecht: Springer.

Matthiessen, Christian M. I .M. and Kazuhiro Teruya (2015), Grammatical Realizations of Rhetorical Relations in Different Registers. *Word* 61(3), 232–281.

McEnery, Tony, Richard Xiao and Yukio Tono (2006), *Corpus-Based Language Studies: An Advanced Resource Book* (Routledge Applied Linguistics). London: Routledge.

Meteer, Marie, Ann Taylor, Robert MacIntyre and Rukmini Iyer (1995), *Dysfluency Annotation Stylebook for the Switchboard Corpus*. Technical Report, Pennsylvania State University, State College, PA.

Meyer, Charles F. (2002), *English Corpus Linguistics: An Introduction*. Cambridge: Cambridge University Press.

Meyer, Charles F. (2008), Origin and History of Corpus Linguistics – Corpus Linguistics vis-à-vis Other Disciplines. In: Anke Lüdeling and Merja Kytö (eds.), *Corpus Linguistics: An International Handbook*. Vol. 1. Berlin: Mouton de Gruyter, 1–14.

Mitchell, Alexis, Stephanie Strassel, Mark Przybocki, JK Davis, George Doddington, Ralph Grishman, Adam Meyers, Ada Brunstein, Lisa Ferro and Beth Sundheim (2003), *ACE-2 Version 1.0*. Linguistic Data Consortium, Technical Report LDC2003T11, Philadelphia.

Miyagawa, So, Kirill Bulert and Marco Büchler (2017), Utilization of Common OCR Tools for Typeset Coptic Texts. In: *Proceedings of DATeCH 2017*. Göttingen, Germany.

Moretti, Franco (2013), *Distant Reading*. London: Verso.

Müller, Stefan (2015), The CoreGram Project: Theoretical Linguistics, Theory Development and Verification. *Journal of Language Modelling* 3(1), 21–86.

Nagata, Ryo, Edward Whittaker and Vera Sheinman (2011), Creating a Manually Error-tagged and Shallow-parsed Learner Corpus. In: *Proceedings of the 49th Annual Meeting of the Association for Computational Linguistics*. Stroudsburg, PA: ACL, 1210–1219.

Nathan, Geoffrey S. (1981), What's These Facts About? *Linguistic Inquiry* 12(1), 151–153.

Naumann, Karin (2006), *Manual for the Annotation of In-Document Referential Relations*. Technical Report, Seminar für Sprachwissenschaft, Universität Tübingen.

Nerius, Dieter (2003), Graphematische Entwicklungstendenzen in der Geschichte des Deutschen. 2. In: Werner Besch, Anne Betten, Oskar Reichmann and Stefan Sonderegger (eds.), *Sprachgeschichte. Ein Handbuch zur Geschichte der deutschen Sprache und ihrer Erforschung.* Vol. 3. Berlin: De Gruyter, 2461–2472.

Neudecker, Clemens (2016), An Open Corpus for Named Entity Recognition in Historic Newspapers. In: *Proceedings of LREC 2016.* Portorož, Slovenia, 4348–4352.

Newman, John and Christopher Cox (to appear), Corpus Annotation. In: Stefan Th. Gries and Magali Paquot (eds.), *A Practical Handbook of Corpus Linguistics.* Springer.

Nissim, Malvina, Shipra Dingare, Jean Carletta and Mark Steedman (2004), An Annotation Scheme for Information Status in Dialogue. In: *Proceedings of LREC 2004.* Lisbon, Portugal, 1023–1026.

Nivre, Joakim, et al. (2017), *Universal Dependencies 2.0.* Prague: LINDAT/CLARIN Digital Library at the Institute of Formal and Applied Linguistics, Charles University.

Nübling, Damaris and Renata Szczepaniak (2011), Markmal(s?)analyse, Seminar(s?)arbeit und Essen(s?)ausgabe: Zweifelsfälle der Verfugung als Indikatoren für Sprachwandel. *Zeitschrift für Sprachwissenschaft* 30(1), 45–73.

Nübling, Damaris and Renata Szczepaniak (2013), Linking Elements in German Origin, Change, Functionalization. *Morphology* 23, 67–89.

Odebrecht, Carolin, Malte Belz, Amir Zeldes and Anke Lüdeling (2017), RIDGES Herbology – Designing a Diachronic Multi-Layer Corpus. *Language Resources and Evaluation* 51(3), 695–725.

O'Donnell, Michael (2000), RSTTool 2.4 – A Markup Tool for Rhetorical Structure Theory. In: *Proceedings of the International Natural Language Generation Conference (INLG 2000).* Mitzpe Ramon, Israel, 253–256.

O'Keeffe, Anne and Michael McCarthy (eds.) (2010), *The Routledge Handbook of Corpus Linguistics.* London: Routledge.

Orfanidou, Eleni, Bencie Woll and Gary Morgan (eds.) (2015), *Research Methods in Sign Language Studies: A Practical Guide.* Chichester: Wiley Blackwell.

Osborne, John (2013), Fluency, Complexity and Informativeness in Native and Non-Native Speech. In: Gaëtanelle Gilquin and Sylvie De Cock (eds.), *Errors and Disfluencies in Spoken Corpora* (Benjamins Current Topics 52). Amsterdam and Philadelphia, PA: John Benjamins, 139–162.

Pascanu, Razvan, Tomas Mikolov and Yoshua Bengio (2013), On the Difficulty of Training Recurrent Neural Networks. In: *Proceedings of the 30th International Conference on Machine Learning.* Atlanta, GA, 1310–1318.

Paul, Douglas B. and Janet M. Baker (1992), The Design for the Wall Street Journal-based CSR Corpus. In: *Proceedings of the Workshop on Speech and Natural Language, HLT '91.* Stroudsburg, PA: ACL, 357–362.

Payne, John, Geoffrey K. Pullum, Barbara C. Scholz and Eva Berlage (2013), Anaphoric One and Its Implications. *Language* 89(4), 794–829.

Pearson, Hazel (2011), A New Semantics for Group Nouns. In: Mary Byram Washburn, Katherine McKinney-Bock, Erika Varis, Ann Sawyer and Barbara Tomaszewicz (eds.), *Proceedings of the 28th West Coast Conference on Formal Linguistics.* Los Angeles, CA, 160–168.

Pedregosa, Fabian, Gaël Varoquaux, Alexandre Gramfort, Vincent Michel, Bertrand Thirion, Olivier Grisel, Mathieu Blondel, Peter Prettenhofer, Ron Weiss and Vincent Dubourg (2011), Scikit-learn: Machine learning in Python. *Journal of Machine Learning Research* 12, 2825–2830.

Pennington, Jeffrey, Richard Socher and Christopher D. Manning (2014), GloVe: Global Vectors for Word Representation. In: *Proceedings of EMNLP 2014*. Doha, Qatar, 1532–1543.

Perret, Jerémy, Stergos Afantenos, Nicholas Asher and Mathieu Morey (2016), Integer Linear Programming for Discourse Parsing. In: *Proceedings of NAACL 2016*. San Diego, CA, 99–109.

Petrova, Svetlana, Michael Solf, Julia Ritz, Christian Chiarcos and Amir Zeldes (2009), Building and Using a Richly Annotated Interlinear Diachronic Corpus: The Case of Old High German Tatian. *Traitement automatique des langues* 50(2), 47–71.

Petukhova, Volha and Harry Bunt (2009), Towards a Multidimensional Semantics of Discourse Markers in Spoken Dialogue. In: *Proceedings of the 8th International Conference on Computational Semantics*. Tilburg, the Netherlands, 157–168.

Piotrowski, Michael (2012), *Natural Language Processing for Historical Texts*. San Rafael, CA: Morgan & Claypool.

Plag, Ingo (2010), Compound Stress Assignment by Analogy: The Constituent Family Bias. *Zeitschrift für Sprachwissenschaft* 29(2), 243–282.

Poesio, Massimo (2004), Discourse Annotation and Semantic Annotation in the GNOME Corpus. In: *Proceedings of the ACL Workshop on Discourse Annotation*. Barcelona, 72–79.

Poesio, Massimo and Ron Artstein (2005), The Reliability of Anaphoric Annotation, Reconsidered: Taking Ambiguity Into Account. In: *Proceedings of ACL Workshop on Frontiers in Corpus Annotation*. Stroudsburg, PA: ACL, 76–83.

Poesio, Massimo and Ron Artstein (2008), Anaphoric Annotation in the ARRAU Corpus. In: Nicoletta Calzolari, Khalid Choukri, Bente Maegaard, Joseph Mariani, Jan Odjik, Stelios Piperidis and Daniel Tapias (eds.), *Proceedings of LREC 2008*. Marrakesh, Morocco, 1170–1174.

Poesio, Massimo, Sameer Pradhan, Marta Recasens, Kepa Rodriguez and Yannick Versley (2016), Annotated Corpora and Annotation Tools. In: Massimo Poesio, Roland Stuckardt and Yannick Versley (eds.), *Anaphora Resolution: Algorithms, Resources, and Applications*. Heidelberg: Springer, 97–140.

Poesio, Massimo, Rosemary Stevenson, Barbara Di Eugenio and Janet Hitzeman (2004), Centering: A Parametric Theory and Its Instantiations. *Computational Linguistics* 30(3), 309–363.

Poesio, Massimo & Renata Vieira (1998), A Corpus-Based Investigation of Definite Description Use. *Computational Linguistics* 24(2), 183–216.

Polanyi, Livia (1988), A Formal Model of the Structure of Discourse. *Journal of Pragmatics* 12(5–6), 601–638.

Pollard, Carl and Ivan A. Sag (1992), Anaphors in English and the Scope of Binding Theory. *Linguistic Inquiry* 23(2), 261–303.

Pörksen, Uwe (2003), Deutsche Sprachgeschichte und die Entwicklung der Naturwissenschaften – Aspekte einer Geschichte der Naturwissenschaftssprache und ihrer Wechselwirkung zur Gemeinsprache. In: Werner Besch, Anne Betten, Oskar Reichmann and Stefan Sonderegger (eds.), *Sprachgeschichte. Ein*

Handbuch zur Geschichte der deutschen Sprache und ihrer Erforschung. Berlin: De Gruyter, 193–210.

Prasad, Rashmi, Nikhil Dinesh, Alan Lee, Eleni Miltsakaki, Livio Robaldo, Aravind Joshi and Bonnie Webber (2008), The Penn Discourse Treebank 2.0. In: *Proceedings of LREC 2008*. Marrakesh, Morocco.

Prince, Ellen F. (1981), Toward a Taxonomy of Given-New Information. In: Peter Cole (ed.), *Radical Pragmatics*. New York, NY: Academic Press, 223–255.

Pulvermüller, Friedemann (1999), Words in the Brain's Language. *Behavioral and Brain Sciences* 22(2), 253–279.

Pustejovsky, James, José Castaño, Robert Ingria, Roser Saurí, Robert Gaizauskas, Andrea Setzer and Graham Katz (2003), TimeML: Robust Specification of Event and Temporal Expressions in Text. In: *Proceedings of IWCS-5, Fifth International Workshop on Computational Semantics*. Tilburg, the Netherlands.

Quirk, Randolph, Sydney Greenbaum, Geoffrey Leech and Jan Svartvik (1985), *A Comprehensive Grammar of the English Language*. London: Longman.

Ragheb, Marwa and Markus Dickinson (2012), Defining Syntax for Learner Language Annotation. In: *Proceedings of COLING 2012*. Mumbai, 965–974.

Ratnaparkhi, Adwait (2000), Trainable Methods for Surface Natural Language Generation. In: *Proceedings of NAACL 2000*. Seattle, WA, 194–201.

Rayson, Paul, Dawn Archer, Scott Piao and Tony McEnery (2004), The UCREL Semantic Analysis System. In: *Proceedings of the Workshop Beyond Named Entity Recognition: Semantic Labelling for NLP Tasks*. Lisbon, Portugal, 7–12.

Recasens, Marta, Zhichao Hu and Olivia Rhinehart (2016), Sense Anaphoric Pronouns: Am I One? In: *Proceedings of the Workshop on Coreference Resolution Beyond OntoNotes (CORBON 2016), Co-located With NAACL 2016*. San Diego, CA, 1–6.

Recasens, Marta, Marie-Catherine de Marneffe and Christopher Potts (2013), The Life and Death of Discourse Entities: Identifying Singleton Mentions. In: *Proceedings of NAACL 2013*. Atlanta, GA, 627–633.

Redeker, Gisela, Ildikó Berzlánovich, Nynke van der Vliet, Gosse Bouma and Markus Egg (2012), Multi-Layer Discourse Annotation of a Dutch Text Corpus. In: Nicoletta Calzolari, Khalid Choukri, Thierry Declerck, Mehmet Uğur Doğan, Bente Maegaard, Joseph Mariani, Asuncion Moreno, Jan Odijk and Stelios Piperidis (eds.), *Proceedings of LREC 2012*. Istanbul, Turkey: ELRA, 2820–2825.

Reid, Wallis (1991), *Verb and Noun Number in English: A Functional Explanation*. London: Longman.

Reinhart, Tanya (1976), *The Syntactic Domain of Anaphora*. PhD Thesis, Massachusetts Institute of Technology.

Reinhart, Tanya (1986), Center and Periphery in the Grammar of Anaphora. In: Barbara Lust (ed.), *Studies in the Acquisition of Anaphora*. Vol. 1. Dordrecht: Reidel, 123–150.

Reppen, Randi, Susan M. Fitzmaurice and Douglas Biber (eds.) (2002), *Using Corpora to Explore Linguistic Variation* (Studies in Corpus Linguistics 9). Amsterdam and Philadelphia, PA: John Benjamins.

Reppen, Randy (2010), Building a Corpus: What Are the Basics? In: Anne O'Keeffe and Michael McCarthy (eds.), *The Routledge Handbook of Corpus Linguistics*. London: Routledge, 31–38.

Reznicek, Marc, Anke Lüdeling and Hagen Hirschmann (2013), Competing Target Hypotheses in the Falko Corpus: A Flexible Multi-Layer Corpus Architecture. In: Ana Díaz-Negrillo, Nicolas Ballier and Paul Thompson (eds.), *Automatic Treatment and Analysis of Learner Corpus Data*. Amsterdam: John Benjamins, 101–124.

Reznicek, Marc, Anke Lüdeling, Cedric Krummes, Franziska Schwantuschke, Maik Walter, Karin Schmidt, Hagen Hirschmann and Torsten Andreas (2012), *Das Falko-Handbuch. Korpusaufbau und Annotationen*. Humboldt-Universität zu Berlin, Technical Report Version 2.01, Berlin.

Richter, Tonio Sebastian (2009), Greek, Coptic, and the 'Language of the Hijra'. Rise and Decline of the Coptic Language in Late Antique and Medieval Egypt. In: Hannah M. Cotton, Robert G. Hoyland, Jonathan J. Price and David J. Wasserstein (eds.), *From Hellenism to Islam: Cultural and Linguistic Change in the Roman Near East*. Cambridge: Cambridge University Press, 401–446.

Rissanen, Matti (2008), Corpus Linguistics and Historical Linguistics. In: Anke Lüdeling and Merja Kytö (eds.), *Corpus Linguistics: An International Handbook*. Vol. 1. Berlin: Mouton de Gruyter, 53–68.

Ritchie, Graeme (2004), *The Linguistic Analysis of Jokes*. London: Routledge.

Ritz, Julia (2010), Using tf-idf-related Measures for Determining the Anaphoricity of Noun Phrases. In: *Proceedings of KONVENS 2010*. Saarbrücken, Germany, 85–92.

Rizzi, Luigi (1997), The Fine Structure of the Left Periphery. In: Liliane Haegeman (ed.), *Elements of Grammar*. Dordrecht: Kluwer, 281–337.

Romary, Laurent, Amir Zeldes and Florian Zipser (2015), <tiger2/> – Serialising the ISO SynAF Syntactic Object Model. *Language Resources and Evaluation* 49(1), 1–18.

Ross, Shawna (2014), In Praise of Overstating the Case: A Review of Franco Moretti, Distant Reading. *Digital Humanities Quarterly* 8(1). Available at: www.digitalhumanities.org/dhq/vol/8/1/000171/000171.html.

Roth, Dan, Mark Sammons, Gourab Kundu, Stephen Mayhew, Chen-Tse Tsai, Ruichen Wang, Shyam Upadhyay and Yangqiu Song (2014), Overview of UI-CCG Systems for Event Argument Extraction, Entity Discovery and Linking, and Slot Filler Validation. In: *Proceedings of the Text Analysis Conference 2014*. Gaithersburg, MD.

Rumshisky, Anna, Nick Botchan, Sophie Kushkuley and James Pustejovsky (2012), Word Sense Inventories by Non-Experts. In: *Proceedings of LREC 2012*. Istanbul, Turkey, 4055–4059.

Russell, Jane and Nina Spada (2006), The Effectiveness of Corrective Feedback for the Acquisition of L2 Grammar: A Meta-Analysis of the Research. In: John Norris and Lourdes Ortega (eds.), *Synthesizing Research on Language Learning and Teaching* (Language Learning & Language Teaching 13). Amsterdam and Philadelphia, PA: John Benjamins, 133–164.

Sabou, Marta, Kalina Bontcheva, Leon Derczynski and Arno Scharl (2014), Corpus Annotation Through Crowdsourcing: Towards Best Practice Guidelines. In: Nicoletta Calzolari, Khalid Choukri, Thierry Declerck, Hrafn Loftsson, Bente Maegaard, Joseph Mariani, Asuncion Moreno, Jan Odijk and Stelios Piperidis (eds.), *Proceedings of LREC 2014*. Reykjavik, Iceland: ELRA.

Sag, Ivan A. (2012), Sign-Based Construction Grammar: An Informal Synopsis. In: Hans C. Boas and Ivan A. Sag (eds.), *Sign-Based Construction Grammar*. Stanford: CSLI, 69–202.

Sag, Ivan A. and Jorge Hankamer (1984), Towards a Theory of Anaphoric Processing. *Linguistics and Philosophy* 7, 325–345.

Säily, Tanja (2011), Variation in Morphological Productivity in the BNC: Sociolinguistic and Methodological Considerations. *Corpus Linguistics and Linguistic Theory* 7(1), 119–141.

Sanders, Ted J. M., Wilbert P. M. Spooren and Leo G. M. Noordman (1992), Towards a Taxonomy of Coherence Relations. *Discourse Processes* 15, 1–35.

Santorini, Beatrice (1990), *Part-of-Speech Tagging Guidelines for the Penn Treebank Project (3rd Revision)*. Technical Report, University of Pennsylvania.

Sauer, Simon and Anke Lüdeling (2016), Flexible Multi-Layer Spoken Dialogue Corpora. *International Journal of Corpus Linguistics, Special Issue on Spoken Corpora* 21(3), 419–438.

Sauerland, Uli (2003), A New Semantics for Number. In: *Proceedings of SALT 13*. Ithaca, NY: CLC Publications.

Schäfer, Roland (2017), Accurate and Efficient General-purpose Boilerplate Detection for Crawled Web Corpora. *Language Resources and Evaluation* 51(3), 873–889.

Schank, Roger and Robert Abelson (1977), *Scripts, Plans, Goals and Understanding: An Inquiry Into Human Knowledge Structures*. Hillsdale, NJ: Lawrence Erlbaum.

Schembri, Adam, Jordan Fenlon, Ramas Rentelis, Sally Reynolds and Kearsy Cormier (2013), Building the British Sign Language Corpus. *Language Documentation and Conservation* 7, 136–154.

Schiel, Florian, Susanne Burger, Anja Geumann and Karl Weilhammer (1998), The Partitur Format at BAS. In: *Proceedings of LREC 1998*. Granada, Spain.

Schiller, Anne, Simone Teufel, Christine Stöckert and Christine Thielen (1999), *Guidelines für das Tagging deutscher Textcorpora mit STTS*. Technical report, Universität Stuttgart, Institut für maschinelle Sprachverarbeitung & Universität Tübingen, Seminar für Sprachwissenschaft.

Schmid, Helmut (1994), Probabilistic Part-of-Speech Tagging Using Decision Trees. In: *Proceedings of the Conference on New Methods in Language Processing*. Manchester, UK, 44–49. Available at: www.cis.uni-muenchen. de/~schmid/tools/TreeTagger/data/tree-tagger1.pdf.

Schmid, Helmut (2008), Tokenizing and Part-of-Speech Tagging. In: Anke Lüdeling and Merja Kytö (eds.), *Corpus Linguistics: An International Handbook*. Vol. 1. Berlin: Mouton de Gruyter, 527–551.

Schmidt, Thomas (2004), Transcribing and Annotating Spoken Language With Exmaralda. In: Andreas Witt, Ulrich Heid, Jean Carletta, Henry S. Thompson and Peter Wittenburg (eds.), *Proceedings of the LREC-Workshop on XML Based Richly Annotated Corpora, Lisbon 2004*. Paris: ELRA, 69–74.

Schmidt, Thomas and Kai Wörner (2009), EXMARaLDA – Creating, Analysing and Sharing Spoken Language Corpora for Pragmatic Research. *Pragmatics* 19(4), 565–582.

Schroeder, Caroline T. and Amir Zeldes (2016), Raiders of the Lost Corpus. *Digital Humanities Quarterly* 10(2). Available at: http://digitalhumanities.org/dhq/vol/10/2/000247/000247.html.

Shisha-Halevy, Ariel (1986), *Coptic Grammatical Categories: Structural Studies in the Syntax of Shenoutean Sahidic*. Rome: Pontificum Institutum Biblicum.

Silveira, Natalia, Timothy Dozat, Marie-Catherine de Marneffe, Samuel R. Bowman, Miriam Connor, John Bauery and Christopher D. Manning (2014), A

Gold Standard Dependency Corpus for English. In: *Proceedings of LREC 2014*. Reykjavik, Iceland, 2897–2904.

Sinclair, John (1991), *Corpus, Concordance, Collocation* (Describing English Language). Oxford: Oxford University Press.

Skopeteas, Stavros and Gisbert Fanselow (2010), Effects of Givenness and Constraints on Free Word Order. In: Malte Zimmermann and Carolin Féry (eds.), *Information Structure: Theoretical, Typological, and Experimental Perspectives*. Oxford: Oxford University Press.

Skopeteas, Stavros, Ines Fiedler, Sam Hellmuth, Anne Schwarz, Ruben Stoel, Gisbert Fanselow, Caroline Féry and Manfred Krifka (2006), Questionnaire on Information Structure (QUIS). *Interdisciplinary Studies on Information Structure* 4.

Smith, Neil V. (1990), Observations on the Pragmatics of Tense. *UCL Working Papers in Linguistics* 2, 82–94.

Snow, Rion, Brendan O'Connor, Daniel Jurafsky and Andrew Ng (2008), Cheap and Fast – But Is It Good? Evaluating Non-Expert Annotations for Natural Language Tasks. In: *Proceedings of EMNLP 2008*. Honolulu, HI, 254–263.

Sobin, Nicholas (1997), Agreement, Default Rules, and Grammatical Viruses. *Linguistic Inquiry* 28(2), 318–343.

Socher, Richard, John Bauer, Christopher D. Manning and Andrew Y. Ng (2013), Parsing With Compositional Vector Grammars. In: *Proceedings of ACL 2013*. Sofia, Bulgaria, 455–465.

Spalek, Katharina and Amir Zeldes (2017), Converging Evidence for the Relevance of Alternative Sets: Data From NPs With Focus Sensitive Particles in German. *Language and Cognition* 9(1), 24–51.

Sparks, Randall B. (1984), Here's a Few More Facts. *Linguistic Inquiry* 15(1), 179–183.

Speas, Margaret (2006), Economy, Agreement and the Representation of Null Arguments. In: Peter Ackema, Patrick Brandt, Maaike Schoorlemmer and Fred Weerman (eds.), *Arguments and Agreement*. Oxford: Oxford University Press, 35–75.

Springmann, Uwe and Anke Lüdeling (2017), OCR of Historical Printings With an Application to Building Diachronic Corpora: A Case Study Using the RIDGES Herbal Corpus. *Digital Humanities Quarterly* 11(2). Available at: www.digitalhumanities.org/dhq/vol/11/2/000288/000288.html.

Stalnaker, Robert (1974), Pragmatic Presuppositions. In: Milton Munitz and Peter Unger (eds.), *Semantics and Philosophy*. New York, NY: New York University Press, 197–213.

Staub, Adrian (2009), On the Interpretation of the Number Attraction Effect: Response Time Evidence. *Journal of Memory and Language* 60(2), 1–39.

Stede, Manfred (2004), The Potsdam Commentary Corpus. In: Bonnie Webber and Donna K. Byron (eds.), *Proceeding of the ACL 2004 Workshop on Discourse Annotation*. Barcelona, Spain, 96–102.

Stede, Manfred (2008), Disambiguating Rhetorical Structure. *Research on Language and Computation* 6(3), 311–332.

Stede, Manfred (2012), *Discourse Processing* (Synthesis Lectures on Human Language Technologies 4). San Rafael, CA: Morgan & Claypool.

Stede, Manfred and Yulia Grishina (2016), Anaphoricity in Connectives: A Case Study on German. In: *Proceedings of the Workshop on Coreference Resolution Beyond OntoNotes (CORBON 2016)*. San Diego, CA, 41–46.

Stede, Manfred and Chu-Ren Huang (2012), Inter-operability and Reusability: The Science of Annotation. *Language Resources and Evaluation* 46, 91–94.

Stede, Manfred and Arne Neumann (2014), Potsdam Commentary Corpus 2.0: Annotation for Discourse Research. In: *Proceedings of the Language Resources and Evaluation Conference (LREC 2014)*. Reykjavik, 925–929.

Steels, Luc and Joachim de Beule (2006), Unify and Merge in Fluid Construction Grammar. In: Paul Vogt, Yuuga Sugita, Elio Tuci and Chrystopher L. Nehaniv (eds.), *Symbol Grounding and Beyond: Proceedings of the Third International Workshop on the Emergence and Evolution of Linguistic Communication* (Lecture Notes in Artificial Intelligence 4211). Berlin: Springer, 197–223.

Stefanowitsch, Anatol (2008), Negative Entrenchment: A Usage-based Approach to Negative Evidence. *Cognitive Linguistics* 19(3), 513–531.

Štěpánek, Jan and Petr Pajas (2010), Querying Diverse Treebanks in a Uniform Way. In: *Proceedings of LREC 2010*. Valletta, Malta, 1828–1835.

Stieglitz, Stefan, Christoph Lattemann, Susanne Robra-Bissantz, Rüdiger Zarnekow and Tobias Brockmann (eds.) (2017), *Gamification: Using Game Elements in Serious Contexts* (Progress in IS). Cham: Springer.

Stolcke, Andreas, Klaus Ries, Noah Coccaro, Elizabeth Shriberg, Rebecca Bates, Daniel Jurafsky, Paul Taylor, Rachel Martin, Marie Meteer and Carol Van Ess-Dykema (2000), Dialogue Act Modeling for Automatic Tagging and Recognition of Conversational Speech. *Computational Linguistics* 26(3), 339–371.

Surdeanu, Mihai, Thomas Hicks and Marco A. Valenzuela-Escarcega (2015), Two Practical Rhetorical Structure Theory Parsers. In: *Proceedings of NAACL 2015*. Denver, CO, 1–5.

Sweetser, Eve (1990), *From Etymology to Pragmatics: Metaphorical and Cultural Aspects of Semantic Structure*. Cambridge: Cambridge University Press.

Szmrecsanyi, Benedikt (2006), *Morphosyntactic Persistence in Spoken English: A Corpus Study at the Intersection of Variationist Sociolinguistics, Psycholinguistics, and Discourse Analysis* (Trends in Linguistics: Studies and Monographs 177). Berlin and New York, NY: Mouton de Gruyter.

Taboada, Maite (2011), Stages in an Online Review Genre. *Text and Talk* 31(2), 247–269.

Taboada, Maite and Debopam Das (2013), Annotation Upon Annotation: Adding Signalling Information to a Corpus of Discourse Relations. *Dialogue and Discourse* 4(2), 249–281.

Taboada, Maite and Julia Lavid (2003), Rhetorical and Thematic Patterns in Scheduling Dialogues: A Generic Characterization. *Functions of Language* 10(2), 147–179.

Taboada, Maite and William C. Mann (2006), Rhetorical Structure Theory: Looking Back and Moving Ahead. *Discourse Studies* 8, 423–459.

Tang, Duyu, Bing Qin, Ting Liu and Yuekui Yang (2015), User Modeling With Neural Network for Review Rating Prediction. In: *Proceedings of IJCAI 2015*. Buenos Aires, 1340–1346.

Telljohann, Heike, Erhard W. Hinrichs, Sandra Kübler, Heike Zinsmeister and Kathrin Beck (2012), *Stylebook for the Tübingen Treebank of Written German (TüBa-D/Z)*. Technical report, Seminar für Sprachwissenschaft, Universität Tübingen.

Tetreault, Joel and James Allen (2003), An Empirical Evaluation of Pronoun Resolution and Clausal Structure. In: *Proceedings of the 2003 International*

Symposium on Reference Resolution and Its Applications to Question Answering and Summarization. Venice, Italy, 1–8.

Timmis, Ivor (2015), *Corpus Linguistics for ELT: Research and Practice.* London: Routledge.

Toldova, Svetlana, Dina Pisarevskaya, Margarita Ananyeva, Maria Kobozeva, Alexander Nasedkin, Sofia Nikiforova, Irina Pavlova and Alexey Shelepov (2017), Rhetorical Relation Markers in Russian RST Treebank. In: *Proceedings of the 6th Workshop Recent Advances in RST and Related Formalisms.* Santiago de Compostela, Spain, 29–33.

Torallas-Tovar, Sofia (2010), Greek in Egypt. In: Egbert J. Bakker (ed.), *A Companion to the Ancient Greek language.* Oxford: Willey-Blackwell, 253–266.

Traugott, Elizabeth C. (1999), The Rhetoric of Counter-Expectation in Semantic Change: A Study in Subjectification. In: Andreas Blank and Peter Koch (eds.), *Historical Semantics and Cognition* (Cognitive Linguistics Research 13). Berlin: Mouton de Gruyter, 177–196.

Trnavac, Radoslava and Maite Taboada (2012), Backwards Anaphora Marking in Coherence Relations. In: *11th Conceptual Structure, Discourse and Language Conference.* Vancouver, Canada.

Truscott, John (1996), The Case Against Grammar Correction in L2 Writing Classes. *Language Learning* 46(2), 327–369.

Uhrig, Peter (2015), Why the Principle of No Synonymy Is Overrated. *Zeitschrift für Anglistik und Amerikanistik* 63(3), 323–337.

Van Deemter, Kees (2016), *Computational Models of Referring: A Study in Cognitive Science.* Cambridge, MA: MIT Press.

Van den Bosch, Antal (2009), Machine Learning. In: Anke Lüdeling and Merja Kytö (eds.), *Corpus Linguistics: An International Handbook.* Vol. 2. Berlin: Mouton de Gruyter, 855–874.

van der Vliet, Nynke and Gisela Redeker (2014), Explicit and Implicit Coherence Relations in Dutch Texts. In: Helmut Gruber and Gisela Redeker (eds.), *The Pragmatics of Discourse Coherence: Theories and applications* (Pragmatics & Beyond New Series 254). Amsterdam and Philadelphia, PA: John Benjamins, 23–52.

Van Valin Jr., Robert D. (1999), A Typology of the Interaction of Focus Structure and Syntax. In: Ekaterina V. Raxilina and Jakov G. Testelec (eds.), *Typology and the Theory of Language: From Description to Explanation.* Moscow: Languages of Russian Culture, 511–524.

Venhuizen, Noortje J., Valerio Basile, Kilian Evang and Johan Bos (2013), Gamification for Word Sense Labeling. In: *Proceedings of the 10th International Conference on Computational Semantics.* Potsdam, Germany.

Verhagen, Arie (2005), *Constructions of Intersubjectivity: Discourse, Syntax, and Cognition.* Oxford: Oxford University Press.

Vyatkina, Nina, Hagen Hirschmann and Felix Golcher (2015), Syntactic Modification at Early Stages of L2 German Writing Development: A Longitudinal Learner Corpus Study. *Journal of Second Language Writing* 29, 28–50.

Wagers, Matthew W., Ellen F. Lau and Colin Phillips (2009), Agreement Attraction in Comprehension: Representations and Processes. *Journal of Memory and Language* 61, 206–237.

Wang, Jianxiang and Man Lan (2015), A Refined End-to-End Discourse Parser. In: *Proceedings of CoNLL 2015.* Beijing, China, 17–24.

Watson, Robin Montgomery (2010), *Epicene Pronoun Use in Modern American English*. MA Thesis, Brigham Young University.

Webber, Bonnie (1991), Structure and Ostension in the Interpretation of Discourse Deixis. *Language and Cognitive Processes* 6(2), 107–135.

Weber, Andrea and Karin Müller (2004), Word Order Variation in German Main Clauses: A Corpus Analysis. In: *Proceedings of the 5th International Workshop on Linguistically Interpreted Corpora (LINC-04)*. Geneva.

Webster, Jonathan, Angela Chan and John Lee (2011), Introducing an Online Language Learning Environment and Its Corpus of Tertiary Student Writing. *Asia Pacific World* 2(2), 44–65.

Weischedel, Ralph, Sameer Pradhan, Lance Ramshaw, Jeff Kaufman, Michelle Franchini, Mohammed El-Bachouti, Nianwen Xue, Martha Palmer, Jena D. Hwang, Claire Bonial, Jinho Choi, Aous Mansouri, Maha Foster, Abdel-aati Hawwary, Mitchell Marcus, Ann Taylor, Craig Greenberg, Eduard Hovy, Robert Belvin and Ann Houston (2012), *OntoNotes Release 5.0*. Technical Report, Linguistic Data Consortium, Philadelphia.

Wu, Dekai (2010), Alignment. In: Nitin Indurkhya and Fred J. Damerau (eds.), *Handbook of Natural Language Processing*. Boca Raton, FL: CRC Press, 367–408.

Wulff, Stefanie (2006), Go-V vs. go-and-V in English: A Case of Constructional Synonymy? In: Stefan Th. Gries and Anatol Stefanowitsch (eds.), *Corpora in Cognitive Linguistics: Corpus-based Approaches to Syntax and Lexis* (Trends in Linguistics Studies and Monographs 172). Berlin and New York, NY: Mouton de Gruyter, 101–125.

Yang, Charles (2015), Negative Knowledge From Positive Evidence. *Language* 91(4), 938–953.

Yimam, Seid Muhie, Iryna Gurevych, Richard Eckart de Castilho and Chris Biemann (2013), WebAnno: A Flexible, Web-based and Visually Supported System for Distributed Annotations. In: *Proceedings of ACL 2013*. Sofia, Bulgaria, 1–6.

Zaenen, Annie, Jean Carletta, Gregory Garretson, Joan Bresnan, Andrew Koontz-Garboden, Tatiana Nikitina, M. Catherine O'Connor and Tom Wasow (2004), Animacy Encoding in English: Why and How. In: *Proceedings of the 2004 ACL Workshop on Discourse Annotation*. Stroudsburg, PA: ACL, 118–125.

Zeldes, Amir (2013), Komposition als Konstruktionsnetzwerk im fortgeschrittenen L2-Deutsch. *Zeitschrift für germanistische Linguistik* 41(2), 240–276.

Zeldes, Amir (2016a), Probabilistic Pragmatics and Probabilistic Experience. *Zeitschrift für Sprachwissenschaft* 35(1), 109–116.

Zeldes, Amir (2016b), rstWeb – A Browser-based Annotation Interface for Rhetorical Structure Theory and Discourse Relations. In: *Proceedings of NAACL-HLT 2016 System Demonstrations*. San Diego, CA, 1–5.

Zeldes, Amir (2017a), The GUM Corpus: Creating Multilayer Resources in the Classroom. *Language Resources and Evaluation* 51(3), 581–612.

Zeldes, Amir (2017b), A Distributional View of Discourse Encapsulation: Multifactorial Prediction of Coreference Density in RST. In: *6th Workshop on Recent Advances in RST and Related Formalisms*. Santiago de Compostela, Spain, 20–28.

Zeldes, Amir (2018a), A Predictive Model for Notional Anaphora in English. In: *Proceedings of the NAACL 2018 Workshop on Computational Models of Reference, Anaphora, and Coreference (CRAC)*. New Orleans, LA, 34–43.

Zeldes, Amir (2018b), Compounds and Productivity in Advanced L2 German Writing: A Constructional Approach. In: Andrea Tyler, Lourdes Ortega, Mariko Uno and Hae In Park (eds.), *Usage-inspired L2 Instruction: Researched Pedagogy*. Amsterdam and Philadelphia, PA: John Benjamins, 237–265.

Zeldes, Amir (2018c), A Neural Approach to Discourse Relation Signaling. *Georgetown University Round Table (GURT) 2018: Approaches to Discourse*. Georgetown University, Washington DC.

Zeldes, Amir, Anke Lüdeling and Hagen Hirschmann (2008), What's Hard? Quantitative Evidence for Difficult Constructions in German Learner Data. In: Antti Arppe, Kaius Sinnemäki and Urpo Nikanne (eds.), *Proceedings of Quantitative Investigations in Theoretical Linguistics 3 (QITL-3)*. Helsinki, 74–77.

Zeldes, Amir and Caroline T. Schroeder (2015), Computational Methods for Coptic: Developing and Using Part-of-Speech Tagging for Digital Scholarship in the Humanities. *Digital Scholarship in the Humanities* 30(1), 164–176.

Zeldes, Amir and Dan Simonson (2016), Different Flavors of GUM: Evaluating Genre and Sentence Type Effects on Multilayer Corpus Annotation Quality. In: *Proceedings of LAW X – The 10th Linguistic Annotation Workshop*. Berlin, 68–78.

Zeldes, Amir and Shuo Zhang (2016), When Annotation Schemes Change Rules Help: A Configurable Approach to Coreference Resolution Beyond OntoNotes. In: *Proceedings of the NAACL2016 Workshop on Coreference Resolution Beyond OntoNotes (CORBON)*. San Diego, CA, 92–101.

Zeldes, Amir, Florian Zipser and Arne Neumann (2013), *PAULA XML Documentation: Format Version 1.1*. Technical Report, Humboldt-Universität zu Berlin.

Zhang, Hongxin and Haitao Liu (2016), Rhetorical Relations Revisited Across Distinct Levels of Discourse Unit Granularity. *Discourse Studies* 18(4).

Zhang, Shuo and Amir Zeldes (2017), GitDOX: A Linked Version Controlled Online XML Editor for Manuscript Transcription. In: *Proceedings of FLAIRS-30*. Marco Island, FL, 619–623.

Zipser, Florian (2009), *Entwicklung eines Konverterframeworks für linguistisch annotierte Daten auf Basis eines gemeinsamen (Meta-)Modells*. Diploma Thesis, Humboldt-Universität zu Berlin.

Zipser, Florian and Laurent Romary (2010), A Model Oriented Approach to the Mapping of Annotation Formats Using Standards. In: *Proceedings of the Workshop on Language Resource and Language Technology Standards, LREC 2010*. Valletta, Malta, 7–18.

Index

Note: Page numbers in *italic* indicate figures; those in **bold** indicate tables.